St Antony's Series
General Editor: **Richard Clogg** (1999–), Fellow of St Antony's College, Oxford

Recent titles include:

Mariana Llanos
PRIVATIZATION AND DEMOCRACY IN ARGENTINA
An Analysis of President–Congress Relations

Michael Addison
VIOLENT POLITICS
Strategies of Internal Conflict

Geoffrey Wiseman
CONCEPTS OF NON-PROVOCATIVE DEFENCE
Ideas and Practices in International Security

Pilar Ortuño Anaya
EUROPEAN SOCIALISTS AND SPAIN
The Transition to Democracy, 1959–77

Renato Baumann (*editor*)
BRAZIL IN THE 1990s
An Economy in Transition

Israel Getzler
NIKOLAI SUKHANOV
Chronicler of the Russian Revolution

Arturo J. Cruz, Jr
NICARAGUA'S CONSERVATIVE REPUBLIC, 1858–93

Pamela Lubell
THE COMMUNIST PARTY DURING THE CULTURAL REVOLUTION
The Case of the Sixty-One Renegades

Mikael af Malmborg
NEUTRALITY AND STATE-BUILDING IN SWEDEN

Klaus Gallo
GREAT BRITAIN AND ARGENTINA
From Invasion to Recognition, 1806–26

David Faure and Tao Tao Liu
TOWN AND COUNTRY IN CHINA
Identity and Perception

Peter Mangold
SUCCESS AND FAILURE IN BRITISH FOREIGN POLICY
Evaluating the Record, 1900–2000

Mohamad Tavakoli-Targhi
REFASHIONING IRAN
Orientalism, Occidentalism and Historiography

Louise Haagh
CITIZENSHIP, LABOUR MARKETS AND DEMOCRATIZATION
Chile and the Modern Sequence

Renato Colistete
LABOUR RELATIONS AND INDUSTRIAL PERFORMANCE IN BRAZIL
Greater São Paulo, 1945–60

Peter Lienhardt (*edited by Ahmed Al-Shahi*)
SHAIKHDOMS OF EASTERN ARABIA

John Crabtree and Laurence Whitehead (*editors*)
TOWARDS DEMOCRATIC VIABILITY
The Bolivian Experience

Steve Tsang (*editor*)
JUDICIAL INDEPENDENCE AND THE RULE OF LAW IN HONG KONG

Karen Jochelson
THE COLOUR OF DISEASE
Syphilis and Racism in South Africa, 1880–1950

Julio Crespo MacLennan
SPAIN AND THE PROCESS OF EUROPEAN INTEGRATION, 1957–85

Enrique Cárdenas, José Antonio Ocampo and Rosemary Thorp (*editors*)
AN ECONOMIC HISTORY OF TWENTIETH-CENTURY LATIN AMERICA
Volume 1: The Export Age
Volume 2: Latin America in the 1930s
Volume 3: Industrialization and the State in Latin America

Jennifer G. Mathers
THE RUSSIAN NUCLEAR SHIELD FROM STALIN TO YELTSIN

Marta Dyczok
THE GRAND ALLIANCE AND UKRAINIAN REFUGEES

Mark Brzezinski
THE STRUGGLE FOR CONSTITUTIONALISM IN POLAND

St Antony's Series
Series Standing Order ISBN 0-333-71109-2
(*outside North America only*)

You can receive future titles in this series as they are published by placing a standing order. Please contact your bookseller or, in case of difficulty, write to us at the address below with your name and address, the title of the series and the ISBN quoted above.

Customer Services Department, Macmillan Distribution Ltd, Houndmills, Basingstoke, Hampshire RG21 6XS, England

Privatization and Democracy in Argentina

An Analysis of President–Congress Relations

Mariana Llanos

palgrave

in association with
St Antony's College, Oxford

First published 2002 by
PALGRAVE
Houndmills, Basingstoke, Hampshire RG21 6XS and
175 Fifth Avenue, New York, N.Y. 10010
Companies and representatives throughout the world

PALGRAVE is the new global academic imprint of St. Martin's Press LLC Scholarly and Reference Division and Palgrave Publishers Ltd (formerly Macmillan Press Ltd).

ISBN 0–333–92052–X

This book is printed on paper suitable for recycling and made from fully managed and sustained forest sources.

A catalogue record for this book is available from the British Library.

Library of Congress Cataloging-in-Publication Data

Llanos, Mariana, 1967-
Privatization and democracy in Argentina : an analysis of President-Congress relations / Mariana Llanos.
p. cm. — (St. Antony's series)
Includes bibliographical references and index.
ISBN 0–333–92052–X (cloth)
1. Privatization—Argentina. 2. Executive power—Argentina. 3. Legislative power—Argentina. I. Title. II. St. Antony's series (Palgrave (Firm))

HD4084 .L47 2002
338.982′05—dc21

2001057525

10 9 8 7 6 5 4 3 2 1
11 10 09 08 07 06 05 04 03 02

Printed and bound in Great Britain by
Antony Rowe Ltd, Chippenham, Wiltshire

To my daughter

Contents

List of Tables

List of Graphs

List of Abbreviations

Acc.Chaq.	Chaqueña Action Alliance
Band.Blanc.	White Flag Provincial Defence
CGT	General Confederation of Workers
Cons.Pop.	Popular Conservative Party
C.R.	Congressional Reports
C.R.D.	Congressional Reports, Chamber of Deputies
C.R.S.	Congressional Reports, Senate
Cruz.Renov.	Renovator Crusade
F.Rep.	Republican Force
Hum.y Lib.	Social Front of Humanism and Liberation
MAS	Movement to Socialism
MID	Integration and Development Movement
MODIN	Movement of Dignity and Independence
MOPOFU	Fueguino Popular Movement
MOSP	Ministry of Public Work and Services
MPJ	Jujeño Popular Movement
MPN	Neuquino Popular Movement
PAC	Corrientes Autonomous Party
P.Bl.Jub.	Pensioners' White Party
PBSJ	San Juan Bloquista Party
PDC	Christian Democratic Party
PDCF	Federal Christian Democratic Party
PDM	Mendoza's Democratic Party
PDP	Progressive Democratic Party
P.D.Pop.	Popular Democratic Party
PF	Federal Party
PI	Intransigent Party
PJ	Justicialist (Peronist) Party
PLC	Corrientes Liberal Party
PRS	Salta's Renovator Party
P.S.Unif.	Unified Socialist Party
UCeDé	Democratic Centre Union
UCR	Radical Civic Union
US-HTE	Honesty, Work and Efficiency Socialist Unity

Acknowledgements

I am extremely grateful to many persons and institutions who, in different ways, helped me in the writing of this book. As the book is a revised version of my doctoral thesis, the first person I wish to thank is my supervisor in the University of Oxford, Alan Angell, who encouraged me to work on the politics of privatization and who gave me permanent support for the completion of this task. I also owe special gratitude to Ana María Mustapic, in the Universidad Torcuato Di Tella, for once having introduced me to the study of political institutions, and having always helped me with her intellectual support, friendship, and many other kindnesses. Both of them patiently read several versions of the manuscript and greatly contributed to its improvement. I am also grateful to Juan Carlos Torre, from whose writings and conversation on Argentine politics I have learned so much, and to Ana Margheritis and Vicente Palermo, colleagues, friends, and partners in the difficult task of disentangling the recent developments in Argentine politics. St Antony's College, in Oxford, and Universidad Torcuato Di Tella, which kindly received me during my stay in Buenos Aires, were the most stimulating environments in which to write and conduct research: warm thanks to all the friends and colleagues who gave me unstinting intellectual support, wise advice on my work, and invaluable practical help. I equally wish to thank Peter Waldmann and the Institut für Spanien- und Lateinamerikastudien at the University of Augsburg, since without their support the latest corrections of this manuscript would have not been possible. I am also greatly indebted to Ruth Hodges at the Latin American Centre in Oxford, who made most of the language and style corrections. Finally, I am eternally grateful to my family and friends, whose love, company and moral support always accompanied me in the long process of writing.

Indeed, all responsibility for errors is mine alone.

1
Introduction

In returning to democratic rule in December 1983, Argentina became part of the world-wide trend initiated in the 1970s, which Samuel Huntington labelled 'the third wave of democratisation in the history of the modern world'.[1] Argentina mounted the wave with the election of President Raúl Alfonsín, after seven years of severe military dictatorship and a longer term of political instability, which extended throughout the century. After this, ten national elections were held in the country at regular intervals, as well as a great number of others at the provincial and local levels. In 1999, a fourth presidential period was initiated with the election of President Fernando de la Rúa, the candidate of the opposition Alliance who put an end to the Peronist Carlos Menem's ten years in government. During these almost twenty years of democratic rule, regular, free and fair electoral processes took place and the other core features of democracy were also well respected: extensive protection for civil and political rights, freedom of the press and civilian control over the military.[2]

Thus, Argentina's political development at the end of the twentieth century evinced a considerable amount of progress compared to the country's previous experience with democracy. Nevertheless, assessments on the functioning of the Argentine democratic regime have been predominantly negative. As most works on democratization have pointed out, during the previous decades but especially in the 1990s, Argentina exhibited the same weaknesses and vulnerabilities as many other countries of the third wave. In this sense, the problems of Argentine democracy often ran parallel to those experienced by other Latin American countries. Thus, Argentina became one of the many cases which seemed to fulfil the conditions for an electoral democracy, but which failed to qualify as a 'liberal democracy'[3] or where the 'liberal and republican components' of the regime were not functioning well.[4] As a corollary, a pessimistic view about the prospect of democracy in the country often accompanied the analyses.

Indeed, these views were not unanimous and a debate unfolded throughout the past decade about the real nature and features of the Argentine democratic regime. But it was especially with the national electoral results of 1999, which ended ten years of Peronist government, that those negative assessments began to be more openly regarded as 'overly pessimistic'.[5] Furthermore, from then on there was reason to state with greater confidence that political developments during the 1980s and the 1990s had been both complex and diverse, perhaps also contradictory or insufficient in many ways, but by no means only negative.

This book intends to contribute to a re-assessment of the performance of the first two decades of the Argentine democratic regime by concentrating on the elected institutions of government: the Presidency and Congress. It produces empirical information to give a better understanding of the functioning of the Argentine political institutions and other related current political developments. Therefore, this study focuses on some of the most criticized aspects of the Argentine regime, those concerning the operation of the principle of separation of power, the relative stature of the governmental institutions, and the capacities exhibited by these institutions in the processes of policy making. This topic is approached by showing the institutions at work, specifically while dealing with the process of state reform and privatization on which Argentina, like many other countries, embarked at the end of the 1980s. The adoption of a new model of growth that discarded 'inward-oriented state-dominated import-substitution industrialisation toward outward-oriented, private-sector-dominated growth',[6] posed privatization policy as one of the most important issues of the previous decade, the approval of which mobilized the whole institutional apparatus of the regime. It is through the lenses of this policy process which completely changed the character of the Argentine state that the institutions of the Presidency and Congress are analysed in the following chapters of this book.

This introduction is divided into two main sections. The first is concerned with relating the topic to the broad framework of analysis provided by the literature on democratization in Latin America, as well as with explaining the reasons for the approach adopted in this book. The second part concentrates on the particulars of the argument, clarifies some conceptual and methodological points, and anticipates the general structure of the book.

1.1. Evaluating the functioning of new democracies

Among the many weaknesses which the literature on democratization has observed in the functioning of the Latin American democratic regimes during the past decades,[7] two acquire particular prominence and are especially relevant for this study: on the one hand, the inability evinced by these regimes to impose institutional checks on the Executive; on the other, and closely related to the previous point, a political style of policy implementation which pays little attention to the search for political consensus.[8] These problems have been noted in almost all Latin American re-democratization cases, the only exceptions being Chile and Uruguay, and also in the older democracies – Colombia and Venezuela – the exception here being Costa Rica. Thus, as has been explained, most Latin American countries – Argentina, Bolivia, Brazil, Colombia, Ecuador, Nicaragua, Panama, Peru and Venezuela – have exhibited serious problems in their institutional functioning.[9]

In effect, as the first point indicates, most criticism on the operation of new democracies stresses their difficulty in curtailing the Executive's wish for unrestrained action and points out the problems that these democracies face with the operation of the rule of law. The argument states that, whilst a lawful state has well-defined legally established boundaries to delimit the exercise of power as well as institutions empowered to control trespasses of these boundaries,[10] freely elected governments in new democracies normally disregard the constraints established by the constitution and the laws of their countries and do not render themselves accountable to other institutions. Guillermo O'Donnell, and others after him, have pointed out that the 'horizontal accountability', which depends on the existence of a network of state agencies committed to upholding the rule of law, is extremely weak or non-existent in these democracies.[11] In effect, the agencies forming this network – that is, the executive, legislative and judicial branches, as well as various overseeing agencies, such as ombudsmen, accounting offices and *fiscalías* – are normally ignored by the Executive, which even displays strategies that seek their elimination, cooptation, or neutralization. The absence of horizontal checks gives way to a system of plebiscitary features, a 'delegative democracy',[12] where the President is the embodiment of the nation, only constrained by societal power relations. Since without the rule of law citizens are not able to exercise their political and civil rights in full, the unbounded Executive has been regarded as one of the most serious threats to third-wave democracies[13] and as one of the obstacles to democratic consolidation.[14]

A corollary of this type of regime characterized by the concentration of political power has been an autocratic style in the adoption of policy decisions. It has been often pointed out that the unilateral propensities of the Executive, combined with acquiescent legislatures and weak political parties, have confined the formulation of policies to the technical teams of the executive branch and favoured their adoption by decree, without previous consultation and negotiation with other social and political forces. Then, policy changes in new democracies – remarkably those related to structural reforms – have been implemented swiftly and decisively, in contrast to the complicated and limited decision-making processes that characterize representative democracies. This particular style of governing has been regarded as negative for the consolidation of both policy reforms and democracy. On the one hand, it has been argued that in the absence of institutionalized consultation and debate with legislators and interest groups, decision makers have been deprived of feedback that might have been essential for correcting mistakes, as well as for finding durable compromises for social and economic conflicts. In other words, an Executive-dominated policy style has been hindering the construction of a democratic consensus.[15] On the other hand, it is argued that this policy style erodes democratic institutions and procedures. This is especially so in the countries where the weakness of representative institutions of the state and the civil society is the norm, but also where sectoral organizations are too strong and prone to act outside the framework of political institutions.[16] Conversely, a policy style characterized by consultation and negotiation among representative organizations within the framework of representative institutions has been regarded as necessary to channel political conflicts towards them and to teach political actors where the real centre of power is.[17]

In giving reasons for these weaknesses of the Latin American democratic regimes, the literature has frequently pointed out a number of causes, which we shall illustrate with the Argentine case, but which are also normally used to explain similar tendencies in other Latin American countries. Most works emphasize the impact of the critical socio-economic conditions of the 1980s and early 1990s. Some, however, consider that the country's long-term and deep authoritarian legacies also had a crucial influence.

Many studies have indicated that the tremendous economic and social crisis that Argentina faced at the end of the 1980s initiated the move towards a concentrated and unilateral style of government.[18] Furthermore, the emergency context of hyperinflation opened a 'maximum window for reform'[19] and helped to empower the new government with an overwhelming mandate that, at the level of governmental institutions, was expressed in the Executive's capacity to move forward by using emergency powers that bypassed normal legislative procedures. A unilateral, centralized and personalized approach to decision-making was a direct consequence of the crisis and helped to avert economic collapse and initiate structural adjustment.

As these studies illustrate, the Argentine case exhibited a political logic which could be repeatedly found in countries involved in the initiation of far-reaching economic reforms,[20] and, more generally, could well exemplify how the institutions of a democratic regime function in times of emergency. In effect, if Executives normally share legislative prerogatives with Legislatures, in times of crisis equilibrium breaks down in favour of the first. Crises are primarily and often exclusively the business of presidents and prime ministers and it is they who exert most legislative powers. Apart from the routine forms of legislative authority, in most democracies, either the Constitution or informal understanding provide Executives with some emergency powers to respond to national crises in ways that bypass normal legislative procedures. A classic measure is the delegation of power to legislate on issues that are normally subject to legislative approval. In these cases, Legislatures lose (for a fixed period of time) their prerogative of participating in the rule-making process of government, at the same time maintaining their supervision and controlling powers. There are other emergency powers that usually take the form of urgency decrees. They can either be written into constitutions to cope with severe external and internal security challenges, or imply broad interpretations of the constitutional powers of the Executive during emergencies and be used to authorize major economic policy initiatives. Such broad grants of emergency powers by definition permit heads of government to supersede the normal channels of representation and decision-making that new democracies seek to institutionalize. Furthermore, since they are not the product of a circumscribed delegation, even the supervisory powers of Legislatures can seriously be restricted. In these extraordinary circumstances of 'constitutional dictatorship'[21] or 'liberal dictatorship',[22] the potential for abuse is obvious. Then, the question remains as to whether the democratic regime will be able, once the emergency is over, to return to a stage of normal politics, because those charged with carrying this out will probably seek to preserve the extraordinary powers they enjoyed during the crisis.

On this subject, a large number of studies have questioned the capacity of the Argentine regime to restore a democratic pattern of policy making. Rather, the economic crisis has been regarded as the opportunity that facilitated the re-emergence of the country's deep authoritarian traditions: majoritarianism, populism, hyperpresidentialism. As we have already noted, Argentina has been one of the cases (Brazil and Peru being the others) used by O'Donnell to support his argument of the *delegative democracy*. In his view, the country's delegative propensities surfaced when the heavy legacy of past majoritarian tendencies combined with the deep social and economic crisis. The authoritarian inheritance has been identified as one of the main causes of difference between policy implementation processes in the above-mentioned cases, and other countries, such as Uruguay and Chile. The latter two nations experienced a process of re-democratization, so that the adoption of economic reforms could be made within the framework of already established institutions. As they already had strong institutionalized restrictions and historically embedded practices, governmental institutions in Chile and Uruguay began to work effectively as soon as democracy was restored, and the policy-making process adopted the features of already consolidated democracies. Argentina, on the other hand, became part of the 'new democratic species' which O'Donnell called delegative democracy, but which has also been referred to as *low-intensity democracy, democracy by default*, and *empty democracy*.[23]

Some works have also shown that, in countries where expansionary policies ended up causing hyperinflationary crises, the subsequent implementation of market-oriented reforms went hand in hand with populism. Thus, *neopopulism* seems to have been one of the important political features of the new democratic regime, which also had a long-standing tradition. Carlos Menem – like Alberto Fujimori and Fernando Collor de Mello, for example – has been considered one of the leading figures of this tendency. He enacted economic policies diverging from those of traditional populism but by means of using old populist strategies of winning mass support. These strategies have consisted of a personalist style of leadership appealing directly to a heterogeneous mass of followers, a fragmentation of the social movement, a personalization of the leadership of the Peronist Party, and a search for personal bases of support outside the party. In other words, the leader has sought to implement neoliberal reforms by bypassing or personalizing intermediary organizations, that is, the party and interest associations. Likewise, autocratic rule and concentration of authority in the Executive have been the corresponding strategies of this neopopulist style at the level of state institutions.[24]

Finally, some authors have argued that the tendency of those in power to undermine the rule of law and concentrate political power comes from another long-established feature of Argentine politics: *hyperpresi-*

dentialism.[25] According to this view, the re-establishment of democracy in 1983 helped to reduce abuses of power from the Executive by constraining it to constitutional rule, but did not put an end to the centralization tendencies of the country. This has been so because 'the roots of Argentine hyperpresidentialism, both *de jure* and *de facto*, lie in the 1853 constitution'.[26] This constitution established a strong Presidency and, thus distanced itself from the model of the American constitution which it was attempting to copy.[27] Critics of the Argentine constitutional system have therefore advocated an abandonment of the presidential regime as the unique solution to centralizing tendencies and, in so doing, have coincided with the views of other critics of the performance of presidentialism in Latin America.[28] The latter have especially pointed out that systems based on the doctrine of the separation of power normally experience difficulties in generating the consensus needed to govern because, in these systems, presidents fail to secure cooperative legislative majorities. Thus, presidential systems have exacerbated governmental paralysis and ungovernability in the region.[29]

As a consequence, from different perspectives, many analysts have agreed in negatively assessing the performance of the Argentine regime during the past decades. They have contributed to moulding a dominant view according to which the misfunctioning of political institutions, the predominance of the executive office, and a version of democracy that is far from being based on participation, deliberation and the search for consensus, are considered central features of the regime. Indeed, this literature has been a great contribution to the understanding of many of the endemic problems and weaknesses evinced by new democratic regimes, but, in my view, several shortcomings of the approach have misled its understanding of Argentine democracy in particular: the characteristics of a particularly critical moment have normally been dealt with as permanent features of the political regime; the features of the institutional system have often been deducted from the leadership style displayed by an incumbent president; the persistence of long traditions has been overstated and, then, the possibility of change and innovation in the behaviour of political actors neglected; the treatment of the institutional developments has been simplified in order to make broad comparisons among countries.

In recent years, this dominant view began to be contested by several works that have pursued the avoidance of the shortcomings pointed out above. This has resulted in a strong criticism to the central idea that Argentine presidents are capable of governing without restrictions. Several empirical studies, especially (but not exclusively) those concentrating in the processes of formulation and implementation of the structural reforms in the 1990s, have shown that although structural reform policies were the Executive's initiative, their pace and scope could not always be imposed from above.[30] Rather, in order to see the reforms implemented, the Executive had to become involved in complex negotiations with the political and social interests affected by their implementation, that is, the protected local business interests, the unions, the president's party, the provincial supports, which, in many cases, considerably curtailed the Executive's original ambitions.[31] Likewise, analysts of Congress have stressed that the use of autocratic resources to adopt political decisions did not suppress the normal production of legislation.[32] In effect, Congress passed Executive initiatives as well as many of those submitted by legislators. It considered and approved legislation that was crucial for the programme of economic reforms and, finally, it modified many of the bills presented by the Executive. Therefore, these works bring about empirical data that contradict the Executive-dominated views and confirm the relevant role played by institutional checks and political negotiations in the past decades. Moreover, they have led some analysts to affirm that Argentina entered the twentieth century being one of the countries where 'political institutions are most highly developed'.[33]

This book adheres to this critical perspective and adds substantial empirical information to temper the view of the irrelevance of the Argentine political institutions in general and Congress in particular. The evidence here provided is connected to the process of rule making of an important policy that put the whole institutional system to work: the policy of privatization. By following this policy, this book aims, first, to examine the interaction between the two elected institutions of government, the Presidency and Congress, during the 1980s and 1990s in Argentina; and, second, to re-assess the role and stature of these institutions in the political system. In the next section, an explanation of why the policy of privatization is especially useful to serve these goals is provided.

1.2. The book

The centrality of the privatization policy over past decades in Argentina perhaps should not need further clarification. It became known worldwide for its scale and scope, and has been referred to as 'one of the broadest and most rapid in the Western Hemisphere'[34] as well as 'one of the most ambitious and quickly undertaken by the economies that implemented structural reform programmes from the end of the sixties'.[35] Although some privatization was implemented during Alfonsín's government, it was President Menem who carried out the massive privatization programme, as a result of which foreign and local private investors currently operate all traditional public utilities. The programme progressed through his first six years in office (although it was mostly accomplished during the first four years), and extended even further during his second term.

> In 1990, television stations, petrochemical enterprises, a branch railway, the national telecommunication company, the public aviation enterprise, and some oil wells were transferred to private hands. Moreover, the most travelled highways were given in concession to be exploited by toll. In 1991 the transference of oil reserves continued. During 1992, steel companies, electricity generation and distribution companies, the local waterworks enterprise, the national gas company, the Buenos Aires underground and new oil wells were privatised. In 1993, the state oil company was privatised, accesses to the city of Buenos Aires were given in concession to be exploited by toll, and the privatization of electricity continued.[36]

Between 1994 and 1995 the privatized pension system began to work in practice, the privatization of the *Caja Nacional de Ahorro y Seguro* took place, in addition to other areas such as petrochemicals, electricity, gas, transport, and defence. The privatization of the post-office, airports, and nuclear plants was approved and implemented in the following years.

The privatization programme has impressed the world because of its depth. But the final outcome has not been the only subject of particular interest; the formulation, adoption and implementation processes connected to the policy have deserved special attention as well.[37] I shall argue here that such a process of policy implementation can also help to illuminate many aspects of the institutional functioning of the democratic regime.[38] In effect, as the literature on the political economy of structural reforms has highlighted, the formulation of the policy of privatization needs to overcome particularly difficult obstacles at the social, political and governmental levels. First, it requires a governmental disposition to adopt it since privatization is not the product of a social movement. Privatization is a governmental reform pushed forward by politicians and public officials rather than by social groups or classes.[39] Second, its adoption affects deeply entrenched interests favoured by the old system of state regulation and ownership, which will show reluctance to accept any change in their power situation. Third, its formulation does not take place at one point in time, but rather extends over a longer period, obliging policy-makers to devise strategies that could help to maintain control over the policy-making process in the long run. Fourth, privatizing involves contradicting the existing legal and sometimes constitutional norms created to protect the previous state-centred development strategy, so that battles also have to take place in institutional arenas.[40]

In short, privatization is normally a piecemeal process, the success of which depends on the ability to overcome obstacles distributed at different points in time and affecting a variable set of interests at every turn. It demands a change of rules and, thus, mobilizes the framework of governmental institutions – executive power, legislature, courts, central and local government agencies – which normally makes the process slower and also exposes it to the influence and veto-power of other non-governmental actors.[41] As a consequence, given the extensive and indiscriminate character of the privatization process in Argentina, it might well be assumed that a unilateral non-consultative Executive-centred style of policy-making accompanied the policy implementation process: only a policy style of this kind would have permitted to supersede the many obstacles that its implementation aroused. This would, in turn, help to confirm the thesis of the irrelevance of the institutions other than the Executive and the existence of a pattern of institutional relations dominated by the Executive. Nevertheless, I shall argue that a study of the rule-making process of the policy based on institutional dynamism would lead us to different conclusions. In effect, the implementation of the privatization policy was extensive and indiscriminate but it also extended over ten years, so that its study can help to clarify whether the role and relative position of the two institutions in the political system was immutable or changed over time. In other words, the presence of a somewhat irrelevant legislature incapable of either imposing checks or participating in the policy-making processes may well have been a feature of the political regime, although not necessarily a permanent one. If and how Congress was able to exercise its control and legislative powers at any point in time is a matter of concern in many of the chapters of this book.

The remainder of this section defines the scope of the book with more precision, presents a scheme of chapter contents, and evaluates some conceptual and methodological concerns.

1.2.1. A working definition of privatization

Privatization has received various academic definitions and interpretations. They vary between the two extremes of privatization as a single policy, concerning the sale of a state-owned asset to a private sector enterprise; and privatization as a wide range of policies, designed to limit the state's scope and functions, as well as to reduce the weight of the public sector in the economy. A wide definition of privatization would include operations that do not necessarily imply the whole or partial change of ownership. For instance, a privatization movement would include the introduction of private sector personnel and notions of efficiency and of management techniques into the public sector; private sector competition with the public sector by a policy of liberalization and deregulation; contracting out public services to private agents; selling land and publicly-owned housing stock;[42] and, finally, a number of political and social reforms associated with decentralization, in other words, with the devolution of political and administrative authority to elected local officials.[43]

This study acknowledges that aspects embraced in a wide definition of privatization have been carried out in Argentina as much as privatization in its limited definition has been taking place at provincial and local levels of government. Nevertheless, it focuses on the policy of selling and conceding public assets in which the institutions of the central government engaged between the late 1980s and the 1990s. It adopts, then, a quite restrictive definition of privatization. The fact is that this book is based on a working definition of privatization. This does not mean that what is left beyond the boundaries established here is not considered privatization, but rather it implies that it is outside the scope of this study. In any case, the cases included in this analysis are those of most importance in terms of their size and weight in the public sector. They are those state entities that, regardless of their different institutional status, had been created by law and, thus, required the passage of special legislation in order to be sold. Congressional ratification turned out to be an unavoidable step in the process of property change.[44] All the major privatization cases fall under this rule.

Thus, this book begins by considering privatization as a governmental legislative programme, and concentrates on the legislative proposals stipulating the total or partial sale or concession of the Argentine state-owned companies. In other words, this book considers a number of privatization initiatives put forward by the Executive (which sought their approval for different reasons that will later be clarified), the adoption of which also involved legislative innovation.[45] Therefore, these initiatives constitute an interesting common ground where president–Congress interactions can be observed.

1.2.2. Analytical concerns

This study takes as units of analysis the privatization bills submitted by the Executive – or induced by the Executive via members of its party – to

Congress during Alfonsín's administration and the two administrations of Menem. It also considers the unilateral resources of the Executive with similar legal status, that is, necessity and urgency decrees. There is an important temporal dimension to this approach since the initiatives did not all occur at a definite point in time, but rather extended throughout the presidential periods under study. Indeed, there is an imbalance towards the beginning of Carlos Menem's first administration (when an important body of legislation was approved), which reveals the importance that the policy acquired during this period. The following pages study the privatization initiatives from two perspectives. On the one hand, the units of analysis are individually explored. This means that there are sections dedicated to telling the story of a bill going through the legislative process. On the other hand, conclusions from the individual cases are considered in the general context of the administration driving the process. The focus here is the government in office, and the set of resources and constraints it is dealing with while managing the policy. Let us explore these two approaches in more detail.

Concerning the first one, it should be pointed out that every single story of a privatization proposal has its own particular characteristics and this is the reason why it is interesting to trace the individual cases. The way in which the Executive approaches and presents the issue, as well as the way in which Congress, political parties and congressmen individually position themselves around it mark the peculiarities of the process. However, the range of actions that these institutions and people can adopt regarding a particular case can somehow be anticipated by taking into account the powers granted to them by the Constitution.[46] In this sense, with respect to the presidential power, the Argentine constitution of 1853 secured its participation in the legislative process with the resources of legislative initiative and veto. Political practices, situations of extreme necessity and, finally, the constitutional reform of 1994, gave them further important legislative resources: delegation of power, necessity and urgency decrees and partial-veto power. Regarding Congress, the Constitution established its right to supervise the rule-implementation aspect of governmental activity (investigation committees, interpellations), and guaranteed its full involvement in the rule-making process of government. In relation to this second role, congressional resources can be classified under headings.[47] The first one is the power of *initiation*, which could be defined as the possibility Congress has to introduce legislation of its own, and, therefore, topics for discussion that do not have to be related to those demanded by the Executive. The converse of this is the second *preventive* power, by means of which Congress prevents the Executive from presenting bills by making it obvious that they will not be passed, or that their passage will demand significant energy. The third role of Congress is as a *reaction* to the initiative of the Executive, by approving, rejecting, amending or delaying governmental rules. This distinction proves to be very useful for exploring the path followed by the privatization bills in Congress. Indeed, as pointed out before, privatization did not give Congress great powers of initiation, since this policy was an initiative from the Executive.[48] Congress was, however, entitled to use its preventive and reactive powers. Preventive powers are difficult to reveal since they refer to everything which does not reach the chambers because the Executive is prevented from introducing it, but they are captured in these pages through press information, statements by legislators, and proposals that were submitted, but later withdrawn. Most of this work, though, is concerned with the third power of Congress, in other words, with what Congress was disposed to do with the privatization initiatives of the Executive. The range of reactive possibilities (approval, rejection, delay, amendment) shows that much can still be expected from Congress-president relations throughout a presidential period.

From the second general perspective, the aim is to explain why presidential initiatives and congressional reactions resulted in a particular outcome. Under this approach, individual legislative processes and outcomes are placed in the broader context of the administration involved in putting the policy forward.[49] As has been explained, 'An analysis of the political background to privatisation reveals the importance of the interplay of constitutional and institutional arrangements with policy aspirations.'[50] Therefore, a far-reaching policy change would suggest that a resolute government worked under propitious political and institutional circumstances or, in other words, that political leadership, institutional resources, and favourable exogenous conditions combined to produce full implementation results. These three conditions should then be carefully analysed.

Firstly, political leadership conditions include both leadership aspiration and leadership skills. The motives and ambitions of the privatizers contain various mixtures of ideological, economic, political and financial objectives that can either motivate or discourage radical policy change. Besides, the adoption of the policy also requires the capacity to find out the appropriate instruments to put it into practice. This is why leadership skills in coalition building, government unification around the policy, and public persuasion should be taken into account as well. Secondly, institutional resources are available to the political leadership when the complex institutional structure in which it has to operate proves to be favourable. The most obvious institutional resource is a favourable distribution of power within the legislative branch: one in which the Executive can count on a secure majority in both houses over the whole period of the administration. Whether this condition is going to be present or not depends, of course, on the electoral results, but also to a great extent on the nature of the party political system, the potential of party coalition building, the character of the relationships between the president and his own party, and the strength and cohesion of parties in opposition. Besides, Congress is the arena in which partisan conflict and cooperation take place, but also where interest group pressures are magnified or muted during the processes of law making. Military, provinces, unions and any other affected organized interests will probably make an attempt to influence the process in their favour. As a consequence, the enactment of a new policy programme demands the reformers' capacity to neutralize veto-players[51] and muster assenting votes at the many decision points involved in the process. Thirdly, favourable exogenous conditions help to create an environment in which institutional processes take place. Comprehensive reform efforts are more likely to occur when the profound economic failure of early reforms creates a sensation of crisis, strengthening broad public support for drastic action and weakening organized opposition. The deterioration of public services at a time when the state is financially unable to maintain decent levels of investment can be the trigger for public support for a privatization programme. Thus, if present, public authorization enhances the legitimacy of the leaders to put reform into practice.

As a consequence of the above, this book does explore the process of formulation and approval of the privatization policy in Argentina, but it does not deal with the subsequent implementation of the policy. I have given pre-eminence to a study extending in time, whilst a study concentrating on policy implementation would have further reduced the case studies and replaced the horizontal temporal dimension by a vertical structural approach in which other institutions, such as the bureaucracy, would come to play a central role as well. In search of an answer for the question of the institutional functioning of the democracy, its quality and prospect, which has already received considerable opinion and analysis but still remains significantly untested, I have opted to concentrate most of my research on the nature of the Executive's relationship with Congress and the political forces and interests represented in it.

1.2.3. *The organization of the book*

Chapter 2 presents the general features of the Argentine presidential system. It begins by describing the main characteristics of the institutional design as established in the Constitution, then it moves on to describe the political parties and the party system to show, finally, how presidentialism has been working in the context of the current party configuration. Social actors are also incorporated into the analysis, and their contact with, and influence on political parties are explored. Finally, an appendix is dedicated to describe the law-making process as it is established in the Constitution and in the congressional statutes in order to facilitate the reading of future chapters.

Chapter 3 deals with the privatization process under Alfonsín's administration. The main characteristics of the Argentine state in the 1980s are also advanced in this chapter. At the same time that this chapter explores how this policy came to be part of the presidential agenda, it also studies the factors that blocked its approval. It attempts to raise the points on which the relative position of Menem later changed, modifying substantially the outcome of the policy. Chapters 4, 5, 6 and 7 are concerned with the Menem Presidency. The first focuses on the critical period of transition from one government to the other, the emergence of structural reforms on the presidential agenda, and the construction of presidential power to pursue the implementation of these reforms. Diverse movements tending to concentrate political power in the Executive (and, within the Executive, in the agencies in charge of the reform decisions) are described as central features of Menem's presidential leadership. Chapter 5 presents the main characteristics of Menem's privatization policy, and follows party reaction in Congress to Menem's privatization bills. Chapter 6 describes several processes of law making and the negotiations taking place in Congress. With the analysis of these processes, the relative positions of both the Presidency and Congress are assessed. Whether the prominence of the former meant the subordination of the latter, and what the consequences of this were for the policy under discussion, are the objects of analysis. Chapter 7 concentrates on the privatization cases during Menem's second presidential period.

Finally, the Conclusion of this book tries to analyse what the outcome of the privatization policy-making process has been in terms of institutional functioning of the democratic regime. This outcome is compared to that reached by other case studies on public policies, and conclusions are drawn on the question of democracy in Argentina.

2
The Argentine Presidential System

Introduction

This chapter outlines the main features of the Argentine presidential system. It is divided into two sections with an appendix. The first section describes the most relevant Argentine institutional traits, those established in the Constitution of 1853 as well as those which developed throughout the twentieth century. It states that the centrality of the Presidency is a distinctive feature of the Argentine political system and is a crucial factor in explaining the way in which policy-making processes have taken place in this country. Therefore, it focuses on the Presidency, its legislative powers, and the historical reasons for the enlargement of its prerogatives *vis-à-vis* the other institutions of government. The effects of constitutional arrangements, political instability, 'movimientism', and state growth on the institutions of government are weighed and assessed. The second section concentrates on the democratic regime inaugurated in 1983. It explores the chief characteristics of the political parties and the party system, and outlines the main features of the presidential regime in the context of this party configuration. It is argued that, despite being constrained by strong historical legacies, this regime exhibits its own novel characteristics, which constitute a dividing landmark. Finally, an appendix containing the main stages of the procedures for law approval has been included, and is intended to facilitate comprehension of the legislative processes described in the following chapters.

2.1. The presidential features of the regime

'Having no counterpart in the democratic pluralist world, Argentina is at the head of the presidential scale: we are in the presence of hyperpresidentialism.'[1] Carlos Nino's words synthesize what has been regarded as one of the main features of Argentine politics, namely, the centrality of the Presidency in the political system. This section describes, first, the institutional powers which both the Constitution and political practice granted to those occupying the presidential role. Emphasis is put on the resources available to presidents to participate in the legislative process. Second, it presents some of the important political developments of the twentieth century which intervened to define the main institutional traits of Argentine politics. As will be seen, the pre-eminence of the Executive has been the product of a number of factors, the incidence of which is assessed in various ways by scholars and specialists. I am inclined to maintain that this pre-eminence has been the result of a complex combination of causes, which came together to stress the exercise of unilateral political power and simultaneously discourage the cooperative practices which were also a possibility within the constitutional framework.

2.1.1. *On presidential powers*

The Argentine Constitution of 1853 was inspired by the Constitution of the United States and, like it, it adopted the principles of a presidential system of government. In effect, the Argentine Constitution displayed both the essential and non-defining characteristics of a pure presidential system.[2] It was based on a separation of power among the three branches of government, the relationship being regulated by a system of mutual checks and balances (the President's veto power – Article 72 of the Constitution; the Senate's consent for official appointments, such as those in the Judiciary – Article 86, subsection 5; the Senate's prerogative of impeachment – Article 51). Separation of power was guaranteed by two essential principles, on the one hand, the 'dual democratic legitimacy' which stipulated that both the president (elected by an electoral college that was elected, in turn, by the people for that sole purpose – Article 81) and an elected bicameral legislature (Articles 37 and 46) enjoyed a separate democratic legitimacy; on the other hand, the 'rigidity of the system', characterized by the fact that both the president (Article 77) and Congress (Articles 42 and 48) were elected for a fixed term, the president's tenure in office being independent of the legislature, and the survival of the legislature independent of the president. Some other non-defining features were also included in the Argentine Constitution: the one-person character of the presidential office (Article 74), automatic succession by the Vice-President (Article 75), no re-election clause (Article 77), fusion of the head of state and the head of government (Article 86, subsection 1), and the freedom to appoint and dismiss members of the cabinet (Article 86, subsection 10).[3]

The horizontal separation of power described above was supplemented by a vertical division of power between the central and provincial governments. Both the Argentine federal system and the presidential regime corresponded to the model provided by the American Constitution. However, some authors have noted that there were some crucial points of difference where the 1853 constitutionalists preferred to distance themselves from the American model in order to incorporate some centralizing elements present in the Chilean Constitution.[4] They argue that Argentine constitutionalists differed from the Americans when it came to defining the presidential role. They followed the intellectual influence of Juan Bautista Alberdi, who wished to strengthen the functions of the executive power. Alberdi's model was the Chilean republic of Portales, where a strong government had become the solution to anarchy and the guarantee of political order. With his preoccupation for territorial order and integrity, Alberdi maintained that a vigorous President, empowered by the Constitution, would have the strength and energy 'to make effective the constitutional order and the peace without which liberty, the institutions, wealth, and progress are impossible'.[5] As a consequence, Argentine presidents were granted resources not available to their American colleagues: the power to declare a state of siege (Article 86, subsection 9), the power of federal intervention (Article 6), and other broad legislative and regulatory powers.

The first two resources were mainly conceived as instruments to respond to threats of sedition in the provinces. The state of siege had the effect of suspending constitutionally guaranteed individual rights in the event of internal disturbance or external attack, and authorized the Executive to arrest or move people from one part of the country to another. State of siege was a decision to be adopted by Congress, but the Executive could also take it unilaterally when Congress was not sitting. Likewise, the ambiguous constitutional clause for federal intervention, which stated that 'The federal government intervenes in the territory of the provinces either to guarantee the republican form of government or to repel external invasions . . . ' allowed the central power to exercise political control over provincial governments. Finally, the 1853 constitutionalists conceived the Presidency as the engine of government. They gave it, first, the power shared with Congress to present legislative initiatives for congressional consideration, which implied that the president was meant to head the process of governing (Article 86, subsection 3). Second, the constitutional provisions on the power of veto allowed the president to participate in the legislative process after congressional approval (Article 72). Furthermore, Argentine presidents did not need to seek legislative confirmation when appointing members of their cabinet or other executive offices; they had broad regulatory powers by means of decree; they combined the positions of head of state, the government, the public administration and the armed forces (Article 86, subsections 1 and 15).[6]

All these presidential prerogatives appear to conclude that the superiority of the Executive in Argentina was enshrined in the Constitution. However, this becomes debatable if one considers strictly the constitutional presidential powers to intervene in the legislative process. In this respect, Shugart and Mainwaring have explained that, in a presidential system, presidents may have a veto and may have decree powers.[7] The veto is a reactive legislative power because it permits the president to defend the *status quo* by reacting to Congress's attempt to alter it. The decree power is, instead, a proactive power because the president can establish a new *status quo* by legislating without the consent of Congress. Since the Argentine Constitution does nor refer to decree powers, the presidential resources would then be 'reactive' and so relatively weak in terms of constitutional powers over legislation.[8]

The fact is that from 1853 to the present, Argentine presidents have used both reactive and proactive powers. They have favoured a loose interpretation on the use of the resources established in the constitutional text and have also added some powers not mentioned in the Constitution. So, when evaluating the presidential powers over legislation, political practices cannot be left aside. It is because of this, that Argentine presidents' powers over legislation have almost unanimously been regarded as broad, and their constitutional legislative authority assessed as 'potentially dominant.'[9] The most important resources incorporated through political practice have been the power of partial veto and the necessity and urgency decrees.

According to the Argentine Constitution of 1853, vetoes could be used to make objections to a bill approved by Congress in whole (full veto) or in part (partial veto). Such a bill would then be returned to the Chamber where it was introduced for reconsideration. If the two Chambers of Congress (with a majority of two-thirds) confirmed their version of the bill, then the veto would be overridden and the bill had to be promulgated by the Executive. Throughout the twentieth century, particular constitutional controversy surrounded the power to veto parts of a bill and promulgate others. Until the 1940s, the partial veto was scarcely used, of them mostly to object to budget bills, and its constitutionality was not generally accepted.[10] From President Perón onwards, presidential practices changed. The use of the partial veto became more frequent and extensive, and was eventually accepted as constitutional by the Supreme Court in 1967. However, the decision of the Court was vague since it only established that the partial veto should not substantially alter the 'unity' (the legislators' original intention) of the bill. Thus, the ambiguity of this decision still permitted the Executive a wide margin of manoeuvre to affect considerably the contents of the bills and so to act in a discretionary manner.[11]

Similarly, the Argentine Constitution did not grant the Executive the power to enact decrees that became law at the moment of signature. In other words, the Constitution did not allow presidents to legislate by means of decree. In effect, the Executive's decree powers involved other functions: regulatory decrees to implement existing legislation and administrative decrees to perform functions within the bureaucracy. Presidents could also have legislative powers delegated by Congress, that is, decree authority circumscribed to the topics and periods previously defined by Congress. Thus, the power to legislate unilaterally was not present in the Constitution, but it became in practice another resource available to Argentine presidents. As a matter of fact, during the twentieth century these decrees were rarely enacted, only under special circumstances of extreme economic or institutional crisis that demanded extraordinary solutions. The president's incursion into the sphere of legislative decisions, without demanding subsequent congressional approval, was a presidential prerogative in effect introduced during the democratic regime inaugurated in 1983. Molinelli has stated that 'before 1983, one could write a book on constitutional law without mentioning the topic and, if it was mentioned, it was only in relation to "political" decisions, exceptional events which, moreover, were generally assessed as being irregular'.[12] By asserting their right to issue 'necessity and urgency decrees' – as they are known in Argentina – Argentine presidents assumed prerogatives of legislation belonging to Congress, those of adopting a new piece of legislation, and of modifying or even repealing prevailing laws. Indeed, Congress could always reject a necessity and urgency decree by passing a law for this purpose, but the Executive still held the power to veto the law.[13]

Having said this, there is probably no doubt that the institutional resources that Argentine presidents have to participate in the legislative process are many and broad. This wide range of presidential resources seems to confirm the thesis of *hyperpresidentialism* as stated above: the president has so many institutional weapons that he can easily dominate the political process. Nevertheless, some authors have preferred to speak about a *limited centralism*, since the centrality of the Presidency still does not cancel out the restraints arising from the separation of power.[14] According to this view, in the system of checks and balances set out in the Constitution, the role of Congress in the legislative process cannot be underestimated. It has the prerogative to initiate, approve, delay, amend and reject the Executive's initiatives, as well as the power to override the Executive's vetoes with a special majority, so that conflicts between president and Congress are always a possibility within the institutional framework. Thus, the dilemma lies in what model is chosen to solve political conflicts: either governing by applying the majority rule – thereby, transforming the Presidency into the exclusive decision-making authority – or by seeking consensus through negotiation, agreement and compromises – and, as a consequence, establishing a formula of cooperation with the other institutions of government.[15] To summarize, it can be argued that we are dealing with an institutional framework which allows for both cooperative and unilateral action. It has been the tortuous history of Argentina in the twentieth century that has led us to forget that the search for consensus is an alternative method of conducting the political process.

2.1.2. Historical developments

Instability has been the dominant feature of contemporary Argentine political history, at least until 1983. Between the democratic elections of 1916 and 1983, the latter inaugurating the current democratic regime, legitimately elected civilian governments held office for three separate periods: the first corresponded to the three consecutive Radical governments (those led by President Hipólito Yrigoyen, 1916–22; President Marcelo T. de Alvear, 1922–28; and again by President Yrigoyen, 1928–30); the second comprised the two administrations of President Juan Domingo Perón (1946–55); and, finally, a third democratic experience took place in the 1970s with Juan Perón again occupying the Presidency (1973–76). All these democratic periods were interrupted by military coups. The military coup of 1930 ended the democratic regime inaugurated in 1916, and became the first in a series (1943, 1955, 1962, 1966 and 1976) that interrupted the constitutional order. At other times, Argentina was governed by unlawfully elected politicians, who presided over regimes that restricted electoral participation through fraud or political proscriptions (1931–43; 1958–62; 1963–66).

Thus, twentieth-century Argentine political history demonstrates not only its inability to solve political crises through constitutional mechanisms but also persistent conflict affecting the political regime and disagreements about the institutional rules regarding the distribution of power between majority and minority sectors. In a political context of disagreement about the fundamental rules for governing the country, a succession of democratic, semi-democratic and authoritarian regimes diminished the stature of institutions like Congress and the Judiciary, and enhanced that of the president. During *de facto* governments, the institutions that imposed control on the executive power were suppressed or restricted, which resulted in the accumulation of prerogatives in the central office of state. The return to short periods of restricted democracy was insufficient to recover the powers of the other institutions of government, or to impose a deliberative and consultative method of making decisions. Similarly, the absence of parliamentary representation of some of the political forces (particularly Peronism) did not favour the institutional channelling of conflicts.

Indeed, it was the non-democratic regimes that exhibited the most extreme centralizing tendencies. However, these tendencies were not interrupted during the constitutional interregnums. As stated before, the authors of the Constitution gave a position of pre-eminence to the Presidency, but also dictated that it had to operate within a system of checks and balances. As in every presidential system of government, both president and legislators enjoyed democratic legitimacy, so it was possible that the majority of the legislature might represent a different political choice from that of the voters supporting the president. When this happened (and the president lacked the institutional resources to govern) the dangers of stalemate surfaced, unless the two institutions were able to establish some kind of political cooperation. The experience of President Hipólito Yrigoyen (1916–22; 1928–30) demonstrates that the latter was not the path chosen in Argentina during those years, but rather that the resolution of conflicts tilted the balance of power towards the Executive.[16] Thus, the first Argentine democratic experience in 1916 already showed that unilateral action by the Executive was the preferred solution to problems arising from the implicit paradoxes of the Constitution.

Yrigoyen began his administration with an unfavourable distribution of power in the Senate, which put the first democratic experience in Argentina in a situation of institutional conflict. The president's approach to the conflict involved the denial of both the powers of Congress and the rights of the conservative opposition both inside and outside his party, by using federal interventions as instruments for the control of opposition and for the concentration of power. Interventions were used to eject the conservative opposition from their provincial offices in order to neutralize their influence in the Senate and, as a consequence, on governmental policies.[17] The result was a reduction in political opportunity for adversarial forces, confining them to the margins of the system. As sectors of conservatism found that they had little chance of winning by playing the democratic game, they were ready to actively participate in the coup of 1930.

The preference exhibited by President Yrigoyen for the unilateral resources of the Constitution is an example of how, throughout the twentieth century, constitutional rule lived alongside hegemonic political tendencies. As has been maintained elsewhere, the strengthening of presidential authority at the expense of the opposition was not only a direct consequence of the unfavourable institutional distribution of political power, but also the result of Yrigoyen's conception of the origins of popular sovereignty.[18] He was convinced that the executive power embodied the will of the people and, therefore, that the other institutions (those only contributing to the technical tasks of government) should not present obstacles to its centralization. A couple of decades later, Peronism would maintain a similar interpretation, but the centralizing tendencies would strengthen considerably. Peronism attained the Presidency after its electoral triumph in February 1946. In contrast to the Yrigoyen years, this party came to power backed by a majority which was consolidated in successive elections. Despite this, the Peronist government began to promote institutional reforms that emphasized the predominant character acquired by the popular vote, thus lowering the opposition's opportunities to gain access to representative offices and, consequently, its capacity to translate its electoral force into political decisions.[19] The extension of voting rights to women (part of the electorate mainly inclined to support Peronism), the statutory reform of the political parties (imposing restrictions on the formation of coalitions), the constitutional reform of 1949 (which, among several provisions strengthening the president's role, allowed his re-election), and the electoral reform of 1951 (which redrew the existing electoral districts), demonstrated that the party of government was capable of increasing its already strong electoral support by institutional changes that damaged the opposition as well as the governmental institutions other than the Presidency.[20] Once more, the practices of the party in power drove the opposition to the margins of the political regime.

Hence, the combination of political instability, periodic suppression of legislative activity and hegemonic projects was a configuration of power in which the prerogatives of government were concentrated in the Presidency. Congress was the weakest institution, in its functions of legislating and controlling the Executive's activities. Other parallel developments contributed to further strengthening the position of the Presidency in the political system. The following subsections are dedicated to comment on problems related to political representation and the development of the state.

2.1.2.1. Parties and groups: If political parties are the institutions in charge of organising, channelling, and representing the interests of the various classes and actors in a democratic regime, Argentine political parties have performed these functions only marginally. In many senses, they have failed to act as mediating channels between society and government. In fact, Argentine parties have borne little resemblance to real political parties. Peronism and Radicalism – the major Argentine political forces – have each revealed 'movimientist tendencies'[21] (although exhibiting also important differences between them), and remained considerably under-institutionalized.

On the one hand, parties view themselves as 'parts' of a 'polity conceived of as a pluralist whole',[22] in which opposition is regarded as permanent and legitimate. Movements, instead, seek a form of national unity for which opposite forces must be defeated. This friend–enemy conception of political relations necessarily leads to conflict, and leaves little room for negotiation and compromise. One of the consequences of this conception is the tendency to increase hegemony while in power. As has been said before, both Peronism and Radicalism displayed such a tendency, by reducing space for: the exercise of political opposition, the systematic competition of parties and the search for some basis for political consensus. Another consequence is that those excluded from power did not find a vehicle to express their interests. In particular, the popular anti-elite character of the Argentine movements did not attract the support of conservative economic interests (such as those of large landowners), who also did not manage to forge ties with a conservative party capable of winning lawful elections. So, they often sought to influence political decisions through social organizations (for instance, the powerful *Sociedad Rural Argentina*), or resorted to military support in order to end their exclusion from power. Therefore, Argentine parties did not enjoy a monopoly in expressing, organizing and channelling social interests and demands.

On the other hand, Argentine parties were born with a catch-all-party format, so that leadership was exalted from the very beginning of their existence. Thus, parties in Argentina have always given their leaders great flexibility when devising programmes and procedures. Within this format, the party organization was conceived as an electoral machine, and its functions confined to the recruitment of political personnel and the organization of elections. If the party managed to get in power, then it was ill-prepared to play a role in the formulation of policy, and became dependent on the presidential leadership of the policy-making process. If it is further taken into consideration that elections were often irregular, then parties also underplayed this basic function. Therefore, the two main parties remained considerably under-institutionalized, although there were important differences between them. In effect, under-institutionalization was not so pronounced in the Radical Party as it was in Peronism, because the first had been built on the basis of a decentralized and relatively autonomous structure that managed to impose some checks to the central leadership, and, since early, had established internal elections for the nomination of candidates. Besides, Radicalism's dislike for social organizations and its ethical principles indicating a direct relationship between people and government, contrasted with the concept of political representation maintained by Peronism. The Peronist view included capitalists and workers, and acquired a corporatist profile. Perón and the Peronists always regarded the unions as the 'backbone of the movement', which added to Perón's plebiscitary style of leadership, further weakened party institutionalization: first, Perón and the unions, not the party, were the main political actors of the movement; second, the unions, which also had economic resources of their own, shared with the party the right to organize elections; third, Perón exercised direct influence on the nomination of candidates, so that the party remained too weak to generate a middle level political elite by itself; fourth, restrictions on electoral participation from 1955 to 1972 did not suppress the Peronist sentiment, but contributed to diminishing the role of the party.

Under Peronism, movimientism developed to become populism. Perón sought to incorporate the growing labour urban and popular sectors in political life, by linking them to a cross-class coalition of support, in which the popular sectors were crucial but which also included the industrial sectors that provided the jobs and goods demanded by the working classes. Within this social framework, the organization called the Justicialist Party built up two distinctive structures to gain electoral support: the urban labour organizations, which provided the corporatist and mobilization machinery, and provincial party organizations, clientelistic and conservative but necessary to mobilize votes outside the working class, especially in the less developed regions of the country.[23] Perón controlled his broad coalition with an authoritarian style, but also legitimized his leadership by using the resources of the state to respond to heterogeneous demands. Thus, he promoted a model of development based on the expansion of the state both as an employer and a regulator of the socioeconomic life.

2.1.2.2. The state: By the late 1940s and early 1950s, a development model based on protectionism and state intervention in the economy was well established and constituted the dominant pattern in Argentina.[24] The establishment of this model had begun in response to both external and internal triggers. In effect, with the adverse world shocks of first, the Great Depression of 1929–30, and then the outbreak of World War II, Argentina and other Latin American countries, had to resort to protectionist and inward-looking policies. Similarly, the political response to increased participation (resulting from the incorporation of previously excluded social actors) was the enlargement of the functions of the state.

Throughout most of the century, the state occupied a central position in the economy of the country by gradually taking on new roles. In so doing, it took charge of at least three kinds of societal demands.[25] First, the state provided (or was supposed to provide) the goods indispensable for the development of societal life: defence, security, justice and administration, which can be considered as the minimal commitment of the state to society and, therefore, as the earliest developed functions of the state. Second, especially from the 1940s onwards, the state became responsible for capital accumulation, the level of employment and the level of economic activity. This role encouraged the formation of mixed economies dependent on public sector leadership. On the one hand, the state leadership was clearly seen in its ownership of strategic economic sectors; on the other, in a number of price subsidies, and tax and financial incentives for private companies. Also, a welfare state was created to assist marginal sectors of society as well as the middle classes by providing access to social services and housing.

The institutional dimension of this state-centred development model was an increase in the size of the executive branch and its bureaucratic apparatus. Consequently, the regulatory and administrative powers of the president were enlarged as well. Cavarozzi has pointed out that the political formula accompanying the economic developments of the twentieth century was as follows: 'politics . . . was primarily organised around the actions of the state. In this respect, the role played by the Presidency and its executive agencies was quite exclusionary . . . political action was channelled and organised around the Executive to filter and eliminate strong democratising elements.'[26] Moreover, a sizeable executive branch provided innumerable opportunities for lobby activities that could be exercised in both democratic and non-democratic periods, so further undermining the legitimacy of Congress to express societal interests and demands.

Sooner or later, though, the implicit paradoxes of the state-centred development model would become apparent. In effect, this large state had to resort to various methods in order to finance its multiple activities. Besides the implementation of the classical tax system (including direct and indirect taxes, as well as taxes on specific consumer goods), and the capture of the domestic savings of middle and high income sectors, the inward model of development provided the state with the resources produced by external trade. For several decades, this system of fiscal and financial resources seemed to operate smoothly, although not always covering the full range of state needs. On those occasions, inflation and the foreign debt were the state's complementary methods of obtaining money. The gradual increase in the inflation rate since the end of the 1940s has, thus, been seen as an indicative of the increasing financial as well as political difficulties of the state. Inflation revealed the pressures on the state accounts. Simultaneously, it disclosed the weakness of the political consensus achieved during both democratic and authoritarian regimes, since the state was forced to resort to inflation in order to blur the expropriatory and redistributive effects of public policies.[27] This resulted in a weak state, large in size, but in practice unable to mediate among the disparate claims of interest groups, the military, political parties and leaders. This also often resulted in formally strong Presidents, who could use their unilateral resources to deliver policy decisions, but simultaneously revealing their incapacity to produce these kinds of decisions through political consensus.

The minimal availability of financial resources probably explains the fact that, despite increasing political and economic difficulties, the model of growth consolidated after World War II did not change until the 1980s. Initially, it was Peronism that embodied the country's commitment to state-led economic development. As has already been pointed out, beginning with the incorporation of the labour and popular sectors into political life, Peronism built a cross-class coalition for a state-guided import-substitution model of capitalist development. The social groups whose organization was vital for the implementation of the model, labour groups and inward-looking entrepreneurs, were its most important constituents. However, the removal of the Peronists from power in the 1950s did not alter the general commitment to the model. During the period of Peronist proscription, civilian governments maintained the policies of state strengthening, by integrating or negotiating with those organizations linked to that movement. Although the process of import substitution became less dynamic during the 1960s, and although it was generally recognized that there were serious obstacles to resuming growth, only isolated attempts were made to reduce state intervention and to introduce a greater reliance on market forces. The stabilization programmes under military regimes, devised by Adalbert Krieger Vasena in 1967 and by José Martínez de Hoz in the late 1970s, were feeble efforts which left the established model basically unquestioned. Furthermore, the role of the state in economic affairs expanded during the 1970s. The sector of state-owned enterprises grew very fast, controls and regulations became generalized, and fiscal assistance to private capital commonplace, in the context of a favourable international lending situation. Once this favourable situation changed at the beginning of the 1980s, it became more apparent that although the state had grown considerably it had not managed to become more powerful. Rather, it could be seen that this state was gradually losing the capacity to control its immense apparatus as well as the multiple activities there unfolded.

2.2. The 1983 democratic political regime

A historical legacy of political instability, hegemonic projects, and institutional weakness did not prevent the political regime inaugurated in 1983 from exhibiting important new elements. The most obvious of these elements were: consensus on the rule of the 1853 Constitution, full political participation, inter-party competition and political alternation in power. In effect, the new regime was based on the old Constitution of 1853, which after a long period of disagreements about the fundamental rules for leading the country, was generally accepted as the basic norm for the distribution of power between majority and minority forces. Thus, the conservative attitude of resorting to the nineteenth-century Constitution worked together with the new feature of consensus on its functioning.

Likewise, other changes operated in the political context of the regime. As has been explained above, apart from the short democratic interregnums, Argentine twentieth-century political history was characterized by the absence of a system of total political participation. If political activity was not totally suppressed, candidates and political parties would normally be subjected either to proscriptions or to restrictions on their political activities. From 1983 onwards, a high level of participation and party competition took place, under the guarantees provided by prevailing laws.[28] First, the Electoral Law regulating national deputy elections established that seats would be allocated using a formula of proportional representation (the D'Hont system) with a low barrier of 3 per cent. This electoral formula facilitated the participation of a large number of parties and alliances.[29] Second, the Political Parties Law gave them the monopoly of representation without exerting controls or imposing restrictions on their organization and programmes. Finally, the ruling constitutional federal system multiplied the areas in which competition could be carried out. The consolidation of parties with federal, provincial and local representation was encouraged by this system.

Within the normative framework established by the Constitution and the above-mentioned laws, systematic party competition put an end to an era of incumbent party hegemonies (Radicalism after 1916, Peronism after 1946), and the alternation of parties in power marked the beginning of a time when this could be achieved without resorting to military intervention. The first step in this direction came with the victory of the Radical candidate, Raúl Alfonsín, in the presidential elections of 1983. This triumph returned Radicalism to its ruling party status, which had lastly been enjoyed under the leadership of Illia in the 1960s, although under the conditions of Peronist proscription. In so doing, it put an end to forty years of Peronist predominance in the Argentine political scene after demonstrating that, for the first time in history, Peronism could be defeated in an electoral contest. It was a hard blow for the Peronist quest for hegemony, and pushed the party into a process of profound internal reorganization. Conversely, as could be foreseen, Alfonsín's victory was interpreted as a new and enduring political phenomenon by his fellow party members. Many of them, who thought that the outcome of a single election would be a permanent element of the new democracy, began to talk of Alfonsinism, and encouraged the vision of a 'third historical movement'.[30] Against their expectations, future electoral results demonstrated that the persistence of popular loyalty to a single leader had become just another chapter in history. First, congressional elections, and then presidential ones not only showed that Peronism was capable of recovering from defeat, but also that hegemonic ambitions were not compatible with democracy's unpredictable electoral arena. These lessons (taught by an increasingly independent electorate) had also to be learnt by the Peronist Party which came to power in 1989. Its hegemonic ambitions led it to seek a constitutional reform that would allow Menem's re-election for a second term. This was successful, and, as a consequence of the 1995 electoral results, Menem became the first Argentine president to be re-elected. However, at times when the political scene seemed to be delineated by the old traditional elements of hegemonism, the 1997 elections for congressional renewal (and then the presidential elections of 1999 that gave the presidential prize to the candidate of the Alliance, the Radical Fernando De la Rúa) reminded the ruling Peronist party of the contingent nature of its support.

2.2.1. Parties and party system

As explained above, in 1983 the democratic regime began to function on the basis of an accepted set of rules and a system of party competition. This section concentrates on the electoral results and the distribution of seats in Congress between 1983 and 1999. Table 2.1 shows the results of presidential elections. It is noticeable that, whilst the Peronist Party managed to retain the support of 38 per cent of the electorate throughout those years, the Radical Party experienced a dramatic fall in terms of votes. In the 1995 election, the Radical Party was relegated to third place (the worst election result in the history of the party) by the remarkable electoral performance of a new electoral alliance called *Frepaso*, the strength of which seemed to come especially from opposition voters, who disliked the way the Radical Party was playing its role.[31] Thus, the weakness of Radicalism in the early 1990s and, then, the

Table 2.1 Presidential elections results (1983–95)

Political party	*1983*	*1989*	*1995*	*1999*
Justicialist Party (*PJ*)	40.1	47.5	45.0	38.1
Radical Civic Union (*UCR*)	51.7	32.4	16.8	—
Alliance (*UCR – Frepaso*)	—	—	—	48.5
Total	**91.8%**	**79.9%**	**61.8%**	**86.6%**
Republican Action	—	—	—	10.1
Frepaso	—	—	28.5	—
Centrist Alliance (includes *UCD*)	—	6.9	2.6 (*UCD*)	—
Independent Federal Confederation	—	4.6	—	—
Other parties	8.2	8.6	7.1	3.3
Total other parties	**8.2%**	**20.1%**	**38.2%**	**13.4%**
Positive votes	97.0	98.0	95.6	96.0
Blank ballots	3.0	2.0	4.3	4.0
Total Voters	85.61%	85.34%	83.34%	80.54%

Source: The Table has been prepared on the basis of data provided by the Direction of Parliamentary Information belonging to the Chamber of Deputies.

fragmentation of the opposition front encouraged, for some time, a pessimistic view about the consolidation of a predominant party system in Argentina. It was only towards the end of the 1990s that this view proved to be groundless. In 1997, the formation of the *Alianza por el Trabajo, la Educación y la Justicia* (the Alliance), between old Radicalism and new Frepaso, and its immediate electoral success, set limits to the expansion of Peronism. The formation of two electoral poles again made possible the alternation of parties in power.

Until the formation of Frepaso, no third party had managed to play a substantive role at presidential elections. During the first ten years of democracy, the probability that undecided Radical and Peronist voters would switch to the other major party rather than to any minor one, was very high, so that some authors pointed out that Argentina had moved toward bipolarism.[32] Others, instead, indicated that the combined share of votes for Peronism and Radicalism had actually dropped in that period. Argentina was therefore a system of 'moderate pluralism' in which two major parties battled over a common electorate, but also faced competition from smaller parties.[33] However, before Frepaso appeared, the role of these third parties seemed to be confined to the regional level,[34] and, as a consequence, they also had a role to play in the National Congress. Tables 2.2 and 2.3 give information on the distribution of seats in the two congressional Chambers.

These Tables demonstrate that, in the past decades, both the Chamber of Deputies and the Senate have been dominated by the major Argentine political parties, Radicalism and Peronism. Until 1995, these two parties together held more than 80 per cent of the seats in the two Chambers. The remaining seats corresponded to a large number of very small parties, most of which were geographically circumscribed to one particular district. (This situation changed in 1995 with Frepaso forming a bloc of 22 deputies.) As a consequence of this distribution of the institutional power, both President Alfonsín and President Menem could count on an important base of legislative support. In the Chamber of Deputies, the two presidents were always supported by a plurality of seats. This plurality even became an absolute majority during Alfonsín's first four years in office, until he lost it as a result of the partial renewal of the Chamber in 1987. Menem was very close to an absolute majority during his first presidential term, and he finally obtained it during the first two years of his second Presidency, but lost it again with the partial renewal of the Chamber in 1997. In the Senate, on the other hand, the Peronists always had a majority, so that the situation there greatly favoured President Menem but was quite restrictive for President Alfonsín.

Table 2.2 Composition of the Chamber of Deputies (1983–99)

Political	*1983–85*		*1985–87*		*1987–89*		*1989–91*		*1991–93*		*1993–95*		*1995–97*		*1995–97*	
party	*Seats*	%	*Seats*	%	*Seats*	%	*Seats*	%	*Seats*	%	*Seats*	%	*Seats*	%	*Seats*	%
PJ	111	**43.7**	101	**39.7**	96	**37.8**	120	**47.2**	117	**45.5**	128	**49.8**	131	**51.0**	119	**46.3**
UCR	129	**50.8**	129	**50.8**	114	**44.9**	90	**35.4**	84	**32.7**	83	**32.3**	68	**26.4**	66	**25.7**
Frepaso	—	—	—	—	—	—	—	—	—	—	—	—	22	**8.6**	38	**14.8**
UceDé	2	**0.8**	3	**1.2**	7	**2.7**	11	**4.3**	10	**3.9**	4	**1.5**	2	**0.8**	—	—
PI	3	**1.2**	6	**2.4**	5	**2.0**	2	**0.9**	2	**0.8**	1	**0.4**	1	**0.4**	—	—
Others	9	**3.5**	15	**5.9**	32	**12.6**	31	**12.2**	44	**17.1**	41	**16.0**	33	**12.8**	34	**13.2**
Total	254	**100**	254	**100**	254	**100**	254	**100**	257	**100**	257	**100**	257	**100**	257	**100**

Source: The Table has been prepared on the basis of data from Cámara de Diputados. Su Composición y Comisiones. Note that the total number of deputies increases from 254 to 257 due to the establishment of Tierra del Fuego as a new province.

Table 2.3 Composition of the Senate (1983–98)

Political party	*1983–86*		*1986–89*		*1989–92*		*1992–95*		*1995–98*	
	Seats	%	*Seats*	%	*Seats*	%	*Seats*	%	*Seats*	%
PJ	21	45.7	21	45.7	26	56.5	30	62.5	37	57.8
UCR	18	39.1	18	39.1	14	30.4	11	22.9	15	23.4
Provincial parties	7	15.2	7	15.2	6	13.1	7	14.6	10	15.6
Frepaso	—	—	—	—	—	—	—	—	2	3.2
Total	46	100	46	100	46	100	48	100	64	100

Note: The total of senators increases from 46 to 48 due to the establishment of Tierra del Fuego as a new province. The period 1995–98 includes new senators in accordance with the constitutional reform of 1994.

In this context of two-party dominance, which has always offered incumbent governments a plurality of seats, the role of the small parties still could not be underestimated. Since the absolute majority (the *quorum*, 50 per cent plus one member of the chamber), is the minimal number of legislators required both to begin the treatment of a bill and to vote it through at the end of the debates, ruling parties often needed to seek some form of support from the opposition parties. In this situation – that is, when the president failed to obtain an absolute majority of seats, or failed to draw enough support from his legislative blocs, or to reach an agreement with the major opposition party – third parties gained importance as potential allies. In the Senate, it was the provincial parties which held the balance between Peronism and Radicalism. With their small delegations of two senators each, the Liberal Autonomist Party (from Corrientes province) the Bloquista Party (from San Juan province), and the Neuquén Popular Party, became important potential allies when voting. In the lower house, provincial parties were also a major component of the 'other party' category, but they shared it with many others. The latter had normally national aspirations yet, in practice, they managed to gain support only in certain geographic areas. One of those was the UCeDé (Democratic Centre Union). It was founded in 1982 by Alvaro Alsogaray, and attempted to capture the support of the conservatives who had traditionally turned to the Armed Forces. By supporting liberalism and a free-market economic system, it became one of the most ideologically based parties. This party, whose constituency was concentrated in the metropolitan areas, was one of the fastest growing during the period 1983 to 1989 (see Tables 2.1 and 2.2). Some small right-orientated parties also gained some measure of popular support by the late 1980s, with an anti-party, nationalist and populist platform. The first of those was the Republican Force in Tucumán, headed by retired General Antonio Bussi, who had been governor during the military regime. Another interesting phenomenon was that of the Movement of Dignity and Independence (MODIN), created by the former *carapintada* leader Aldo Rico.[35] These parties together with the provincial forces mentioned above formed a centre-right axis with substantial coalition potential in the Chamber of Deputies.

Indeed, there was also room for the centre-left and the left in the Chamber. The Christian Democratic Party (PDC) was part of the centre-left. It never became a cross-class party as in other Latin American or European countries. It advocated strong state intervention, tight regulation of the private sector, and redistribution policies. Sharing the social content of the Peronist doctrine, and unable to obtain enough popular support on its own, PDC joined Peronism in an electoral alliance in 1983. Menem's ideological changes then drove it from the alliance at the beginning of the 1990s. A similar case was that of Alende's PI (Intransigent Party). It gave a good performance on its own at the beginning of the 1980s, then allied with Peronism at the 1989 elections, but left it after Menem's turnaround. The socialist parties were divided into several groups of which the Socialist Unity and the Unified Socialist Party were the main ones. They formed a moderate sector active in Buenos Aires and the central-eastern provinces, and occasionally made electoral alliances with Radicalism. Therefore, the centre-left never exhibited a strong popular appeal in Argentina. It was only with the Frepaso phenomenon in the 1990s that it overcame its historical limitations and became a dynamic and growing force. Finally, with the labour movement totally Peronist, communist parties never had a mass appeal. Indeed, rather than from the workers, communist support came from intellectuals and university students concentrated in metropolitan areas. Moreover, Argentine communism was always deeply divided, but it did manage to obtain some congressional representation through a number of alliances (such as Alianza Izquierda Unida in 1989).

In short, the high number of 'other parties' reflects ideological diversity, as well as other substantial differences (national or provincial aspirations, coalition attitude to the major parties, cultural values, historical trajectories, etc.). It is probably this diversity of interest that kept them small in size and separate.

2.2.2. *Parties and Congress*

The persistence of democratic rule, full political participation and inter-party competition sooner or later had to bear fruit, that is, to give parties and Congress the place they had not managed to have historically. Nevertheless, as is well known, new third-wave democracies had to face difficult times, and Argentina was no exception to this trend. Both the Radical Party and the Peronist Party were faced first with the profound crisis taking place at the end of the 1980s (which was at the same time a political, economic and state crisis), and then with the great and rapid process of structural changes undertaken by Menem's government. Within the framework posed by these critical conditions, institutional developments during the past few years were often contradictory, showing both advances and reversals, and provoking a debate about their implications for the consolidation of the democratic regime. Although these problems are a great matter of concern in this book, in this section I would like to discuss some of them.

With respect to the political parties, the return to democracy had brought a climate of euphoria and mobilization that encouraged political action, and motivated people to join a party, and actively participate in party and general elections. Towards the end of the 1980s, the situation had changed, and a climate of disillusionment accompanied the parties' incapacity to fulfil the great expectations that the democratic regime had raised during the transition years. People–party relationships became increasingly characterized by electoral independence and distrust of parties and politicians. Thus, the political parties' capacity for mediation between the state and public opinion, as much as their capacity to deliver decisions when in government, was challenged, and parties began to suffer from 'a crisis of representation'.[36] The weakness of party structures, the personalization and informalization of politics, were the elements of this crisis which could be observed in the emergence of successful leaders without party, the lost of popular appeal from traditional parties, and the importance acquired by other alternative actors, such as the media, technocrats and business sectors.

If this was the prevailing climate at the end of the 1980s, some years later there were signs that the historical parties had managed to survive the crisis: they were still monopolizing the selection of candidates for public posts, they exerted control on the public administration, and they negotiated the public policies.[37] Their success involved, indeed, a process of internal re-organization and institutional strengthening which was in many ways induced by the framework of democratic stability and institutional competition. On the one hand, the party in government had to learn to assume the responsibility of its actions before the electorate. On the other, the development of opposition parties indicated that the expansion of Peronism had limits. On the opposition front, the recovery of Radicalism from its electoral defeat in 1989 was slow and painful. Meanwhile, it was a new centre-left coalition which became the most attractive shelter for those discontented with Peronist policies. Frepaso (the name it adopted before the 1995 presidential elections) grew rapidly from 1991 onwards as a result of the convergence of different sectors: dissident groups from the two major political parties, the support of other minor groups (Unidad Socialista, Democracia Cristiana, Partido Intransigente, sectors from the Communist Party), and a wide range of people who had previously been active in trade unions and human rights movements.[38] The front expanded considerably with the process of constitutional reform in 1994 and, in the 1995 presidential elections, it almost achieved 30 per cent of the vote. Its agreement with Radicalism in 1997 consolidated the opposition alternative to Peronism.

Like the political parties, Congress began the democratic period by playing a greater role compared to that which it had previously practised throughout the century. As, according to the prevailing constitutional framework, most public policies had to be approved by law, Congress obtained an unusual level of participation in the process of formulating public policies. However, as was also the case with the parties, the role to be played by Congress would not be entirely free from difficulty. This institution's position *vis-à-vis* the Presidency was a major cause of concern. In effect, within the context of democratic uncertainty, lack of absolute majorities, and the ever present possibility of alternation of the parties in power, the ruling Constitution once more demonstrated its implicit paradoxes. At the very beginning of the regime, the plebiscitary character of President Alfonsín's election (with more than 50 per cent of the votes) did not match the amount of institutional resources that he had obtained at the same time, and opened the possibility of deadlock or conflict between president and Congress. In other words, the type of situation that at other times in Argentine history had tended to provoke a concentration of power in the Presidency was repeated.

In this sense, the regime inaugurated in 1983 showed substantial differences to, but also, some similarities with previous situations in Argentina's history. The most important innovations were the cooperative attitude of the parties and their commitment to the democratic regime. It has been maintained that the major parties' commitment to institutional continuity was demonstrated by their determination to prevent governmental paralysis.[39] In the Alfonsín years, they established a pattern of cooperation by means of which 60 per cent of government initiatives were approved by consensus. Their discussions took place in the congressional arena, where agreements were achieved. Simultaneously, a number of initiatives that were central to the government's policy interests remained within the area of political conflict and received no congressional approval. These cases brought about a solution that was in accordance with the historical tendency of concentrated power. Either when consensus did not work or when it could be foreseen that it would not, the government resorted to emergency decrees, the unilateral initiative from the Executive used to avoid congressional obstruction. Thus, the historical tendency favouring executive predominance reappeared in the 1980s, although, this time the goal was not, as in the past, to exclude the opposition from the political system. Instead, the Executive's unilateral actions emerged as a response to the multiple vetoes posed by Congress. They coexisted with a basic institutional game that showed the commitment of the political forces to the democratic regime as well as the incipient role of Congress as an arena of policy discussion and formulation. Under Menem, a similar situation of party cooperation took place under a more favourable distribution of power. At the same time, though, centralizing tendencies increased considerably. This is explored further in Chapter 4.

2.2.3. 1994 constitutional reform

Encouraged by previous electoral successes (the 1989 presidential elections, and the 1991 and 1993 congressional elections) and favourable opinion polls, Menem was determined to seek constitutional reform in order to get himself re-elected. However, to initiate the process of reform, he needed to obtain the support of two-thirds of the two Chambers of Congress, and this was practically impossible without the consent of the Radical Party. Thus, Menem would resort to other means to force a positive vote from the legislators, such as calling a plebiscite and pressing legislators to respect the decision of the people. These were difficult times for the Radicals. Alfonsín saw the dangers posed by Menem's hegemonic pretensions to democracy and to his party, which was close to breaking up because of this issue.

In the middle of this situation, Alfonsín and Menem signed the so called *Pacto de Olivos* (Olivos Pact). It included the basic points of agreement on the contents of reform: the president obtained the Radicals' consent for his possible re-election for a second four-year term, and the Radicals, guarantees for the inclusion of a number of modifications in the constitutional text, as well as Menem's accord for the removal of some members of the Supreme Court and their replacement by agreed appointees. Although Alfonsín's initiative was immediately backed by his party (but not unanimously), and although the proposal of constitutional reform included many interesting issues other than re-election, the perception of the public opinion was that Radicalism had facilitated Menem's re-electoral ambitions. Thus, the pact turned out to be damaging for Radicalism's electoral bases, whilst it widened the way for other forces to appear as channels for the expression of opposition demands.[40] In the 1994 elections of constitutionalists, Peronism obtained almost 38 per cent of the votes, Radicalism 20 per cent, and Frente Grande, 12 per cent.

Despite debates on the subject, it could be argued that the Olivos Pact was more than just a turning point in the Argentine democratic regime inaugurated in 1983. It was a crucial event in Argentine constitutional history: for the first time in this century a constitutional reform was not imposed by a single majority party, but was the product of inter-party consensus.[41] For the first time, a constitutional reform managed to enlarge its basis of legitimacy. On this basis, important amendments were made to the 1853 Constitution, many of them aimed at affecting presidential powers. The presidential term in office was reduced from six to four years, and re-election was to be permitted. The president continued to be both head of state and head of government, but a new executive office – the Chief of Cabinet – was created to carry out the general administration of the country.[42] The president appoints the chief of cabinet without congressional approval, but he/she can be removed by a congressional vote of censure (requiring absolute majorities in both houses). Moreover, the Constitution explicitly regulates some prerogatives of the Executive: its ability to legislate by decree, to use partial vetoes, and the conditions for legislative delegation. Finally, the reform introduced a ballotage system for the cases where no presidential candidate obtained more than 45 per cent of the votes in the first election, or the difference between the two most favoured candidates was less than 10 per cent.

Concerning the legislative powers of the president, a comparison with the previous constitutional text would indicate that those were increased. Delegation of power, necessity and urgency decrees as well as partial vetoes were not mentioned in the 1853 constitutional text, but were explicitly included in the new draft of the Constitution (Article 76, Article 99 subsection 3, and Article 80, respectively). Therefore, the constitutional reform involved the increase of presidential legislative powers at the *de jure* level. However, some comments should be made at this point. Firstly, as Jones has stated, 'while increasing the *de jure* legislative powers of the President the constitutional reform has in fact decreased the President's *de facto* legislative powers', since the inclusion of presidential extraordinary powers in the text was countered by the parallel arrangement of restrictions on their use.[43] Under the new Constitution, a president cannot issue decrees in the areas of criminal law, taxation, electoral law, or party political law. Both necessity decrees and partial vetoes must be submitted to a bicameral commission within ten days of their promulgation. Similarly, legislative delegation is only allowed within fixed terms, on specific topics, and according to the practice established by Congress. Thus, the constitutional acknowledgement of what was happening in practice was probably a way of restraining abuse, since from then onwards there was a norm deciding what was and was not allowed.[44] Secondly, the transference of legislative powers to the Executive seems to have been the consequence of an implicit political and juridical consensus concerning the legitimacy of this type of emergency measures.[45] In fact, before achieving constitutional status in 1994 (coupled with partial vetoes and partial promulgation of laws) necessity decrees had been used by the two presidents from each of the two major parties. Later on, the Supreme Court's *unanimous* resolution (*Peralta case*) accepting their validity for the first time in Argentine history further supported their legitimacy.[46] Finally, the 1994 constitutional reform, although propelled by the overriding ambitions of a successful political leader, was approved by a wide consensus supporting its final draft, and voting favourably for it. This consensus covered the use and operation of emergency resources, and restrictions to prevent their abuse by the president.

Besides legislating on presidential power, the new constitutional text also affected the legislative and judicial powers. Concerning the first, the senators' term of office was reduced from nine to six years, and a new senator was added to each district to represent the first party of opposition. Two congressional bodies were created to exercise control over the administration: the General Audit of the Nation and the Defender of the People (ombudsman). In terms of judicial reform, the most significant change was the creation of the Council of the Magistracy. This body would be responsible for proposing judicial appointments and for the operation of the courts.

Conclusion

The 1983 democratic regime inherited two important legacies from the past. The first was the old Constitution of 1853, which was the only point of agreement among political forces during the times of transition. As has been explained at the beginning of this chapter, the presidential system that this Constitution enshrined was meant to produce formally strong presidents whose power did not necessarily have to have a corresponding measure of institutional and political resources. Thus, the possibility remained open for the existence of a formally vigorous but politically weak Executive, which, under certain circumstances, could still be capable of governing by ignoring opposition views and avoiding agreements and compromises. The second legacy was a considerable history of unilateral executive action. It has also been explained that the use of unilateral presidential resources potentially available to every incumbent was the preferred method used to solve the complicated political conflicts that took place throughout the century. Therefore, presidents coming to power in the 1980s relied on this background of power centralization.

However, after the re-establishment of democracy in 1983, democratic presidents also faced the challenge of playing the institutional game. They had to learn to deal with variable majorities and shortage of institutional resources, that is, situations of potential conflict which could not always be successfully dealt with by governing unilaterally. For this, the search for consensus through negotiation, agreement, and compromise needed to be seriously considered. Within this framework, the presidents of the 1980s were no less powerful than their predecessors. They did, however, face a greater challenge: they had to show an ability to make the democratic system function. When a change of regime was no longer an option, the ability to bring together institutional, political and social resources became a condition for delivering public policies and, therefore, a challenge for the presidential leadership. Similarly, the effectiveness of political decisions began to depend on whether the decisions in question enjoyed a consensus. Thus, it remains to be seen how presidents performed in practice, and what role was occupied by the other institutions of the state. The following chapters are dedicated to exploring the way the presidents in question approached policy-making processes, especially those connected to the case of privatization. The type of resources that the two presidents, Alfonsín and Menem, were ready to use in order to have their decisions adopted and to overcome institutional obstacles are considered and assessed. The role left to Congress and the political parties sitting in it are also an important concern of these pages. The next chapter begins with Alfonsín's Presidency.

Appendix: the legislative process

This section synthesizes the process that a bill must follow in order to be transformed into a law. To begin with, according to the Argentine Constitution, legislative initiative belongs to both Executive and Congress. Bills emanating from the Executive are promoted by a minister or some ministers. Those from Congress can be introduced by any member of either house.

For a law to be made (or enacted), a bill (or draft statute) must be laid before one of the two houses of Congress. To become law, it then passes through an elaborate procedure of scrutiny in both the Chamber of Deputies and the Senate, at the end of which the two of them must agree on an identical text. When this has been achieved, the executive power has ten working days to exercise its veto. After this term, and if the bill has not been rejected, the Executive promulgates it.

The drafting of government bills begins long before they are laid before one of the houses, either in a deputy's office or inside the confines of a ministry in the executive branch. Once the bill has been submitted the process of legislative scrutiny starts, and it consists of at least two readings, one in every house, and a maximum of five, three of them in the house of origin. But before being read by the plenary session, a bill automatically goes to the committees selected for its treatment. At the committee stage a bill is examined in detail, clause by clause, almost invariably by one or several committees of some twenty congressmen. Committee members are chosen in proportion to the party balance in the house itself. Depending on the type of bill, a standing committee can take anything from a few minutes to months to consider a bill. When two years have passed from its submission, and the bill has not received approval (*dictamen*) in the committees, it expires. If it has received some consideration, its term is extended for another year. Committees can amend bills as they see fit. This is where most of agreements are reached within the governing party and with opposition.

When committees have completed their task, the bill is considered in the plenary assembly where further amendments can be added during voting. Although the committee procedure is the regular one, there are cases in which the bill is taken directly to the plenary session and discussed there. These are normally the cases where there is very little opposition to a subject, or the government feels that it has a safe majority to pass it. Either of the procedures (regular or *on the floor of the house*) give way to the *first reading*. Once a bill has passed its first reading, it automatically proceeds to the other house, where it goes through a broadly similar process. A bill can become a law after the *second reading* if the Chamber in charge of dealing with it does not modify the draft coming from the other. If any amendments have been made, the bill goes back to the original Chamber for consideration at a *third reading*. Thus, amendments are considered in the plenary session of the original Chamber, which can do one of two things: it may agree to them (and the bill then becomes law, and is forwarded to the Executive); or it may disagree outright. If it opts for the latter course, the bill is returned to the other House for its *fourth reading*, which can prevail with the consent of the present two-thirds. If this is the case, the bill is sent again to the original Chamber. This Chamber needs the consent of the present two thirds majority to reject the amendments in a *fifth reading*. This process of creation of a law was amended by the constitutional reform of 1994. First, it added the possibility that each Chamber delegated in its committees the approval of a bill with the consent of the absolute majority of its members (Article 79). Second, it reduced from five to three the number of readings required for the approval of a bill (Article 81).

3
Privatizations in Alfonsín's Agenda

Introduction

The promotion of a privatization policy in Argentina during the 1980s challenged well-established practices and conceptions concerning the traditional function of the Argentine state. Throughout the twentieth century, the state had undertaken various activities and responsibilities. It was supposed to provide not only the necessities for the development of public life (defence, security, justice), but also the accumulation of capital, employment and a high level of economic activity. Thus, the economy became greatly dependent on public sector leadership, which concentrated a high percentage of production and capital in industrial and service enterprises. By owning these enterprises, the state tried to guarantee the development of strategic economic activities, a public presence in the absence of private risk, and the correction of monopolistic inefficiencies. In addition, the entrepreneurial role of the state was a well-established value for the major political parties. They strongly supported the model of growth based on the state's leadership and distributive, industrialist and nationalist policies. Therefore, in the view of the parties, the state ownership of public enterprises, contributed to national growth, guaranteed economic independence in the face of foreign interests, and maintained a sense of social responsibility in the administration of service enterprises.

Against this background, any attempt at transforming the economic model that had prevailed for decades would demand much public authority, political will, and political resources to counterbalance the numerous emerging opposing forces. President Raúl Alfonsín's privatization plans came to be part of the presidential agenda only gradually and in a limited way. Despite the restricted character of Alfonsín's approach to the policy, privatization provoked a huge opposition front, which included, among many other actors, Congress and the political parties. As a result, most of Alfonsín's privatization plans were killed in some of the many arenas of negotiation. This chapter explores how and why the logic of opposition prevailed in the president–Congress relationship. Since congressional participation was unavoidable in the formulation of the privatization policy, the institutional constraints had a direct influence on the destiny of the policy.

The chapter is divided into five parts: the first one provides information about the Argentine state in the 1980s; the second explains how privatization appeared in the presidential agenda and presents the general characteristics of the four privatization bills sent to Congress; the third part concentrates on the history of the processes of law-making, demonstrating the reactions of both Radicals and Peronists in Congress to the Executive's initiatives; the fourth part analyses how social groups and public opinion reacted to the privatization policy; finally, the conclusion tries to make some general comments on president–Congressional relations as revealed by the privatization case-study.

3.1. The Argentine state in the 1980s

As in the rest of Latin America, state regulation of the economy was already noticeable in Argentina in the 1930s, but from the 1940s onwards, a decisive increase in direct public control of the means of production took place, regardless of the ideological orientation of the government in power (see also Chapter 2, subsection 2.1.4). During the 1930s, regulatory monetary policies led to the creation of the Central Bank. In a similar way, the need for regulation of production led to the establishment of a number of demand and supply regulatory organizations, such as *Junta Nacional de Carnes* and *Junta Nacional de Granos*. In the 1940s, public enterprises became the main instrument of investment and accumulation of capital. In the following decades, they continued to be a central part of the development model based on internally-oriented import-substitution industrialization. As a result of this historical development, the state became highly involved in almost every sector of the economy. It controlled the total production and distribution of electricity and gas, some two-thirds of oil production, almost every activity relating to communications (post-office, telephones, telex and satellite connections, ports, railways, half of the air and maritime transport). The state also exercised control over steel production, and the military chemical and hardware industries. On top of all this, it owned banks, financial institutions and insurance companies.[1]

Therefore, in the early 1980s, 'there were between 900 and 1000 enterprises in which the state had partial or total ownership. Of that group only fourteen (among them, YPF, Segba, Gas del Estado, and Aerolíneas Argentinas) represented between two-thirds and three-quarters of the total economic activity of state-owned enterprises.'[2] In 1985 companies defined under statute as 'public' totalled around three hundred, of which 117 companies were national in scope. In terms of a legal-institutional classification, at a national level there were 20 decentralized organizations, seven state enterprises, eight mixed companies, 20 *sociedades anónimas* with the state as majority shareholder, eight *sociedades anónimas* with majority or total state control, nine state corporations, five bi-national corporations, one meat-packing operation, and 39 radio and television stations.[3]

As pointed out in the previous chapter, throughout the century, the growth of the state apparatus was accompanied by increasing tensions in the financial resources of the respective companies. This was mainly the consequence of the use of state enterprises not only as economic engines, but also as political instruments. As a matter of fact, efficiency and profit maximization were rarely considered part of the goals of public enterprises.[4] Normally, enterprises suffered from increasing bureaucracy, were greatly over-capitalized, over-employed, and operated under a system of distorted prices. As a consequence, their productivity as well as the quality of their services was always in decline. Furthermore, these companies provided a market for all kinds of rents: subsidized inputs for national companies, protected markets for the production of national companies, employment opportunities, and economic opportunities for marginal regions of the country. This reflected the weakness of the Argentine state – great in size, but impotent to mediate between contradictory interests – and exhibited the importance of inflation as one of the main sources of financing multiple activities.

This tendency increased during the 1976–82 military regime. It advocated a 'neoliberal' economic orientation, and sought to roll back the developmentalist model by launching a programme of economic restructuring to dismantle the apparatus of public welfare and state intervention.[5] In practice, however, this regime only increased the degree of state intervention and assistance. On the one hand, there was no serious engagement in a privatization programme, only the concession of some peripheral activities that had no impact on the structure of the public sector. On the other, local major economic groups were especially favoured with subsidies and tax promotions, an internal monopolistic and protected market, subsidized external production, as well as other kinds of protection. Eventually, this protection came to include the nationalization of their external debt. Thus, during the military regime, the economic and fiscal problems of the state were exacerbated: the autonomy and capability of the state were reduced, its private colonization was increased, and its existing financial difficulties were increased when external indebtedness occurred in the absence of its conflict-management capacities. The 1982 international crisis made the long-term and recently-accelerated deterioration evident, and left the Argentine state, along with most others in Latin America, as one of its most important victims.

In effect, Mexico's debt moratorium crisis in August 1982 made apparent that Latin American countries could no longer count on international capital as a way to supplement scarce domestic resources used to run states overloaded with all kinds of economic burdens. The large-scale loans from private banks going to the Third World during the 1970s were at an end. They had in fact led to expansionist policies mainly because of being detached from stabilization requirements, as was the case with credits from the international financial institutions. This permissive international environment grew restrictive after 1982, and at the same time other negative shocks also appeared. Actually, the debt crisis came on top of other difficulties already under way. In industrial countries interest rates were being raised to fight inflation, bringing recession as a consequence. Debtor countries were forced to pay more interest on their debt when their export revenues were in decline. Therefore, declining terms of trade combined with higher financial outflows for debt servicing put acute pressure on the balance of payments. International pressures emerged for both debt service and stabilization, and the IMF became the most important transmission agent as the policy-oriented loan provider.

The debt crisis and the reappearance of conditional loans in the 1980s motivated the diffusion of a set of policies concerned with deficit reduction and the containment of inflationary pressures. Sooner or later, however, it became obvious that external shocks were not temporary deviations, but rather elements of a new international political economy. Macroeconomic stabilization began to be regarded as insufficient to deal with this environment, and claims for structural adjustment to complement stabilization were raised. The World Bank, the loans of which were based on these policy conditions, played a major role in this respect. Other political and ideological factors taking place in the international environment also contributed to giving an impulse to economic liberalization policies. On the one hand, the general decline of the statist ideologies that had prevailed during the 1970s, was counterbalanced by the new intellectual trends of neo-classical economics that began to occupy the academic world, and also the World Bank, the IMF and other multilateral institutions. Governments with fiscal constraints would find it difficult to pursue policies other than those dictated by the international lending organizations,[6] especially since alternative sources of financing from socialist countries were no longer available for those favouring other heterodox courses of action. On the other hand, there was the 'successful-country-example'. Most of the nations that were doing economically well in the continent had adopted orthodox strategies (Chile being the main example), while the others were undergoing severe economic problems. Most importantly, the diffusion of the contemporary experiences of some developed countries with conservative policy agendas – Britain and the United States in the 1980s – created pro-reform models that spoke by themselves with the strength of what had been achieved in practice. Consequently, the restrictive conditions posed by the international context first raised concerns with fiscal discipline and, then, urged the roll-back of the state, both in terms of its ownership of industries and financial institutions, and its regulatory activities in trade, industry, agriculture, credit and foreign investment.

Therefore, Latin American governments coming to power in the wake of crisis found out sooner or later that they needed to undertake the policy initiatives indicated by the international context. However, the way in which they responded to the external trends varied in terms of timing, speed, scale and contents. The next section will show how one of these structural policies, the privatization of public enterprises, became part of the agenda of the first Argentine president of the democracy inaugurated in 1983. It is emphasized that this was not the policy with which the president arrived in power. Instead, price adjustment and expense reduction were the first mechanisms chosen to deal with the shortage of resources. However, the persistence of the fiscal crisis would lead to more drastic measures.

3.2. Privatization in the president's agenda

The policy of privatization during Alfonsín's Presidency was not part of the programme with which the president had won the elections. Neither was it a relevant issue in the policies the president implemented immediately after his election. Rather it was the result of the exercise of power and the consequent discovery of the needs and difficulties of the economy at that time. It involved a great amount of political learning and could never be interpreted without considering the context of institutional political reconstruction that was at the centre of the government's preoccupations. As stated above, the fact that the centrality of the economic problem and the state crisis were not identified as such until the Alfonsín period was well advanced does not mean that they did not exist in October 1983, when Argentina began a new era of democratic political life. Nevertheless, the state crisis was not that obvious to a leader assuming power after the breakdown of the previous authoritarian regime. At that time, the focus was on the re-establishment of democracy after a tough dictatorship. This objective strongly influenced the analysis of the crisis, and determined the views of the necessary reconstruction in the political, social and economic fields.

3.2.1. The beginning of democracy

In October 1983, Argentina began a new era of democratic political life with the victory of the Radical candidate, Raúl Alfonsín, in the presidential elections. The triumph of Radicalism indicated the extent of the citizens' expectations of the new political regime, and the breadth of the role which they hoped the Radical leader would fulfil. In effect, Alfonsín had based his political campaign on a range of promises, from the re-establishment of the *estado de derecho* to the reinstallation of the concept of social justice. On many occasions, he explained that he understood the Argentine post-authoritarian reconstruction in the following terms:

> We are going to live in freedom. No doubts about that. There should be no doubt that this freedom is going to be useful in building, creating, producing, working, claiming justice – all justice, that of ordinary laws and that of social laws – in maintaining ideas, organising in defence of the legitimate interests and the rights of the people and of every particular sector; in total, in living better, because we have said many times from the political tribune that the Argentine people have learnt, in the light of the tragic experiences of recent years, that democracy has a value even higher than that of a mere form of legitimacy of power, because with democracy one not only votes, but one also eats, educates and cures.[7]

Therefore, democracy embraced, in the leader's view, a kind of expansive movement through which justice would be brought to all levels of society. The military regime had illegitimately concentrated both political power and economic wealth in the hands of the privileged few. The democratic regime would have the task of dispersing what had been unfairly concentrated. Framed in this context of social reparation, politics as well as economics would acquire distributive features. On the political front, the firm establishment of democracy in Argentina implied, for the Radical leader, not only the conservative alternative of rule by the Constitution,[8] but also positive governmental action that would ensure the greatest respect for basic individual rights. In order to do so, the newly elected constitutional government would have to concentrate its efforts on solving problems occuring in the recent past as well as preventing them from recurring in the future. Leaving the terrorist and counter-terrorist human rights violations of the past years unpunished meant, in Alfonsín's view, abandoning fundamental ethical principles and jeopardizing the prevention of future violations. Therefore, the establishment of the rule of law led to the promotion of both general standards (laws) and specific actions (trials) that would give effective validity to it. Likewise, the extension of democratic procedures to those sectors in society that did not make clear use of them was seen as an imperative mandate:

> I continue fighting to recover democracy and I am not going to strike the fundamental flag of the democratisation of unions, because I think that, in our country, we cannot seriously talk about integral democracy if we do not recover the right to intervene in union organisation for the Argentine workers...[9]

The political contents of the Radical platform took centre stage in the presidential campaign debate and in public attention.[10] However, democratization, the constitution, and human rights were not divorced from economic issues. Indeed, the electoral campaign demonstrated that the interpretation of the economic problems of the time was basically political; consequently, economic arguments were framed in the context of justice and solidarity that the advent of the new democracy had created. The Radicals started from the assumption that the former dictatorship was the main force responsible for the evils in Argentina. If the military had left the economy in ruins, the solution would be democracy itself, reversing the process that had taken place up to then. So, the party did little to define the terms of an economic programme. Rather it embraced old state interventionism, and proposed to counterbalance the unfair elements of the monetarist policies of the military with a distributive programme. Actually, there were not many chances for the party to attempt a different response. On the one hand, no structural reform was possible, since neoliberal reformist strategies had become discredited by the military experience. On the other hand, since party life had been frozen by dictatorship, the politicians leading the transition were much the same they had been, and still held their old ideas and conceptions, that is, distributive and interventionist policies that were also linked to firm ideas on industrialism, nationalism, and anti-imperialism.[11]

Consequently, in its proposal for economic policy, the Radical political platform acknowledged that 1983 'will be the third year with three digit inflation', which was why 'the first commitment that UCR assumes in its economic platform is to attack poverty'.... 'So much urgent and legitimate demand needs an immediate and efficient answer from democracy because if it fails in this field, it will not survive.'[12] The distributive elements of the Radical economic programme were complemented by another policy, which was also introduced after the experience of the military regime. Based on a politics of privilege, the military had administered the country with no rational pattern. With this background, the new government was obliged to attempt the difficult combination of solidarity and austerity:

> we have to achieve objectives that are apparently contradictory, such as containing inflation and increasing the buying power of the population.... We are going to meet the most profound crisis in Argentinian history, but the Radical Civic Union has already prepared a programme for the emergency.... to contain inflation, we are going to change the financial system, and lower interest rates. We shall conjugate the verbs 'to grow' and 'to contain' at the same time: we shall grow economically without exacerbating inflation. We shall increase the buying capacity of the people, which will bring an increase in effective demand, and this will bring an increase in production, which will simultaneously allow us to reduce unitary costs and create new employment. In short, this means putting in motion the apparatus of production. We are not going to define ourselves as monetarists, but as structuralists with great fiscal and monetary discipline.[13]

It was in this context that the problem of the state was raised, and the vision of how it should be faced was put forward. As could be expected, the issue of public expenditure did not produce any major innovative proposals other than austerity and reallocation of resources. The Radical platform laid down the necessity of reallocating resources on the basis of new priorities, according to the determinations of the political power;

the need to improve efficiency in expenditure and contribute to the growth of the economy, to obtain a reasonable balance between the financial needs of the public sector and the credit requirements of the private sector in a growing economy, and to reduce expenditure whilst acknowledging the need to make the economy recover and develop. As well as this, the Radicals also argued that all companies in charge of providing essential public services should be kept under state control, in order to secure critical supplies and other goals of national interest.[14] The sale of public companies was not even contemplated, with the exception of those companies that had been seized by the military in order to protect them from bankruptcy. They were the only enterprises that had to be returned to the private sector.[15]

Above all, this shows how the experience of the former military dictatorship affected the interpretation of the economic difficulties of the time, as well as the solutions proposed to deal with them. The economic programme carried out by Bernardo Grinspun (Alfonsín's first Minister of Economy and an old member of the Radical Party) did not produce any major surprises.[16] The minister adopted a neo-Keynesian approach, which attempted to tackle simultaneously income distribution, low inflation, and economic growth. He also boldly opposed the IMF solutions for economic stabilization.[17] In the particular case of public enterprises, the government started to implement the policy of re-privatization that had been promised in its election campaign. An inter-ministerial commission was set up by Decree 414 as early as January 1984 aimed at identifying those enterprises that did not provide services which were of national interest, or social benefits that justified state ownership and, therefore, could be returned to the private sphere. However, only a few minor privatizations were effectively carried out: SIAM (an industrial conglomerate), Opalinas Hurlingham (ceramics), Sol Jet (a travel agency), whilst the Austral Airlines privatization (the small domestic airline) was only concluded in 1987.

Contrary to the expectations that the advent of democracy had raised, Grinspun's economic programme turned out to be unsuccessful. Thus, a new stage began in Alfonsín's administration, featuring gradual acknowledgement of the size and sources of the economic crisis. This new stage would also enlarge the scope for innovative responses and solutions.

3.2.2. The Austral Plan

As inflation would not stop rising, it became obvious that the extent of the economic problems had been underestimated. It was in this context that the president appointed his new economic team. With this new appointment, the president dismissed the party economists from office, putting Juan Sourrouille and his team of *técnicos* in charge of the ministry.[18] The new economic team prepared its strategy in secret and adopted by necessity and urgency decree a stabilization programme which was launched in June 1985. This was the Austral Plan, the first in a series of heterodox packages implemented in Latin America. The decision to face the crisis with a new plan did not relegate the concept of reparation that the government had developed as being central to the management of the economy. The plan aimed at stopping inflation whilst maintaining levels of employment and economic activity. In contrast to orthodox plans, it tried to avoid regressive re-distributions. The plan included a price and wage freeze, the creation of a new currency (the *austral* replaced the *peso*), and the de-indexation of the economy. It also drew attention to the connection between inflation and imbalance in public accounts and, therefore, to the necessity of complementing the plan with fiscal measures. Thus, it was planned to reduce the deficit by adopting some urgent taxation measures (a reform of the tax system was sent to Congress), reducing public expenditure, and increasing efficiency in the management of state enterprises.[19] All this was complemented by a renegotiated agreement with the IMF.

Within this framework, the government developed some new ideas regarding privatization. These did not point directly to the idea of selling to cover the deficit, but to the restructuring of the public sector, which would therefore have fewer resources than before. These ideas were an alternative to promoting efficiency in the functioning of the companies as well as in the economic sectors where those companies existed. In a public statement in February 1986, the Minister of Economy declared that the government's privatization plans embraced enterprises belonging to the petrochemical and steel industries, in other words, the privatization policy would probably be extended to areas where the state had historically performed functions of production.[20] The objective was efficiency: 'the transfer to the private sector will run parallel to the fixing of the rules of the game, removing the negative aspects of the national steel industry, with the aim of eliminating the monopolistic features that hinder competitiveness, winning flexibility to operate in a very demanding market, and obtaining greater efficiency to make the enterprise's competitive appearance in the world possible.'[21] In the same speech, Minister Sourrouille announced the government's intention to send a privatization bill to Congress in order to obtain the resources that 'the magnitude and significance of the aimed operation require for its success'.

The bill was submitted to the lower house in October 1986. It proposed the creation of a general legal framework to conduct and regulate privatization operations. Its objective was to extend the already existing legal procedures in order to facilitate the private sector's access to public enterprises[22] as well as to confirm the Executive's powers to conduct any process of privatization.[23] Together with the arguments about improving economic efficiency, the Executive stated that the state had to continue to play its leading role in the economy, and privatization was the right means to do this.[24] In effect, one of the objectives of state intervention in the economy was to guarantee national development through activities considered strategic for the growth of the country. However, these strategic areas of the economy changed according to the pace of technological transformation. Because of these changes, 'many goods that until recently were directly connected to national defence' now had 'other uses'. As a consequence, the entrepreneurial state had to adjust to this by reallocating resources from the older strategic areas (such as the petrochemical industry) to new ones (biogenetics, cybernetics, etc.). In a context of a shortage of resources, privatization of the older sectors would hopefully provide the necessary funds for the development of the new national priorities.

With these provisions, the government attempted to demonstrate that the historical role of the state was not being challenged. Moreover, the bill was not presented to Congress as a privatization bill, but as one aimed at the creation of a National Fund for Industrial Development. Such a fund was meant to include different kinds of resources, such as those obtained through privatization. Likewise, the bill included an appendix containing a list of enterprises which, because of 'their particular characteristics, the role they are playing today and their significance to the public sector and the community in general', needed to be excluded from the scope of this law.[25] These enterprises were involved in public services (telephones, postal services, the rail system, television) and basic production (gas, oil, coal, hydroelectric power). In general, these areas of economic activity had a strong symbolic meaning and were, in the traditional view of the political parties, part of the state patrimony. Considered together, the characteristics of the bill watered down the objectives of state transformation, by guaranteeing by law the destiny of future privatization income, and by restricting the extent of the sale of companies in advance.[26]

Therefore, the bill showed that the view of the major public-service companies had not changed at all: 'none of the state's public-service enterprises will be privatised. Besides the public service companies, those involved in exploitation of natural resources, critical supply, and activities of general interest will be maintained within the state's orbit. *Agua y Energía, YPF, Gas del Estado, SEGBA, Encotel* amongst others, approximately twenty four, that depend on the MOSP and the Secretariat of Energy, are untouchable.'[27] These enterprises produced a 'social benefit' that was very difficult to measure and, therefore, had to remain within the state's jurisdiction. Their critical financial situation was not a determining factor in promoting their sale. Instead, the cooperation of private capital was welcome, but ownership had to remain in the hands of the state. In effect, the government invited the private sector to participate in the provision of some public services (a considerable number of new telephone lines were financed with private capital, like *Plan Megatel*), as well as in the exploration and exploitation of oil producing areas (after a presidential announcement in mid–1985).

To summarize, the first privatization bill developed by the Radical government revealed a cautious and timid attitude to the introduction of the privatization issue into the political arena. Both the decision to restrict the application of the law to a small area of the economy and the careful arguments supporting the bill underscored the limited scope of the privatization project. This agreed with the spirit of the Austral Plan. Like the Austral Plan, the policy towards private capital demonstrated no will to incur great expense either on the social or political fronts. It aimed at restructuring the public sector, but avoided alterations involving great risk. Additionally, in the context of the Plan, fiscal balance was understood as a condition with a complementary (not a central) character.[28] Furthermore, it has been argued that a clear diagnosis of the problems of the public sector was not possible in 1985. Machinea has written that the announcement of the privatization of the steel and petrochemical plants came more as an attempt to show that the government was ready to address the issue of structural reforms than as part of a well-thought-out plan. The economic team knew that 'something else' had to be done in the public sector, but did not know exactly what.[29]

3.2.3. Attempting structural reforms

Despite the fact that the Austral Plan did achieve some success for more than a year, from the middle of 1986 onwards, inflation proved to be persistent and even worsened.[30] Exposed to multiple demands from various interest groups (both the unions and entrepreneurial sectors), the government gradually began to release the fiscal and monetary restraints, which sooner or later would lead to another overheat of the economy. From then on, several stabilization shocks were implemented, each one having less and less success. Amidst increasing economic difficulties, the exhaustion of the old state model became apparent, and the government faced the need to tackle the structural problems of the public sector. In a public message in July 1987, Minister Sourrouille warned of the existence of a crisis caused, among other factors, by the lack of resources necessary to finance the state's traditional functions. For this reason, 'The state, impoverished and driven by social pressures, while it is stifling social initiatives, is always about to collapse into fiscal deficit.'[31] Since obtaining extra resources was a fairly impossible task, there were no longer any 'imaginative responses' to such a crisis. Therefore, the only available solution consisted of the construction of a new state which, according to the minister's words, should be supported by the new pillars of 'integration into the world, deregulation and rationality'.[32]

Some new privatization bills were drawn up within the framework of the 'structural reform' that the Ministry of Economy had decided to put into practice. Disregarding the first privatization bill (which had not received congressional approval), three new bills were sent to the Senate. They were introduced in 1988 by Rodolfo Terragno, the new Minister of Works and Services and, like most of the economic team, a figure from outside the party. Two of the bills concerned the privatization of Aerolíneas Argentinas, the other, the privatization of ENTel. The aim of the ENTel and Aerolíneas bills was to sell 40 per cent of Aerolíneas Argentinas' stock to the Scandinavian Airways System (*SAS*) and a similar proportion of ENTel to the Spanish company *Telefónica de España*.[33] The state would thus relinquish part ownership of the two enterprises (as well as their management), but would still maintain control as majority shareholder. Moreover, the bills provided for the possibility of granting the concession of 9 per cent of the companies' stock to the workers. By this measure, the government pursued the idea of an organizational design that consisted of the state's majority presence, private capital and the participation of the work-force.

The method chosen by the government to carry out both sales was a direct contracting procedure, based on agreements made earlier with the partner enterprises.[34] These agreements involved companies that had previously been considered central to the public sector, and had then been excluded from the first privatization bill. Nevertheless, the agreements only implied commitment if congressional approval was obtained. In effect, the deadline for the agreement involving Aerolíneas Argentinas was set for 15 December, 1988, and it was expected that the bill would have obtained congressional approval by that time. But as the date approached, the bill had not even begun to be considered in the Senate. Because of this, the second bill concerning Aerolíneas Argentinas was presented to the Senate on 16 December, after this Chamber had refused to consider the first one. This bill also proposed the sale of 40 per cent of the company but, this time, through a public bidding procedure. Just like the three previous bills, this also failed to receive congressional approval.

The change of perspective in the government's privatization policy as shown in its later bills dramatically altered the enterprises that were to be affected by the privatization programme. While the telephone and airline industries were untouched by the first privatization bill, Terragno began his privatization programme with them. Two conclusions can be drawn from this: first of all, by the end of its mandate, the government progressively moved toward the adoption of an economic programme that had at first been avoided. This movement was accompanied by the heightening economic crisis as well as the increasing acknowledgement of the causes of the crisis, which pointed to state reform as the last solution. In this process, the Austral Plan was an intermediate stage in which the government, as it had done in the first year of the administration, again underestimated the level of the crisis, assuming that it could be solved without taking major incisive decisions. Nevertheless, the Austral Plan had already introduced an element of discontinuity, which leads to the second point of this conclusion: that the government closed ranks to protect itself when the plan was being designed. The Ministry of Economy's technical team formulated the plan, separating itself from other members – and even branches – of the government. This process developed further when Terragno was appointed Minister of Works and Services. Thus, the two ministries in which the state reform was conducted were meant to be far removed from the growing sociopolitical pressures and demands.

3.3. The privatization bills in Congress

That the four privatization bills were never approved does not mean that Congress did not consider them at all. In fact, an important discussion did occur, indicating that the lack of approval was due more to a situation of conflict than to congressional inactivity. For instance, in 1988, Rodolfo Terragno, the Minister of Public Works and Services, had to attend three interpellations by the Senate. He was asked for information about the letters of intent that had been signed with SAS and Telefónica de España. On those occasions, he was also asked to comment on the oil and gas programmes undertaken by the government, which, although they did not involve the transfer of property to the private sector, put forward the participation of private capital in the exploration and exploitation of these resources. Besides Terragno, the Minister of Defence, José Horacio Jaunarena, was asked by the Justicialist Party to appear before the Senate in order to give information on probable privatization in his area. The following subsections comment on how the two major political parties positioned themselves with respect to the Executive's bills.

3.3.1. The Radical Party

The Radical Party did not go along with the gradual movement towards the adoption of a privatization policy by the government. The party interpreted the first distributive policy as its own, and from the Austral Plan onwards, the party viewed the economic decisions of its own government as alien, and never really understood the purpose of the changes. It rejected the privatization policy for two reasons: one was ideological, and the other was its lack of participation in the definition of the programme.

As has been explained above, the first movement towards a policy of privatization took place some months after the launching of the Austral Plan. In February 1986, the Minister of Economy incorporated some related proposals in a public speech. These were received with a mixture of surprise and dismay within the Radical Party. Using populist arguments, party members manifested their displeasure. Objections concerned the probable sale of steel as well as petrochemical companies, areas of production traditionally owned and developed by the state. The companies SOMISA, the petrochemical General Mosconi and petrochemical Bahía Blanca were the centre of attention since Minister Sourrouille had declared the government's wish to privatize them. Even party members in the cabinet did not hide their anxieties. Newspapers reported, for instance, that Conrado Storani, the Secretary of Energy, accepted that 49 per cent of the petrochemical company Mosconi could be sold because the state would maintain the remaining 51 per cent. However, he refused to accept the privatization of the petrochemical company Bahía Blanca because the state only owned 51 per cent, so that the sale would involve the loss of state control.[35] Younger party members in particular expressed their disagreement: 'the defence of the nation's wealth, the development of an economy that favours the popular sectors, and the opposition to the parasitic oligarchy and the interest of multinational corporations' should have been, in their view, the guiding principles of the government, by which it would face 'firmly the pressures of usurious organisations such as the International Monetary Fund, encouraging internal development on the basis of control of the financial sector and basic industries like steel and petrochemical production that must be in the hands of the people'.[36]

Despite these public declarations, the feeling of unease was mostly expressed only within the confines of the party. However, it was important enough to push the Radical National Committee to organize some control over the dissidents. With this in view, the Committee worked out a document whereby the party declared its 'organic support' for the government's privatization policy, and whereby it tried to demonstrate that such a policy was based on Radical principles regarding the functions of the state. Adopting the government line on the issue, the National Committee emphasized that the policy in question did not challenge state control of economic activity. It simply implied a reallocation of resources in order to adapt state functions to the technological developments of the time. Likewise, it stressed that the Radical demands 'concerning the decisive role that the state must play in the economic emancipation and autonomous and continuous development of the country'[37] were being ratified.

Nevertheless, the party's opposition persisted and was also expressed in the lower house. Even before the arrival of the Executive's bill, some party members had already been working on the privatization issue. Discussions had been led by the chairman of the Committee of Industry, the Radical Hugo Socchi, who – in opposition to the majority of his own party – advocated an assertive policy towards privatization. He had declared that 'last July I understood that together with the frontal fight against inflation starting with the Austral Plan, it was also necessary to make the state efficient enough to put forward the major transformations demanded by our economic system'. Because of this, Socchi had presented his own bill, in which a 'flexible and modern framework'[38] for privatization activities was proposed. However, the deputy also believed that any decision regarding the sale of public companies had to rely on the explicit support of the main opposition party. In his opinion, 'the importance of these matters presupposes the necessity of an unquestionable guarantee of consensus, capable of serving as the foundation for an image of trust and permanence in the economic agents'.[39] Pursuing these ideas, Socchi began to work with the Peronists on a common text (*texto conformado*), in which his bill was being coordinated with a proposal by Peronist Deputy José Luis Manzano. Manzano's bill was intended to defend the labour force by selling the state shares totally or partially to the workers.

At the end of these negotiations, Socchi drew up a new bill of his own, the presentation of which coincided with the one emanating from the Executive. Socchi's bill intended to find a consensual solution so that it included a list of 29 enterprises that could only be privatized by means of specific laws and which, therefore, were not affected by the bill under discussion. The idea went beyond the issue of privatization, 'to give the National Congress its due participation in decisions of such importance',[40] transforming it into the arena where the political debate on the role of the state would take place. Thus, the cost of the inter-party negotiations in Congress had been the drawing up of a bill with a general framework which did not allow for innovation in the functions of the state, and which practically eradicated any privatization attempt. The bill differed from that simultaneously submitted by the Executive, which, as previously stated, allowed for the privatization of the petrochemical and steel companies. The Executive had taken a long time to define it, while seeking a draft that could receive the support of the political forces in Congress. In fact, the first announcement regarding privatization had been made in February 1986, and it took the government eight months to produce a bill. In the statement accompanying the bill, Minister Sourrouille admitted to having used the Socchi and Manzano common text as background. Despite these efforts, Congress had produced another bill with clauses that denied support to the privatization programme.

Socchi's position in favour of privatization was really a minority view within the Radical Party. In fact, the party rejected both the Executive's programme and Socchi's original bill.[41] However, his concern about the necessity of the participation of both Congress and the party in the definition of the policy was shared by many of his *correligionarios*. In fact, many members complained about the absence of an internal debate and the fact that the party was limited to giving its consent to pre-formulated decisions. In part, the problem was that it was not the party in government, but 'the technical members of the government' who were in charge of creating the new policy. Conflict between the members involved and those who were not increased with the passage of time. When, in 1988, the Minister of Works and Services, Rodolfo Terragno, took the leading role on privatization, many Radicals objected that they could only obtain information regarding the privatization of ENTel and Aerolíneas 'in the newspapers'.[42]

To sum up, it is possible to say that the Radical Party's position on the government's privatization policy was characterized by two features: on the one hand, the majority of the party questioned a policy which, in its view, was in direct conflict with the party's traditional principles; on the other hand, the party complained because it had not participated in such a momentous decision. The distribution of institutional power gave the party direct responsibility for the destiny of the Executive's bill of 1986. Because the Radicals held the majority in the lower house – as they did in the Industry Committee where the bill was sent – the party had enough veto power to stop the advance of the Executive's project. In 1987, the government had already lost interest in pursuing the approval for its first privatization bill.[43] From then on, negotiations related to Terragno's proposals. This time, the Peronists would exercise their veto power in the Senate.

3.3.2 The Peronist Party

The Peronist Party also maintained an unchangeable position of rejection of the privatization policy conducted by the Presidency. The conversations that the Peronist deputy José Luis Manzano and the Radical Hugo Socchi held in the Industry Committee at the Chamber of Deputies during the 1986 legislative period demonstrated that, although approaches were possible between the major political parties, the results would be negative as regards privatization. When the *texto conformado* was produced, the government treated it as a reference from which to draft its own bill but Deputy Manzano did not hesitate to distance himself from it, and declared that his bill 'is opposed to the one that the Executive promotes, because of the enterprises to be privatised'.[44] He did not admit the idea of 'indiscriminate privatisation'. Manzano declared to the press that a policy of privatization should not affect those enterprises

> that possess some of the following characteristics: provision of a public service; operation in monopolistic conditions; industries whose privatisation could generate either new monopolistic conditions or affect the normal development of the market; determination of supply or prices; specific social goals; provision of a strategic service for both development and national security. Besides this, no enterprise could be declared subject to privatization until the conditions under which the enterprise was nationalised had disappeared.[45]

The negative attitude of 1986 was maintained throughout Alfonsín's administration, although opposition was more intense regarding the telephone and airline privatizations. The Peronist senators demonstrated no desire to initiate the treatment of the bills and, instead, requested the presence of the Executive's ministers in the Senate's floor for interrogation. Likewise, some variations were introduced to the arguments used to oppose privatization. For instance, the general ideological references constituted only a small part of the Peronist position in the congressional debates in 1988. Instead, party principles tended to appear behind direct criticism of the way in which the government approached the particular cases under discussion. In this sense, the Peronists expressed their unanimous rejection of the procedure chosen by the government to carry out the privatization of the airline and telephone enterprises (sale by direct contracting). By using this argument, the Peronists affirmed that they were defending the only way recognized by Argentine law for privatization procedures, which was national or international bidding. Eduardo Menem's words illustrate this position: 'public bidding is universally recognised as the best method that the state can use to choose the party to make a contract with. It appears that in the cases of Aerolíneas and ENTel that procedure is not right, but it is in the case of Austral.... It is much more imperative to use the public bidding procedures in relation to Aerolíneas and ENTel, because of the importance of these enterprises and the resources that are being transferred, than it is with Austral, and this is the reason why... I reaffirm the necessity of the bidding procedure.'[46] Additionally, Peronists pointed out some other aspects of the contracts that made the bills unacceptable to them. For instance, it was mentioned that the government was transferring not only public resources to private hands, but also the decision-making power for the future administration of the enterprises.[47] Others complained because Terragno had entrusted the valuation of the enterprises to international companies rather than national ones. In their view, this meant that they were probably undervalued.

The Peronist Party directed its criticisms to the way in which the government was seeking to implement privatization, which allowed them to affirm publicly that 'we never said that we are against privatisation... privatisation itself is a neutral entity; it is neither good nor bad. It is applied according to circumstances.'[48] However, this did not prevent the Peronist Senator Eduardo Menem from mentioning some principles or rules that should be met in any process of privatization. First, the procedures chosen to carry out any process of sale had to be those established by law, namely, 'public bidding, or private bidding in very special cases'. Secondly, companies in economic areas regarded as essential to the country's development should not be privatised. Neither were public services to be sold, because of their 'social profitability' and importance for 'national sovereignty'. Thirdly, the state could sell companies with deficits, but not profitable ones: 'The state, based on a principle of good administration, must do what any individual with two or three different businesses, some in profit and others in deficit, would do: get rid of those with a deficit at once and only later those with profits. Because if he does the opposite, I do not know how he will be able to cope with the losses from the companies that are not profitable.'

Although the Peronist Party had not abandoned its opposition in principle, it was the political context in which the privatization debate was taking place that explains not only the changes of emphasis in the Peronist speeches but also their bitter opposition to the official proposal. On the one hand, it is worth pointing out that political parties knew that the public had adopted an attitude favourable to privatization latterly as this information was being revealed by the public-opinion polls (see next section). Because of this, Terragno had requested that his interpellation in the Senate be televised as a way of putting pressure on Peronist obstructionism and, probably because of this, Peronists preferred to say that they were opposing the government but not the policy. On the other hand, it is only in the context of the presidential election campaign that the increasing intensity of the opposition can be understood.

Therefore, the attempt to sell public companies resulted in a scenario in which the logic of opposition prevailed. If support for the policy did not exist at all amongst Peronists, there was a difference between the disposition to speak and negotiate with the ruling party in Congress in 1986 and the stubborn attitude in the Senate during 1988. The timing of the reforms thus acquires relevance especially because the opposition progressively perceived that reforms were linked to the increasing economic problems and the government's inability to solve them. Indeed, Terragno's bills were proposed shortly before the presidential elections, during a chaotic economic situation that had deepened the government's discredit and enhanced the real chances of a Peronist victory. The scene was set for competition rather than for political agreements.

3.4. Other opposition forces

Congressional opposition to privatization was part of a broader opposition front that included all the relevant social forces. This has also been referred to as a 'huge anti-privatisation coalition', the members of which worked closely to stop any privatization initiative.[49] First, there were the unions which were concerned with the preservation of the labour sources on which their power and strength were based. Second, business sectors accustomed to obtaining all kinds of privileges from their relationship with state-owned companies were also opposed: opposition came from all, private contractors and suppliers, who used to buy and sell under very favourable conditions, as well as private competitors of the state, who favoured from competition against obsolete and poorly managed state companies.[50] As a result, the private sector engaged in all kinds of activities to stop the government's privatization plans.[51] Third, the state bureaucracy in both the central administration and the state-owned enterprises themselves had no incentive to support a policy that involved the withdrawal of the state.[52] Finally, the military opposed the sale of the wide range of military industries run by the state.

Although each of these groups clearly had a particular interest in stopping privatization, it is also true that the evolution in the government's relations towards them did not do much to reverse the situation. As is well known, Alfonsín began his period in office with a confrontational approach to social groups. He was acting within the framework of democratic reconstruction, and he understood that, in order to eradicate the sources of authoritarianism, the old Argentine *corporaciones* had to be reformed. In the president's view, the *corporaciones* (unions, entrepreneurs, military) had a direct responsibility for the recurrent breakdown of democratic rule, so that their reform was an unavoidable step towards strengthening the chances for survival of the new regime. Reviving the old civic tradition of Radicalism, the president believed that democracy's strength came from the people. Therefore, he confronted the military by seeking to punish its human rights violations by laws and judgements. He also confronted the Peronized unions with a bill aimed at the democratization of their internal organization. He did not, however, foresee that these policies were not politically viable: in fact, the Senate did not pass the union bill and the military refused to pass judgement on themselves in the military courts. From that time on, Alfonsín's government was often obliged to retreat from its original positions, which caused great damage to its image and credibility with the electorate.[53] Moreover, the government was no more fortunate in its dealings with the entrepreneurial sector. Although several approaches were tried, it was soon apparent that the sector's heterogeneity and its differences in interest and organization obstructed any general agreement, as well as that the members of the sector seemed more concerned with protecting their income and defending their capacity for veto than with cooperating in the development of an economic policy.

The fact is that when structural reforms came to be part of the presidential agenda, the government had few political resources to implement them, and instead faced serious problems of credibility and governability. In 1987, the unions exhibited a permanent state of mobilization by organizing national and sectorial strikes, while a sector of the Army carry out three insurrections.[54] Furthermore, the government feared the formation of an opposition block instigated by all the *corporaciones*, which could jeopardize the future of democracy.[55] Consequently, the Executive felt reluctant to take drastic economic decisions that might provoke a unified reaction from the major groups so putting democracy in danger. The results were timid and limited reforms, undertaken without conviction, and in fear of dispute and obstruction.

In the conflictive environment of the late 1980s, public opinion had also lost confidence in the capacity of the government to cope with basic social problems. In fact, Alfonsín managed to retain public support for barely half of his administration. Public opinion initially supported the restitution of the Constitution, respect for democratic procedures, and the resolutions against human rights violations, all of which were central to Alfonsín's presidential campaign, and constituted the power of his leadership. The government's subsequent decision to face economic problems with the Austral Plan was also accompanied by a tide of public opinion that put aside institutional, military, and human rights concerns, instead demanding control of inflation and other economic issues. However, in the conflictive context of Alfonsín's last two years, the government only transmitted an image of weakness which was received by the general public with great disaffection. Graph 3.1 traces the movement of the president's image after the launching of the Austral Plan. Graph 3.2 traces the popularity of the economic plan in particular. Both of them were highly popular at the beginning of the Austral Plan and, then, their popularity declined, although Alfonsín always did better than his economic policy.

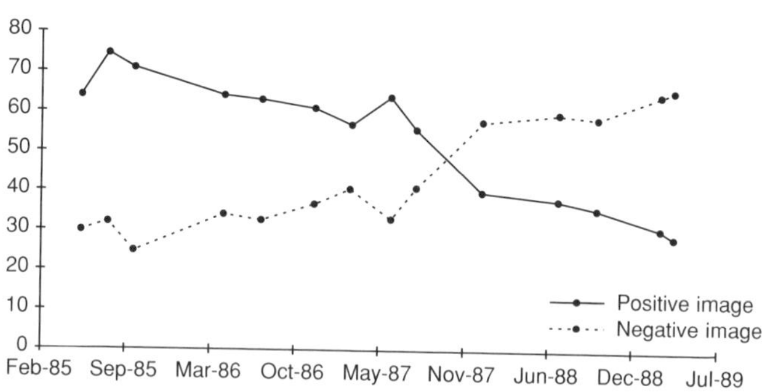

Graph 3.1 Alfonsín: image during his presidential mandate

Source: Estudio Sociológico y Político Mora y Araujo, Noguera y Asociados. National sample of 800 cases: Argentines older than 18 years. Estimated error: 3.5 per cent.

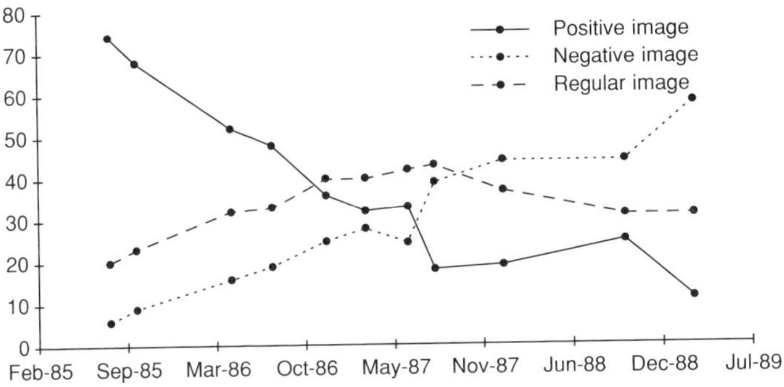

Graph 3.2 Alfonsín: image of the economic programme

Source: Estudio Sociológico y Político Mora y Araujo, Noguera y Asociados. National sample of 800 cases: Argentines older than 18 years. Estimated error: 3.5 per cent.

It should be added here that, despite the diminishing positive image of the economic plan, the public view of the privatization policy first stayed the same, and then slightly increased, between 1986 and 1988 (28.3 per cent, 28.2 per cent, 29.2 per cent, respectively), which would indicate discontent with the administration in charge of dealing with the reforms, rather than with the proposed policies in particular.[56] These figures also show that a considerable proportion of public opinion had begun to regard the reduction of the size of the state as a positive alternative. This was the assessment made by those who suffered from the use of increasingly deteriorating public services, the crisis in the pension and social security systems, as well as the incompetence, politicizing, and corruption of the state bureaucracy. Although this pro-reform attitude in the public became stronger and clearer only after the hyperinflation episode of 1989, many politicians felt earlier that room for ideological and programmatic discussions was gradually narrowing.

Finally, Graph 3.3 shows that the main worries of the Argentine people during Alfonsín's period in office concerned inflation. As long as the Austral Plan could maintain inflation at a lower level, worries about it would remain the same as those about other issues. But the increasing anxiety about inflation, starting about August 1987, contrasts with the declining approval levels of the government's image as shown in Graphs 1 and 2. Public opinion polls – and the government's defeat in the 1987 congressional and provincial government elections – show that, towards the end of the period, the government could not rely on much public support to legitimate its policy decisions.

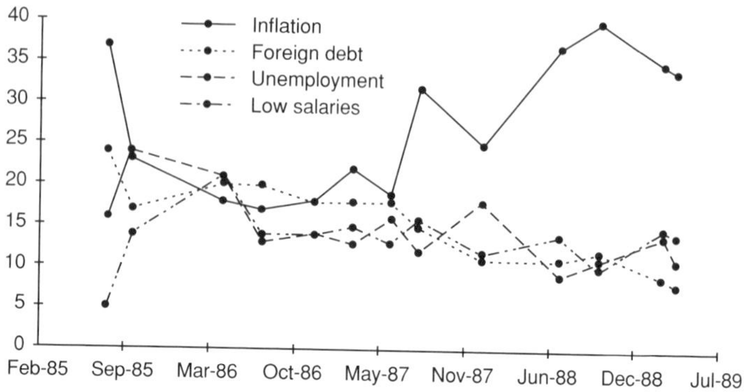

Graph 3.3 Alfonsín: principal problems of the country

Source: Estudio Sociológico y Político Mora y Araujo, Noguera y Asociados. National sample of 800 cases: Argentines older than 18 years. Estimated error: 3.5 per cent.

Conclusion

The failure of Alfonsín's government to obtain the approval of its privatization bills cannot be explained without considering the shortage of institutional resources on which the government could rely as well as the characteristics of the presidential leadership. As regards the first point, it should again be pointed out that the president did not have a solid congressional majority to support his initiatives. Conversely, he had to face a predominantly Peronist Senate throughout the whole period, and the lack of a Radical majority in the Chamber of Deputies from 1987 onwards. The parity of forces gave government and opposition a mutual veto capacity, making any process of policy approval difficult and, thus making it necessary to have some kind of inter-party cooperation to conclude successfully any process of law formulation. However, cooperation on an innovative policy such as privatization was difficult to achieve, and even more difficult because this was the government of the democratic transition. Some authors have emphasized the parties' difficulties in cooperating because this was a transition to democracy characterized by the absence of governability pacts[57] and a political tradition that regarded inter-partisan pacts as 'illicit unions'.[58] In effect, during Alfonsín's years in office, the only possible understanding between the major parties in Congress involved issues unanimously agreed upon by both parties. This *unanimity rule*[59] implied, in practice, that the parties were committed to avoiding a total institutional paralysis by approving an important number of bills, but also that those issues on which there was a serious disagreement would be left aside or postponed indefinitely.

This study reveals that privatization was an example of this practice. As the negotiations over the first privatization bill in 1986 show, a dialogue between the parties was possible, although the common text emanating from it resulted in the prevalence of the *status quo* rather than in any privatization initiative. In any case, this exercise of political dialogue, consultation and agreement which did not favour the approval of some crucial polices in particular (such as privatization), was to be instead fairly positive for the institutional progress of the regime. In effect, two parties accustomed to exclude each other began slowly to learn how to live together in an institutional framework where it was not possible to govern alone. The bitter opposition of Peronism in the late 1980s did not contradict this tendency. It rather showed that the pattern of adversarial relations would prevail in times of electoral campaigns (the three last privatization bills were discussed the year before to the presidential election) when the parties sought to differentiate themselves before the electorate.

Government–opposition problems were not the only ones the Radical government had to face. As this case-study shows, it also had difficulty in convincing its own party in Congress. In effect, Radicalism's control of the majority of seats in the lower house during most of the period did not automatically imply support. On the contrary, the party exhibited a great reluctance to innovate on the traditional functions of the state. Like Peronism, the Radical Party had no consciousness of crisis and, therefore, of the need for economic reform. Moreover, the absence of a clear diagnosis of the economic problems was also shared by the Radical government at the beginning of its mandate. As has been explained before, during the second half of the century, the popular parties could hardly exist as organizations and had not much opportunity to be in power. This fact effected the development of a rather distorted vision of the requirements of the 1980s, and demanded that programmes from the 1960s be applied to the critically changed post-authoritarian situation. In addition, the military dictatorship had critically influenced their views, contributing to the discredit of any attempt at structural economic reform, and therefore, confirming the need to return to the old distributive policies. Consequently, the acknowledgement of the severity and the causes of the Argentine economic crisis was a process gradually experienced by those in charge of taking economic decisions, but not accompanied by the rest of the ruling party. On many occasions, the policy of privatization showed that the line of conflict divided government and Congress, and not government and opposition. Concentrating on the defence of their values – and the values they thought they shared with everyone committed to the defence of the democratic regime – the parties saw the government's economic decisions as a betrayal of well-established party principles and electoral promises. This attitude was maintained without change throughout the decade.

In view of this background, it is not surprising that there was no successful process of policy formulation in Congress. Indeed, the institutional situation was too complicated to handle, and would have represented a challenge for any president. However, the way in which the policy was managed by the government was not conducive to any government–party cooperation. This was in part a product of the way in which the president constructed and interpreted his role. First of all, Alfonsín's primary concern with the establishment of democracy obstructed his view of the economic problems as needing special attention. There were so many other areas of concern, which the president found more crucial for the democratic reconstruction, and at which he was prepared to throw his full political weight (especially the military problem). Thus, this overlapping of problems did not help to give the impression that privatization, among other measures, was *the* policy of the president and deserved a strict party discipline in response. In fact, Alfonsín was personally quite reluctant to implement a wide programme of structural reforms. This was not only because he was afraid of the consequences that attacking the interests of the *corporaciones* could have for the future of democracy, but also because he knew that these measures could be traumatic and painful for society as a whole.[60] The expected social costs of structural reforms were not compatible with his ideas and promises of what democracy would be, so that Alfonsín lacked the political determination to put these policies forward. Instead, he favoured a partial and timid approach to economic reform.

Apart from this, the way in which the leader built up the sources of his political power did not greatly help in making his economic policies politically viable. Based primarily on popular support, the government adopted an attitude of closing ranks, and opted for the formulation of policy in secret and within the confines of the technical teams of the administration. By doing this, it attempted to avoid the pressure from the multiple forces opposing economic changes. However, the strategy did not bring positive results. Although it helped to gain time and resources at the stage of policy formulation, it did not avoid the obstacles which appeared in the following stages of policy approval and implementation. During these stages, the government became vulnerable to pressure from social groups. Although some *concertación* was sought after initial confrontation with the labour unions and entrepreneurial sectors, no general agreement was possible to sustain a programme of structural economic change. On the contrary, the government found itself ceding to social demands which, in turn, only helped to jeopardize macroeconomic stability. Within this context of increasing conflict with the social groups, the ruling party expressed its discontent at being invited to participate only after decisions had already been adopted. Although the party did not abandon the government,[61] support was not easily obtained in these circumstances and, in the case of privatization, it was not given at all. As for the Peronist Party, during the last years of Alfonsín's government it showed mounting opposition, paving its way for the coming presidential elections.

Despite unsuccessful policy implementation, Alfonsín's government managed to include the privatization policy in the presidential agenda. With Menem's arrival in office, the reconstruction of democracy dramatically gave way to the restructuring of the Argentine state.

4
Privatizations in Menem's Agenda

Introduction

In the last chapter it was argued that President Alfonsín's government failed to achieve its goals of implementing a policy of privatization: the shortage of both political and institutional resources, as well as a presidential leadership primarily identified with the reconstruction of the post-authoritarian regime conspired against a successful outcome. Thus, the power necessary to implement the privatization policy was not forthcoming during the years of Alfonsín's administration. This chapter will show that the scene radically changed with the new president's accession in 1989. The following pages describe how President Carlos Menem built up his political power in a manner that would eventually result in the implementation of one of the most extensive and rapid privatization processes in the world. Indeed, privatization and other structural reforms were introduced amidst a context of hyperinflation, which placed the economy at the top of the government's list of priorities. If the state's financial problems were not among those that a democratic transition leader had been prepared to face, a president coming to power in 1989 knew that the economic front was clearly the greatest challenge. Therefore, at the beginning of his Presidency, Menem counted on the fact that critical socioeconomic conditions encouraged comprehensive efforts at economic reform, and at the same time they facilitated the means for the adoption of daring economic decisions by weakening the position of obstructive actors and stimulating a general mood for change.

Despite an environment favourable to reform, the manner and scope of the reform still greatly depended upon the political motivations, perceptions, and interpretations, as well as the governing style of those occupying the presidential office. Thus, the present chapter is concerned with characterizing the presidential leadership that implemented the economic structural policies in Argentina and, particularly, with highlighting its institutional dimensions. Firstly, it focuses upon the president and his approach to the emergency, his adoption of the programme of structural reforms as a crucial component of the presidential agenda, as well as his building up of public, social and institutional support to implement it. Special emphasis is put on how the challenges posed by the critical context favoured the concentration of the political power in the Executive. Secondly, the chapter shows that the tendency to a unilateral exercise of the political power to the detriment of the other governmental institutions, went beyond the period of emergency and became, as is well known, a dominant feature of Menem's leadership.

In fact, these centralizing political strategies, which the Executive gained with the crisis and procured to maintain over time in order to obtain autonomy and expertise in the implementation of the economic reforms, have often been highlighted for their damaging effects on the democratic regime. Over time, the way in which the structural reforms were being implemented began to raise concerns about the prospects of democratic consolidation in Argentina. It was observed, with pessimism, that the attainment of macroeconomic stability and the recovery of economic growth involved a parallel disrespect for the procedures and institutions of democracy. Therefore, it was argued that the transition to market reforms, characterized by the absence of a consultative and deliberative style of policy implementation, seemed unlikely to coexist with a successful regime consolidation. In the following pages, the institutional features of Menem's first Presidency which contributed to this pessimistic view are presented as a distinctive characteristic of Menem's leadership. However, it should be borne in mind that they were not unique. As leadership is a relational concept, a thorough analysis of it needs also to take into account the view of the other political and institutional actors (with their own preferences on public policy and leadership strategies). Thus, as will be shown, their view could favour a centralized pattern of decision-making in times of emergency, but, whether they would continue to accept it in periods of normality or not is something that needs further exploration.

4.1. The hyperinflation context of 1989

A context characterized by a profound economic crisis has been regarded as having a positive influence on the implementation of a successful economic reform.[1] In effect, the literature explains that such a situation both facilitates the adoption of a reform programme by a government, and contributes to the creation of governmental capacities to sustain the reforms.[2] This section will show that the hyperinflationary context that accompanied Menem to power in 1989 pushed him to pursue the full implementation of an economic programme for which he had never had any real preference. It also shows that the crisis provided the Executive with great political and institutional resources for a unilateral exercise of political power, which was crucial for the adoption of the first measures of economic reform.

4.1.1. The outbreak of the crisis

The hyperinflation crisis of 1989 dramatically revealed the collapse of the state, a state that had gradually and increasingly lost its autonomy *vis-à-vis* social, external and private pressures, that was therefore unable to support the national currency and to control the economic variables that affected its own activities.[3] The outbreak of hyperinflation occurred as a result of the conjunction of contingent and long-term, economic and political factors. In effect, at the beginning of 1989, the socioeconomic situation revealed a series of alarming features, which have been described in the following terms: 'a deeply deteriorating fiscal situation, an increasing governmental indebtedness with unfavourable rates and terms, and international reserves at minimal levels, added to the uncertainty provoked by the coming presidential elections'.[4]

The fact is that during the last third of Alfonsín's term of office there was an increasingly deteriorating situation on the economic front, the clearest evidence of which was the return to a high – and gradually accelerating – inflation rate. The government's inability to maintain the level of fiscal revenues achieved at the beginning of the Austral Plan raised the fiscal deficit to 8 per cent of the GNP in 1988, and increased dependency on foreign debt. The incapacity to control the economic indicators made a political impact on the electoral arena, where the ruling Radical Party lost its majority in the Chamber of Deputies in the 1987 parliamentary elections. As shown in Graphs 3.1, 3.2, and 3.3, presented in Chapter 3, the government's declining image was also noticeable in opinion polls, which showed its gradual loss of popular support from late 1985 onwards together with a growing concern about inflation.

In view of this situation, a last attempt at stabilization was made by the Radical government. The *Plan Primavera* was launched in August 1988, with 'the basically limited (objective) of avoiding hyperinflation before the presidential elections scheduled for May 1989'.[5] To implement it, the government managed to obtain some entrepreneurial commitment to control prices and to contain speculative behaviours leading to runs on the currency. Despite an initial phase of declining inflation, the plan's vulnerability was made apparent when the United States government decided to stop supporting Alfonsín's economic policies and, immediately afterwards, the World Bank declared its refusal to grant a requested loan. Facing a demand for US dollars which threatened to exhaust foreign reserves, the Central Bank suspended sales on 6 February 1989. After the rapid increase in the price of the dollar, inflation followed the same path and became hyperinflation a couple of months later.[6]

4.1.2. The Peronist presidential candidate

The political uncertainty which appeared at the end of Alfonsín's presidential period at the prospect of Peronism's return to power can also be regarded as a factor with a negative influence on the stability of the economy. Much of this was due to the political profile of Carlos Menem, the Peronist candidate, and the way he conducted the presidential campaign.

Menem had graduated with a degree in Law from the University of Córdoba. In 1955, after finishing his studies, he returned to his home province of La Rioja, where he combined his first professional experiences with becoming an activist in the Peronist movement. Menem's political career progressed in the province and he was elected governor in 1973. As the 1976 military coup suspended political life in the country, Menem was arrested without having completed his first administration. During the difficult years of dictatorship, he was first placed in prison and later under house arrest. Elections held on the return to democratic rule in the 1980s resulted in Menem becoming governor of La Rioja for a second term. During Alfonsín's government, belonging to a different party from the one controlling the national government was not regarded by Menem as an obstacle to obtaining political benefits. He astutely knew how to profit from Radicalism's need to cultivate ties with Peronists controlling provincial governorships. He took advantage of this situation and asked for federal subsidies in order to finance an overgrown and inefficient provincial state apparatus. Increasing public employment and all kinds of social plans for housing, health and food were used in La Rioja as political instruments of clientelism, but they also left a fiscal deficit and a financial crisis in the provincial bank and the lottery. Moreover, there were suspicions of corruption regarding the use of public funds and accusations of manipulation of control institutions such as the Judiciary.[7] Thus, Menem's political style resembled that of a typical *caudillo*, since it combined populist policies with a feudal administrative style in which the lack of accountability was the norm. He even sought constitutional reform and was re-elected governor in 1987. However, during his second administration, he was too busy putting his presidential aspirations forward to concern himself with provincial issues.

In 1988, Menem won the first internal elections ever held by the Peronist Party, and became the party's candidate for the coming presidential elections. Menem had managed to secure his candidacy over that of Antonio Cafiero, who was then the president of the party. Both Menem and Cafiero were members of *Renovación*, a group of Peronist legislators and governors who started the process of the internal restructuring of Peronism. Their goal was dictated by the political substance of the Radical triumph of 1983 when democracy arrived in Argentina.[8] In order to adapt the Peronist movement to suit the new democratic era, *Renovación* promoted the free internal election of candidates and the ousting of the union leaders from the party's leadership. It emphasized the importance of the party structure (as opposed to the movement), the internal democratization of this structure, and Peronism's participation in electoral contests as one of the parts of the party system. Despite being a member of this movement for renewal, Menem knew how politically convenient it was to play the role of an outsider, and to take advantage of the possibilities that governing a small marginal province offered for a presidential career. This contrasted with Cafiero's double institutional responsibility of being the president of the party and the governor of the densely populated province of Buenos Aires. In effect, Menem could dedicate much of his time to travelling around the country and becoming involved in national problems. He could give shelter to those excluded by the party's leadership during the reorganization process, especially the union leaders and some orthodox sectors. He was not forced to make compromises with the national government, compromises that were crucial to the continuity of the political regime, especially when after the 1987 elections Peronism gained control of most provincial governments. Menem's status of being an outsider, as well as his political style full of traditional elements that awoke the Peronist identity and restored the mystique of the movement, turned to his advantage and helped him to defeat Cafiero.

Later on, this political style would also prove to be successful in arousing public sentiment and winning the presidential prize. As a presidential candidate, he presented himself as a saviour who would change the destinies of his people.[9] By running a presidential campaign based on a direct appeal to the public,[10] Menem avoided being linked with the discredited party organizations.[11] Similarly, by putting emphasis on his personal qualities, he avoided programmatic definitions. He was there to change people's destinies, without having to say much about how he was supposed to achieve such a goal. His speeches were vague, and even contradictory, since Menem would adapt them to suit whoever was listening. Nevertheless, a few propositions came out clearly during the campaign, but they tended to sound like the old populism, especially to the business sectors. Menem for the most part promised debt moratorium, *salariazo*, productive revolution, Latin American unity and national reconciliation.[12] This old-style political discourse, together with Menem's populist image and what his experience as governor of La Rioja revealed of his work in the public sphere, created great uncertainty about what would happen if he was to come to power. Thus, the prospect of a return of Peronism to government left the business sectors greatly concerned and indeed worried. Without offering any credible alternative, Menem's campaign merely contributed to the fears of future fiscal indiscipline and, thus, more inflation.

Despite arousing the distrust of the entrepreneurial sectors, Menem's presidential campaign was effective from an electoral point of view. People seemed to prefer the uncertainty of times to come under Menem, to the poor performance of the ruling party on economic issues. Eduardo Angeloz, the Radical candidate, made a considerable effort to distance himself from both Alfonsín's administration and his Peronist opponent, while formulating a clear programme of government, supporting economic liberalism and capitalism. Nevertheless, he could not counteract the erosive effect that the increasingly deteriorating socioeconomic situation had on the electoral support for his party. Thus, the 14 May elections gave the presidential prize to Carlos Menem.

After this date, inflation, which had followed the path set by the growth of the dollar during the previous months, became hyperinflation. The whole country was shaken by the loss of control over the economic situation,[13] with popular riots taking place in the suburbs of the big cities, amid a general state of emergency and feelings of desperation. With one president still in office and the next one just elected, Argentina suffered from a sharp fall in tax collection and public expenditure, alongside recession, public misery and violence. In this context, the question of the presidential transition arose. The weakness of a president still in office but without any real power to effect a way out of the crisis was coupled with the fact that the newly elected president was due to assume power in December, seven months after the elections had been held and the crisis had erupted. The creation of a political power able to handle the situation was imperative. It involved not only the political survival of the elected figure, whose winning of the popular vote did not help to calm down the financial markets, but also the creation of the conditions which, by smoothing the presidential succession, would secure the continued existence of the political regime.

4.1.3. The presidential transition

The eventual solution to the question of transition was an understanding between the major Argentine political parties, which consisted of both an arrangement for the transfer of the Presidency and the establishment of rules for a period of party cohabitation. The process of political *rapprochement* began at the height of the crisis, when the Radical Party – then in power – witnessed the dissolution of its ability to govern. In order to deal with these circumstances, Radical administrators moved towards a strategy of cooperation with elected Peronist officials.[14] Thus, the political outcome of the crisis was an agreement between the two major political parties, which had two main components. The first was that there was to be a change in the duration of the transitional period. Within the context of the crisis, it was understood that the will to undertake emergency measures was not in itself enough to deal with the situation. The power to put these measures into practice became necessary, and Alfonsín's ability to implement this task was extremely limited. Conversely, the majority of the popular vote that Menem had obtained in the recent elections gave him concrete power to initiate a more daring economic programme. However, he was not expected to assume power until the following 10 December, and the remaining six months appeared dangerously long. In view of this, both major political parties agreed to shorten the transition period from December to July. The president's resignation was the most convenient institutional way out of the crisis and this would still allow for the continuation of the democratic regime.[15]

Other parallel agreements accompanied the one concerning the transfer of the presidential mandate. These arrangements took into account the unfavourable situation that the transfer of the Presidency in July would mean in terms of congressional seats for the new administration. In fact, the shortening of Alfonsín's period in office did not include Congress, which kept December as the changeover date. Since the Radicals had a majority in the lower chamber, Menem would start governing without congressional support. Hence, the Peronists agreed to assume the presidential office before the expected date, but obtained in return the Radicals' commitment to facilitate the approval of all economic laws that the Peronists would send to Congress during the period July to December. The agreement especially affected the Chamber of Deputies, because in political terms it meant that the Radicals would provide the number of legislators necessary to form the *quorum*. Since they had 114 deputies and were, consequently, the first minority, the agreement consisted in guaranteeing their presence to begin the discussion of the bills, but only up to the maximum of 75 people so that the Peronist position would turn out to be predominant.[16]

Consequently, agreements made in 1989 showed the parties cooperating at times when the socioeconomic crisis seemed to put the democratic regime in danger. As will be seen, this disposition to agree provided the Executive with invaluable institutional resources to launch a daring programme of structural reforms. But, first, I shall comment on how this programme came to be part of the agenda of a president who had the most unlikely background to implement it.

4.2. Building presidential power

In July 1989, much of the power of Carlos Menem was due to the extraordinary environment created by the crisis as well as to the great expectancy and hope that the inauguration of a new mandate involved. In other words, the new president could count on the weakness of other political and social actors and the public's approval for undertaking rapid and strong actions to cope with the emergency. Using the power given by these special circumstances, Menem took the lead in trying to build a more solid basis of support. In so doing, the structural reforms became the political instrument of a new daring politics of alliances. Therefore, the Executive invested great political effort in order to obtain a rapid and complete implementation of the reforms on which it relied for its political survival. The delegation of power granted by Congress helped Menem to accelerate their adoption.

4.2.1. *The great turnaround*

Once elected, Menem began to move away from the ambiguous stance of his electoral campaign towards a more precisely defined position. This position was in fact far removed from what his political experience and Peronist affiliation would ever have suggested. It embraced – to the surprise of Menem's opponents and followers alike – the principles of a neo-liberal programme: ending state interventionism and protected capitalism, privatization of public enterprises, fiscal adjustment, the opening up of the economy. Thus, in a matter of days, within the restrictions imposed by the hyperinflation context, Menem put aside the old traditions of Peronism towards state intervention. He learnt that his future capacity to implement public policies and to recover the state's lost governmental resources, depended on the abandonment of criticism of the adjustment policies and the adoption of business-oriented reforms. The structural reforms were regarded as the instrument necessary to obtain political resources, in other words, the only way to calm down the financial markets, obtain some urgently needed external aid, respond to the public demands for urgent solutions, and, finally, gain the support of the predominant business sectors, which, as Alfonsín's experience had illustrated, proved to be crucial for the implementation of any economic plan. Therefore, soon after his arrival in power, Menem began to put in practice a number of emergency measures, similar to stabilizing shock packages (such as an increase in taxation and a currency devaluation), and a programme of structural reforms aiming at eliminating the fiscal deficit.[17]

Indeed, such a sudden change left Menem open to accusations of 'political opportunism'[18] and to a 'problem of political credibility'.[19] The economic orientations of Peronism, the socio-political composition of its bases, Menem's own political profile, the substance of the presidential campaign, were all elements conspiring against the certainty that Menem would be able and committed to maintaining the chosen direction of reform. This fact is very important to our understanding of the dimension of the political operation that Menem undertook after the elections. Indeed, a president having to face a serious crisis needs to take drastic decisions and propose policy changes. However, a president who, besides confronting an emergency has to gain credibility, will go much further, making an abrupt break with the past. As a consequence, Menem's efforts to try to gain credibility greatly affected the pace and scope of the economic reforms: they would be both rapid and profound. They also prescribed that reforms went beyond the range of strictly economic decisions (to involve, for instance, foreign affairs) and meant that, on many occasions, they would be implemented without due consideration of the constitutional limits on the use of political power.[20]

With the adoption of a market economy programme, Menem was able to draw support from the national business sector and international banks and creditors. He also gained the approval of public opinion and, furthermore, he did not lose the backing of his own political movement. As Torre and Palermo have concluded, Menem's turnaround once elected 'was the result of a strategic calculation; more precisely, the choice of market policies was a means to neutralise his political weakness, forge a hitherto unknown social coalition, and maintain himself in power'.[21]

4.2.2. *The social supports*

The alliance with the business sectors was made explicit and put in practice from the very beginning of Menem's administration. This implied a reformulation of the interests that Peronism had previously represented since, although it had historically had links to the capitalist sector through organizations of small and middle-range industrialists, the large economic groups had always been regarded as the enemies of the interests of its members. The first moves in this direction consisted of appointments to public posts, the most remarkable of which was that of Miguel Roig – who had been president of Bunge & Born, the largest Argentine multinational firm – as head of the Ministry of Economy. This made quite a symbolic impact, as did other parallel appointments, such as that of Alvaro Alsogaray – the leading figure of the small centre-right party, UceDé, with a long tradition of support for liberal economic ideas – as the president's adviser for external debt matters.[22] Thus, by means of key cabinet appointments, Menem sought to emphasize his commitment to the newly selected course of action as well as to his new politics of alliances.

However, given the heterogeneity and divergence of its interests, the support of the business sectors was not easily obtained, being at the beginning often more rhetorical than practical. Entrepreneurs approved economic reforms that helped to bring an end to instability and improve the fiscal situation of the state. But, in practice, they were reluctant to accept the withdrawal of the benefits they had enjoyed under the old model of state interventionism: they opposed tax increases, reductions in subsidies, cuts in exports incentives, increases in the prices of the services and products of public companies. Therefore, to transform this diffuse support into an effective alliance, the government decided to offer special incentives, remarkably, those connected to the investment opportunities that the privatization programme provided for local business.[23] As Corrales has pointed out, while Alfonsín would have been content to secure a privatization deal with foreign firms, Menem would do whatever was necessary to persuade the large Argentine entrepreneurial groups to buy state-owned companies.[24] Thus, in almost every privatization that Menem would carry out, a domestic buyer would eventually be included. Sooner or later, the strategy would prove to be effective in weakening business opposition by securing the support of the most important economic groups. However, as will be shown in the next chapter, this strategy would also have negative consequences for the quality of the privatization policy, particularly of those privatizations implemented during the first years of the administration.

Agreements with the new partners did not imply a breakdown in relations with pre-election supporters, but rather the extension of the coalition to include new members. Menem's political strength grew soon after he took office when his party and the unions demonstrated that, despite internal complaint, they would not rebel against him. In fact, Menem could exert an effective control over the Peronist Party because he was its first real political leader since Perón's death.[25] With his electoral victories in 1988 and 1989, Menem legitimized his leadership and, thus, gained the support of the party. As will also be shown in the next chapter, this was functional to the tasks of the government even though his decisions as a president involved the revision of the party's principles. By exercising the leadership of the party, Menem gained autonomy in the adoption of decisions and was able to maintain the economic direction adopted during the hyperinflation crisis.[26]

On the other hand, although the processes of structural reform and industrial restructuring would challenge the institutional influence of unions (as, for instance, unemployment and job loss caused by privatization would diminish union membership and their industrial resources), their opposition to Menem's policy shift was very limited. The confrontational attitude that had characterized the CGT's leadership during Alfonsín's years, leading to 13 general strikes, contrasts with only the one strike that the CGT organized during Menem's first administration. In effect, after announcements regarding market reforms, the CGT split into a supportive confederation, an opposition confederation, and a group of independent unions. As Murillo has explained, the first supported Menem's initiatives in exchange for political appointments and a privileged relation with the Executive. The second was formed by opposition unions (teachers, state employees, metalworkers) which organized several strikes but which represented, nevertheless, a minority of the organized labour sector. The third group included the large unions which, facing the challenges posed by the structural reforms, chose the strategy of organizational autonomy. This strategy consisted of preserving their large organizations (threatened by the reforms) by increasing their reliance on market mechanisms.[27] When the CGT reunited in 1992, these unions joined it and exerted a strong influence on its organization.[28]

The fact is that, given the Peronist identity of the labour movement, Menem's government did not have to face major confrontation from that front. However, its support is not only explicable in terms of old political loyalties, but also, of the selective incentives that the government offered, particularly, the opportunities for market activities that the implementation of structural reforms provided.

Menem also counted on the favourable reaction of public opinion and its support for the economic reforms. As opinion polls indicated, (see Graph 4.1), in July 1989, Menem managed to raise the 47.5 per cent of votes he had obtained in the elections to an 82 per cent approval rating. Thus, the president could present his initiatives as expressions of the people's needs and desires. Public opinion was an 'asset' with which Menem could face resistance from interest groups, bureaucracies and reluctant politicians. But, how could Menem obtain public acceptance of measures that involved social costs? Social acceptance of economic reforms was not the consequence of a firm conviction that they would lead to a better future, but rather, it expressed the people's need to escape from an unbearable present and to avoid its possible repetition in future.[29] The long-term economic crisis, accelerated by the hyperinflationary episode, had raised popular demands for change and economic governability.[30] Therefore, with such a level of public approval, Menem not only managed to legitimize the chosen direction of market reforms, but also to obtain a blank cheque to cope with the crisis, a unique opportunity to succeed in the policy-making process. In effect, hyperinflation was a challenge, but also an opportunity to exercise his political leadership, and Menem knew how to profit from it. Without facing major social and political resistance, Menem opted for a unilateral use of political power, which eventually helped him to launch a profound and wide programme of reforms. At an institutional level, the

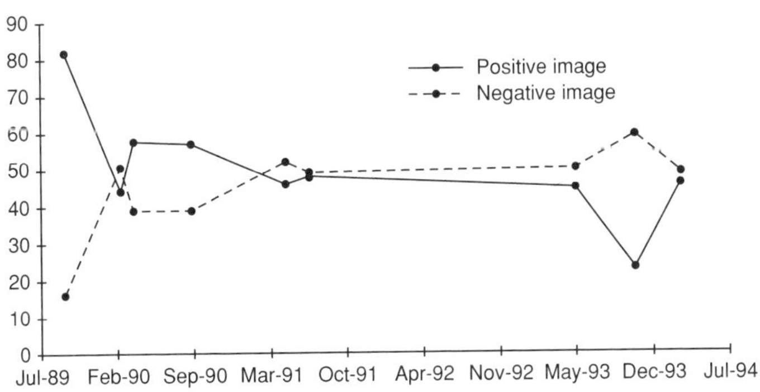

Graph 4.1 Menem: image during his presidential mandate

Source: Estudio Sociológico y Político Mora y Araujo, Noguera y Asociados. National sample of 800 cases: Argentines older than 18 years. Estimated error: 3.5 per cent.

first phase of Menem's Presidency was characterized by the delegation of power from Congress.

4.2.3. *The institutional resources*

This section analyses the main instruments used by the Executive in order to obtain, this time institutionally, the instruments necessary to adopt the decisions to deal with the emergency. As I shall explain in the following subsections, delegation of power was the means selected by the president to consolidate his power *vis-à-vis* Congress. The large amount of unilateral authority that this resource produced was connected with the urgent need of the Executive to prevent the appearance of obstacles to the implementation of its economic reform plans.

4.2.3.1. The delegation of power: In order to manage the crisis the Executive demanded the approval of two bills by Congress: the economic emergency bill and the state reform bill. These bills provided a major framework for future policy actions, in accordance with the programmatic direction followed after the presidential elections. However, they did not restrict themselves to drawing up a programme of government. They were concerned at the same time with the necessity of building a political power-base able to implement it.

Based on the need to overcome the fiscal crisis of the state, the economic emergency bill was aimed at the financial cleansing of the public sector. Its measures attempted an immediate and temporary reduction of public expenditure, mainly expressed in terms of subsidy regimes. In particular, it tried to suspend subsidies and subventions, benefits for industrial promotion, and appointments that could mean the increase of public administration costs; defer debts; sell state properties; and establish the autonomy of the Central Bank, in order to preserve the value of the currency and avoid direct or indirect financing by the national and provincial governments. Concurrently, other measures aimed at modifying market conditions while seeking, for instance, equality between national and foreign productive capital, suspension of preferential treatment for nationally produced goods, and of import permits in the case of either expensive home-produced goods or those in short supply.[31]

The emergency measures adopted by the economic emergency bill were complemented by the provisions of the bill for the privatization and restructuring of public enterprises, which was also sent to Congress in the middle of the phase of hyperinflation, a few days after Carlos Menem's administration took office. This bill had been designed by

Roberto Dromi, the Minister of Public Works and Services, and constituted the starting point of the Menem's privatization policy.[32] In spite of the long-term structural changes that the initiative was seeking, most of its provisions showed that a sense of urgency accompanied the basic reform. In fact, on the one hand, the bill was thought to be the instrument that would allow the government to undertake the reform of the state – the structural part of the government's programme considered essential to starting the 'productive revolution'. As explained in the preamble to the bill, the process of privatization was to contribute to a powerful surge in production in the Argentinian economy, because the participation of private capital in public services would offer the resources that the state was at that time unable to provide. On the other hand, the critical economic situation revealed that the state was not only lacking the necessary resources to carry out a social and economic transformation, its enterprises were also faced with serious financial problems, most of them characterized by increasing deficits as well as unpaid debts and obligations. In the government's view, the critical situation of the state was an invitation to try a pragmatic response, which consisted in setting aside ideologies and prejudices in order to let private capital participate in the process of improving public financial conditions and, therefore, of expanding the country's economic capabilities.[33]

Following these aims, the bill declared a state of emergency affecting all the state's entities, enterprises and societies. To begin their reorganization, the law established that someone would take them over (*interventor*) for a fixed period of time (180 days), which could be extended for a similar term. During that time, those assuming control, according to the instructions sent by the Executive or the minister involved, would basically be in charge of preparing the conditions for the privatization of the enterprise under his/her supervision. However, the bill also stated that the Executive first needed to obtain congressional approval in order to arrange the privatization of any of the entities. In this sense, the declaration 'subject to privatization' made by law was the condition necessary to make a state enterprise transferable to the private sector.

Besides establishing these general rules for privatization, the bill adopted the first concrete measures regarding the policy by incorporating an appendix with an extensive number of enterprises, which were declared 'subject to privatization' under Article 9.[34] The list included public companies that executed a wide range of activities, encompassing public services (such as airlines, telephones, underground, media, cultural activities, ecological maintenance) and basic production (such as the coal and petrochemical industries), and indicated what sort of privatization would apply to each of them (total or partial).[35] The list also made reference to the concession of public works and services. In this way, when the bill was approved, the repair and maintenance of roads, works relating to the infrastructure of the rail network and its services as well as oil exploration and exploitation were, among others, to be conceded to private companies.

Consequently, by means of the sale of state-owned companies or the concession of public works, the state would relinquish many of its economic activities into the hands of private capital. In reality, the bill also incorporated a clause according to which state assets could be totally or partially sold using the system of *propiedad participada*. Under this system, capital assets were represented by shares to be acquired by the workers of the company to be privatized, the users of services provided by the company and the producers of the raw material used by the company. In practice, the 'participated property' system authorized the participation of the unions in the privatization process by the administration of the workers' shares.[36] However, this system also seemed designed to favour the state's private contractors and suppliers. The participated property clause (Article 22 in the bill's final version) and Article 16, which also included private contractors and suppliers among the sectors to be given preference in privatization processes, were criticized for showing that the government had surrendered to the pressure from these entrepreneurial sectors.[37]

Under these conditions, the state reform bill had been designed to deal with the fiscal crisis the state was going through. It did so by setting the basis of the privatization policy, which from then on would be closely linked to the stabilization objectives of the new administration. Furthermore, the critical economic context also dictated how the programme would later be carried out. In effect, both the economic emergency bill and the state reform bill provided a major framework for future policy actions as well as a series of dispositions aimed at guaranteeing the Executive the means to implement those measures without major institutional interference. The government's proposal for state reform made it clear that it was the Executive and its cabinet which would be controlling the process of restructuring the public sector, rather than Congress, for the simple reason that the urgency of the moment did not allow time to discuss each privatization case individually. In this way, the privatization policy would mainly be implemented by means of decrees rather than laws.[38] Whilst the context of the crisis was invoked to justify the delegation of power, the function of controlling the process that was to take place in the executive branch was reserved for Congress. For that purpose, the bill decreed the creation of a *comisión bicameral*, consisting of six senators and six deputies, who would be given all information regarding the bill and who would have the right to ask for further information and formulate proposals, advice and observations. Similarly, the economic emergency bill also delegated legislative powers to the Executive, although to a lesser extent, because some crucial dispositions had already been adopted by the bill itself.[39] Congress also retained prerogatives of control, since Article 88 established the creation of a congressional bicameral commission in charge of controlling the Executive in its use of the functions delegated to it by this bill.

4.2.3.2. The delegative laws in Congress: The approval of the State Reform Law and the Economic Emergency Law created a great imbalance in the relative powers of Presidency and Congress.[40] The reason for this is that Congress agreed to delegate its legislative powers to participate in the policies' design. By delegating to the Executive, Congress resigned its 'legislative powers of reaction' (see Chapter 1, subsection 1.2.2.), that is, the possibility to intervene in the approval processes of several individual privatization laws while solely maintaining its functions of political control. Furthermore, it did so by respecting the timetable set by the Executive. It should be noted, though, that delegation did not prevent Congress from attempting to amend original drafts. Legislators did not try to alter the bill's basic arrangements, but rather to include control mechanisms and, in the case of the state reform, improve privatization conditions. Some of these modifications were successful (such as explicit references to external control organizations, like the *Tribunal de Cuentas* and the *Sindicatura de Empresas Publicas*, which would work in close cooperation with the Bicameral Commission which, in turn, was granted the power to receive data and documents from the Executive whenever it needed them), whilst others concerning the policy's design (such as provisions eradicating the possibility of external debt capitalization) were eventually withdrawn during the rule-making process. To sum up, the government managed to control most of the contents to be included in the final version, so that any delays or threats to the subsequent implementation process could be avoided.[41]

Delegation was possible in 1989 because of the political convergence that the context of hyperinflation had created: Peronists, Radicals, and members of smaller parties facilitated the bill's approval in both Chambers. The first two parties did so in accordance with the arrangements for the transfer of the mandate from President Alfonsín to President Menem, which, as explained before, included cooperation in the passage of economic legislation. Then, UCeDé members and provincial parties completed the support which resulted in the unanimous vote for the bill in the Senate and a wide majority in the lower house. Total cooperation in Congress served, in practice, to confirm the predominance of the president. Therefore, the critical context in which these bills were discussed allowed the recently elected government to obtain great political autonomy. In fact, the amount of delegation that they involved remains as a distinctive feature of the first months of President Menem's administration. In other words, the launch of the structural economic reforms in Argentina could be characterized by Keeler's expression of 'an ideal-typical maximum window:' a severe crisis that helped to empower the new government with an overwhelming mandate, and created an extraordinary policy-making context to produce the reform legislation.[42] As a consequence, all decisions authorized by the delegative laws at this stage were to be made by the Executive. For privatization, the Ministry of Public Works and Services and the Ministry of Defence would be in charge of leading the implementation process. Congress was confined to exercising control functions by means of bicameral commissions.

4.3. Furthering presidential resources

The previous section commented on how the Executive managed to gain power from a delegation that concentrated in its hands the making of decisions necessary to deal with the economic emergency. This section looks at other important measures intended to confirm not only that the formulation and adoption of policy decisions were meant to be prerogatives of the Executive, but also that the Executive would not tolerate interruptions, delays or derailments in the economic implementation process. They show that the delegation of power was regarded as insufficient. Throughout the years of Menem's first administration, a movement to concentrate unilateral resources in the Executive took place. Many of them were connected to policy implementation needs, while others could hardly be justified in terms of urgency, and would be better regarded as indicatives of an autocratic style in governmental leadership. Firstly, the Executive resorted to necessity and urgency decrees. Secondly, it dealt with obstacles coming from the judicial system by controlling the composition of the Supreme Court. Thirdly, it increased the centralization of power within the confines of its own branch of government.

4.3.1. Necessity and urgency decrees

As has been explained before, many of President Menem's economic structural reforms were meant to be approved by means of decrees instead of laws. The use of decrees was authorized by the delegation of power provided for in the Economic Emergency and State Reform Laws. Similarly, some other reforms, such as the policy for the rationalization of public administration, were adopted by decrees that derived directly from the powers granted to the president by the Constitution. Thus, in these cases, the use of decrees in order to make economic policy decisions was based on powers either constitutionally granted or legally delegated. However, Menem also resorted to 'legislate' by means of decree. By using necessity and urgency decrees, the president assumed the prerogatives of legislation belonging to Congress, with no authorization, frequently modifying or even repealing prevailing laws. Menem became noted for the vast amount of these decrees he issued during a single term of office. Ferreira Rubio and Goretti have shown that, between July 1989 and August 1994, President Menem signed 336 necessity and urgency decrees, while between 1853 and July 1989, a total of only 35 had been issued.[43]

As regards subjects, necessity and urgency decrees were mainly connected to economic issues (65 per cent were related to taxation, salaries, public debt, transport, sale of real estate and the restructuring of public agencies). They involved, for instance, the pegging of salaries to the inflation rate in 1989, the restriction of the state's expenditure in 1990 by considering public debt and state structures and organizations, as well as the deregulation of the economy, the core of which was put forward in the mega-decree 2284 in October 1991. However, the use of these decrees was not confined to the period of economic emergency. In fact it covered the whole presidential period, in times of both hyperinflation and macroeconomic stability.[44] This fact, as well as the large amount of decrees issued during Menem's first term in office, reveal a certain autocratic style in the adoption of decisions. They further show that the government made its own assessment of the risks it faced when sending an economic issue to Congress, and that fears of delay or rejection encouraged the use of unilateral resources. Rather than responding to real critical situations, then, necessity and urgency decrees were often the answer to the government's own political need to see its measures implemented rapidly.

4.3.2. *The Supreme Court*

Soon after the approval of the emergency laws, the government began to perceive that justice was another sphere where opposition to the economic reforms could be expressed. A declaration claiming those laws to be unconstitutional was interpreted as disastrous for the future of the economic plan. Similarly, the constitutionality of necessity and urgency decrees was another preoccupying topic for the government. Thus, control of the Supreme Court of Justice was necessary to avoid any challenge to the reforms.[45] With the argument that no obstacles should interfere with the will of the people as expressed through their elected representatives (the Court was not an elected body), the government devised a bill that was meant to create a favourable majority in the Supreme Court by means of increasing the number of members from five to nine. The bill was submitted in September 1989 and passed in April 1990, after a fairly easy passage in the Senate (where the comfortable Peronist majority approved it in only 11 days), and a more complicated one in the lower house.[46] As previously noted, the result was the enlargement of the membership of the Supreme Court, and the appointment of pro-government candidates. In May 1990, Menem had already appointed, with the Senate's agreement, six Supreme Court judges: four in the created posts, and the remaining two replacing those who had resigned.[47]

The effectiveness of the changes was proved immediately. The most eloquent case was that of Moisés Fontela, a Peronist dissident deputy who attempted to call into question the privatization of Aerolíneas Argentinas by resorting to the judicial system. The deputy tried to interrupt the final process of the sale, by using an *acción de amparo* in which objections to the legal procedure of adjudication were presented. The judge allowed the demand, and gave orders to stop the bidding process until the alleged irregularities were clarified. Soon afterwards, the Minister of Public Works and Services, Roberto Dromi, appealed directly to the Supreme Court, and rapidly obtained the Court's suspension of the judge's decision. This case was particularly interesting not only because the government could confirm that the judiciary could have been an obstacle if its reform of the Supreme Court had not been carried out, but also because the controversial *per saltum* resource was used for the first time in Argentine history. The bypassing of the intermediate stages in the judicial process had no clear legislative background, so that the Supreme Court's acceptance of the procedure legitimated what had historically been a matter of controversy and debate.[48]

The Supreme Court's response to necessity and urgency decrees was another demonstration of the effectiveness of the changes in its composition. In a decision taken in 1990 (*Caso Peralta*) the Court's doctrine was established: although these decrees were not mentioned in the Constitution, they could be adopted in 'extremely grave situations'. From them on, the Court had to rule on various questions that had been issued by necessity and urgency decrees, and had stimulated judicial demands. In general, the response was favourable to the executive power's decree ordinances, except in cases directly affecting the Court's own prerogatives.[49]

4.3.3. Inside the presidential branch

It is true that, by using the delegation of power authorized by both the Economic Emergency and the State Reform Laws, and the measures adopted by the unilateral resource of decrees, the president managed to keep all decision-making regarding the economic reform within the executive branch. Nonetheless, it was soon demonstrated that a process of policy implementation concentrated in the Executive would not be exempt from difficulties. To begin with, the government had an extensive and complex structure. It consisted of different ministries and secretariats with competing interests, many of which had a vested interest in opposing state reform. Secondly, the policy decisions had been adopted by a leader who, in difficult circumstances, had been compelled to reverse traditional policies. Thus, the party leaders and teams in charge of the implementation processes might be ready to follow the president's directions, but their philosophical base was rather closer to populism than to adjustment policies. Finally, the executive branch included members of the broad social coalition that had been formed after the elections.[50] The coexistence of old and new members of the coalition in government provoked the natural conflicts of different goals within the confines of the same administration. By having an entrepreneur in charge of the Ministry of Economy and union representatives in the Ministry of Labour, Menem attempted to tackle the problems of governability. However, this strategy soon made the government highly vulnerable to social pressure.

Since this situation conspired against the president's goals of adjustment and structural reform, and could tarnish the public view of the government's capability to address the reform (so increasing problems of credibility), a series of measures were adopted to counterbalance the lack of governmental competency. Consequently, by means of the top-down political strategy headed by the president, a process of concentration of power began to take place within the Executive branch. Firstly, the president began to establish a kind of 'parallel administration'[51] by appointing *interventores* (as authorized by the State Reform Law) to carry out privatizations, replacing those reluctant to cooperate with the adjustment plans with loyal pro-reform appointees, or forming special reform commissions with the participation of groups of interest. Secondly, the president sought to exert direct control over much of what took place within the executive branch by means of weekly meetings of the whole cabinet, a historically unusual practice of regularity. Thirdly, decisions were made concerning the structure and organization of the ministries which were intended to centralize power in the areas in charge of implementing the reforms. The most important decision in that direction was probably the merger of the Ministries of Economy and Public Works and Services, in order to concentrate the reform processes in a single entity.[52] The measure was the initiative of Minister Domingo Cavallo, who had proposed it soon after his arrival in office at the beginning of 1991. It signified an important positive step toward the unification of the leadership of the economic process.

Indeed, these measures contributed greatly to diminishing the levels of dissent within the Executive. But the most crucial move in the Executive's search for autonomy and expertise was the displacement of party officials and the appointment of professional *técnicos* into the key areas of reform implementation. The arrival of technocrats in the Executive occurred gradually. It began with the failure of Minister Rapanelli's administration of the economy. After a few months, the very Peronist decision of selecting an entrepreneur to head the Ministry of Economy proved to have increased the state's vulnerability and its incapacity to deal with the crisis. The administration acknowledged the situation and changed its strategy with the subsequent appointment of an accountant, Erman González, a personal friend of Menem's from La Rioja. With his arrival, professional economists began to be included in the cabinet. During this period, the government continued to respond favourably to the business sector, but decisions were adopted without their direct participation. However, it was only with the appointment of Domingo Cavallo that the party men surrendered the management of economic affairs into the hands of the technocrats.

Cavallo had a Doctorate in Economics from Harvard University. His participation in the last military regime – as president of the Central Bank for a short period – is usually remembered for the nationalization of the external debt of private companies. In the new democratic era, he was, first, elected as a Peronist national deputy for the 1985–89 term, and then appointed Minister of Foreign Affairs by Menem. At the time of his arrival at the Ministry of Economy in January 1991, he was accompanied by a team of specialists that had previously worked with him, or were somehow connected to, his own research and consultancy foundation. This team exhibited a formidable technical education, a strong internal coherence, and an unusual sharing of common understandings and conceptions, so that the minister managed to create a solid bureaucratic nucleus which implied a qualitative change compared to the previous teams in charge of reform implementation. Thus, Cavallo's weapons were knowledge, a homogenous team, and good relationships with both the local and foreign business sectors and the financial world. With this background, his appointment contributed to enhancing the levels of coherence and unity in the execution of the policy-making processes, as well as to closing the credibility gap which Menem's government had faced from the beginning of the mandate.

Like the president and his closest political allies, the *técnicos* in charge of running the economy also tried to centralize power and enact policy reform in an autocratic manner.[53] If the first were interested in the rapid success of the reforms for their own political survival, the latter did so in order to break the resistance of both public agencies and groups that had benefited from state intervention and were, therefore, opposed to the structural reforms. Together they acted as an extremely powerful instrument of government and this had an impact on their relation with the other institutions of government. For instance, Carlos Menem's propensity to enact necessity and urgency decrees was often shared by Cavallo, who later publicly admitted that these resources had been crucial in the implementation of the economic reforms.[54] Nevertheless, this governmental machinery created problems of its own. Cavallo's technical profile, coupled with his successful economic performance (linked to the stabilization achievements of his 'convertibility plan'), became a source of power for him but it also generated rivalries with the rest of the government. Therefore, despite all the efforts at unification, conflicts did not disappear within the executive branch. To state the situation simply, there were two sectors: the '*técnicos*' in charge of running the economy, and the '*rama política*' in charge of providing the political means to make the reforms possible. In principle, this tacit division of labour could be thought of (and certainly was for some time) as being strong and efficient, since the two sectors pointing in the same direction greatly improved the chances of reform implementation. However, increasing power conflicts between president and minister as well as rivalries for the president's favour would sometimes hamper the Executive's capabilities.

Conclusion

This chapter has described the many elements, often cited in the specialist literature, that conformed a tendency towards a unilateral Executive-centred exercise of the political power during the years of Menem's first administration. Concentration of power was made to the detriment of the other institutions of government, Congress and the judiciary, since measures such as the delegation of legislative power, the introduction of changes to the composition of the Supreme Court, and the extensive use of necessity and urgency decrees, considerably reduced their institutional stature and capacities to impose checks on the Executive's actions. It was stated that this tendency was favoured by the context of the hyperinflation in which Menem initiated his mandate because it raised general demands for change and economic governability, and simultaneously weakened social and political opposition to economic reform. Similarly, the extraordinary environment created by the crisis was the starting point on which Menem based to build a more solid basis of support, that is, a new daring politics of alliances, the consolidation of which depended on the progress and success of the implementation of structural reforms. As a consequence, for reasons that involved the president's own political survival, the process of economic restructuring turned out to be both rapid and profound, and carried out without paying due consideration to the constitutional limits on the use of political power. This was especially so for the first years of the administration, when the government was urged to achieve both economic stability and the consolidation of its power base.

However, the tendency to the unilateral adoption of decisions did not stop in those early years. The Presidency exhibited a proclivity to govern unilaterally even in later stages of the administration (when economic stability had already been achieved), as revealed by the continued use of necessity and urgency decrees. This was regarded as an indicative of an autocratic style of presidential leadership, represented not exclusively by President Menem but also by the leadership of his economic team. Therefore, the case of Menem's Presidency reverses the interpretation argument developed in Chapter 3. If, while studying Alfonsín, preoccupations concerned the possibility of constructing a political power that was strong enough to carry on a process of economic transformation, with Menem, worries soon came to be if this political power could be controlled and restrained.

In the next chapters, it will be shown that, despite the Executive's efforts to design, formulate and implement the economic policies without political or institutional interference, this could not always be achieved. Therefore, as in every complex political process, the Argentine process of structural reforms and state transformation cannot simply be read in terms of black and white. Based on evidence drawn from the privatization case-study, these chapters introduce some variations to the understanding of the institutional functioning of the democratic regime in the 1990s, according to which the autocratic tendencies described in these pages combined with other parallel movements resulting in a more institutionalized and consultative style of policy-making.

Appendix: public enterprises included in the State Reform Bill Appendix

Public enterprises included in the bill's appendix	Changes proposed
Aerolíneas Argentinas	TP, PP
Agua y Energía	C
Buenos Aires – Catering	TP
Coordinación Ecológica	
Area Metropolitana (CEAMSE)	TP, PP, C
Conarsur	TP
Dirección Nacional de Vialidad	C
Empresa Federal de Energía Eléctrica	—
Empresa Líneas Marítimas Argentinas	TP, PP
Empresa Nacional de Correos y Telégrafos	C
Empresa Nacional de Telecomunicaciones	TP
Ferrocarriles Argentinos	C
Gas del Estado	C
Media	
L.S.84 – TV Canal 11	TP
L.S. 85 – TV Canal 13	TP
L.R. 3 – Radio Belgrano	TP
L.R. 5 – Radio Excelsior	TP
Other media	TP
L.S. 82 ATC – Canal 7	Excepted
L.R.A.1 – Radio Nacional Bs. As.	Excepted
Radiodifusión Argentina al Exterior (RAE)	Excepted
Servicio Nacional de Radiodifusión	Excepted
Ministry of Defence companies	
Talleres Navales Dársena Norte SACI y N	TP
Forja Argentina Soc. Anónima	TP

Carboquímica Argentina Soc. Anónima Mixta	TP
Petroquímica Río Tercero Soc. Anónima Mixta	TP
Polisur Soc. Anónima Mixta	TP
Monómeros Vinílicos Soc. Anónima Mixta	TP
Petropol Soc. Anónima Mixta	TP
Induclor Soc. Anónima Mixta	TP
Obras Sanitarias de la Nación	C
Optar	TP
Segba	C
Servicios culturales, recreativos y mantenimiento urbano de la Ciudad de Buenos Aires	TP, PP, C
Subterráneos de Buenos Aires	TP, PP, C
Yacimientos Carboníferos Fiscales	TP, PP
Yacimientos Petrolíferos Fiscales	
exploration and exploitation	C
assisted recovery	SM

Source: C.R.S., 19 July 1989, pp. 1100–01

Note: TP: Total privatization; PP: Partial privatization; C: Concession; SM: Mixed society: — Only institutional restructuring.

5
Privatization and Political Parties

Introduction

As is well known, the privatization programme implemented during Menem's years in Argentina became known world-wide for its extensive, indiscriminate and rapid character. In fact, the terms 'extreme rapidity' and 'lack of discrimination' have commonly been used to summarize its characteristics. Similarly, a number of figures have repeatedly been given in confirmation of the programme's success. The World Bank, for instance, has referred to the privatizations in Argentina in the following terms:

> The Argentine privatisation programme initiated in 1989 has been unique in its scope, since it included all the important enterprises, and in its pace, because it was essentially realised in four years. . . . Toward 1993, the market value of privatised assets was estimated to be US$ 18 000 million. The privatisation programme had a significant impact on the economy: until 1993, it had generated more than US$ 8000 million in cash and, concerning public debt reductions, over US$ 10 000 million at a nominal value and US$ 4000 million at a market value.[1]

Because of these features of the privatization process in Argentina – and also considering the Executive-centred style of the presidential leadership described in the previous chapter – it might well be assumed that the success of the policy implementation process involved an extensive use of emergency and unilateral resources of government. This would, in turn, confirm, as a permanent feature of the political regime, the irrelevance of the institutions other than the Executive and the existence of a pattern of institutional relations controlled by the Executive. However, as this and the following chapters will show, the characteristics of the process of adoption of the privatization policy were varied, as well as more institutionalized than is often assumed. Although the privatization programme was mostly concentrated during the first four years of Menem's first presidential period, its implementation persisted throughout the years of both Menem's first and second administrations. As a consequence, the programme had to be carried out under differing external conditions, in times of both hyperinflation and macroeconomic stability. The State Reform Law was a crucial part of the whole divestiture process, but also only the first one. In order to continue moving its policy forward, the Executive worked out further legislative initiatives and, in fact, initiated a second stage in the implementation of the policy which did not include either delegation of power or necessity and urgency decrees. Instead, privatization decisions inaugurated a new phase in president–Congress relationships in which Congress managed to have greater influence on the design of the policy. This chapter, as well as the following one, are concerned with analysing the process of approval of all the laws relating to privatization between 1989 and 1995. Chapter 7 deals with the same laws during Menem's second Presidency.

To summarize, the extensive programme carried out by Menem's government was not the product of the single institutional dynamic revealed by the hyperinflation crisis, but the result of various dynamics taking place both within and outside that context. These dynamics show that the relative position of the two institutions of government was not invariable and permanent, and that Congress was able to move away from the constrained position where the State Reform Law had initially left it. As a matter of fact, Congress did not obstruct the approval of the policy, and, at least until 1995, the government managed to assemble the votes necessary for the passage of all the privatization bills. The current chapter begins by analysing the way in which privatization became part of the president's agenda, the reasons why it was permanently kept as a top priority, and the characteristics of the legislative proposals submitted for the consideration of Congress. Then, it moves on to explore the positions maintained by the political parties towards the Executive's initiatives, and what kind of political support the president's policy in Congress received. This section emphasizes that the ruling party discipline and the cooperative propensity of small opposition parties played a major role in the passage of the bills. However, it also shows that this support was far from being automatic and was instead preceded by a process of substantial negotiation, the details of which are presented in Chapter 6.

5.1. The privatization programme

The government undertook a privatization programme characterized by speed, lack of discrimination, and persistence as a response to two major difficulties: genuine economic problems, and problems of political credibility. In fact, the hyperinflation episode of 1989 was not the only one from which the Argentine state and society suffered; two other periods of high inflation shook the economy during the following eighteen months. Throughout this time, three different ministers of economy tried various methods of control and stabilization.[2] The first two, Rapanelli and González, failed to achieve much success. Indeed, at the beginning of 1991, the economy was characterized not only by recession, but by the third outbreak of hyperinflation, the latter being less intense than the previous ones, but still acute enough to lead to yet another change in the Ministry of Economy, with the appointment of Domingo Cavallo as minister. During these difficult first months of Menem's Presidency, successive stabilization failures were combined with advances in the implementation of structural reforms. Within this context, privatization was directly aimed at macroeconomic stabilization. The sale of public assets implied that the government could either obtain fresh cash or foreign debt papers, the two contributing to cleansing the state and improving the negotiating position with creditors. The intention was to find a temporary way to finance the fiscal gap – aggravated by the hyperinflation episodes – until the adjustment policies produced their full effects.

In addition, during this period, the problems of political credibility that Menem faced at the time of his arrival in power, remained large. Therefore, the privatization policy also served as a political instrument to fulfil the function of legitimization,[3] and privatization efforts were increased as proof of commitment to the economic reforms. The policy was used as the clearest political sign that the government's commitment to economic change was irreversible. First, the business sector was notified that the government was creating some wonderful opportunities for doing business. In other words, the intention was to show businessmen that the loss of state subsidies, subventions and preferential industrial regimes was compensated by the creation of opportunities to own and become partners in the old state companies. Secondly, foreign creditors were notified as well. The implementation of a privatization programme showed Argentina's adherence to the Washington Consensus, and enhanced Argentina's external credibility. Creditors knew that privatization revenues served to cancel debts, and the Argentine government understood that by means of privatization, the probability that it would gain access to new loans and foreign investment was increased.[4] Thirdly, if the government were able to privatize, it could demonstrate its political ability to control its pre-election allies, namely the unions, the support of which was crucial to see the reforms implemented. Unions, on their part, would also have the incentive of doing business through the opportunities provided by market reforms. Fourthly, privatization could produce demonstrable effects, easily perceived by the general public. The government began the programme with the public service enterprises, in order to produce such effects. The simultaneous deterioration in the quality of public goods and the price increase that the 1980s adjustment plans had generated had contributed to creating a public malaise that later on was transformed into demands for more drastic changes. The improvement of public services appeared as a source of public legitimacy for the government. Therefore, it concentrated on the companies, the privatization of which had been authorized by the State Reform Law, rapidly pursuing a process that ended up with almost the total transference of the selected companies to the private sector at the end of 1990.[5]

The tenor of the problems faced by Menem's government changed with the introduction of Minister Cavallo's *Plan de Convertibilidad*. The plan, launched in March 1991, provided the way out of instability. It involved a radical change from earlier plans both in its objectives and instruments. On the one hand, it created a convertible currency on a one-peso-to-one-dollar basis, and required that the Central Bank have gold, foreign exchange, or other external assets (generally foreign government securities) in reserve to completely cover the monetary base. On the other hand, the plan was introduced by means of a law. The government attempted to demonstrate, through its own self-discipline, that its commitment to monetary and fiscal discipline was so strong that it sought permanent, legislated control, as opposed to the type of commitment that could be expected from decrees.[6] The consequence of convertibility was that inflation began to decrease slowly, but sustainably. After eighteen months of instability, accompanied by a gradual loss of confidence in the president's ability to handle the emergency, Menem's credibility weakness was overcome, and the president was able to recover control of the economic and political processes. For the economy, a period of demand-driven expansion commenced, paralleling the excellent results in the fight against inflation. Between 1991 and 1994, GDP increased at an annual rate of

7.7 per cent, consumption grew 40 per cent, and a similar tendency was signified by investments in machinery and equipment that had been postponed during the period of crisis. Because of the political effects of the plan, the government was able to reach its peak of popularity and so regain the public support which had been decidedly unstable during the previous months.[7] Moreover, the government was able to strengthen its majority in the Chamber of Deputies in the congressional elections which took place in 1991.

Although a different economic phase was inaugurated by the convertibility plan, the centrality of structural reform implementation remained. The macroeconomic logic of the plan demonstrated that structural reforms needed to be taken further, and this was the beginning of what can be called the second privatization wave. The commitment to non-devaluation and the refusal to print more money meant public sector finances continued to be in a straitjacket. Only fiscal or commercial policies, or structural reforms, were available to strengthen the fiscal situation. Thus, privatization cash revenues remained central to closing the fiscal gap and reducing the public debt. Additionally, the sale of state assets played a key role in the evolution of external accounts. One of the weaknesses of convertibility was the current account's growing imbalance, which had appeared as a negative result of accelerated economic reactivation. A large amount of capital inflow became crucial to reducing the imbalances, and cash revenue from privatization was an important source of this.[8]

Therefore, either for reasons connected to macroeconomic stabilization or as a consequence of the stabilization plan adopted, privatization always remained central to Menem's administration, and was located at the top of the government's public policy priorities. Moreover, since the president's political survival depended upon closing the credibility gap (and privatization was the policy which provided the greatest demonstrable effects), this policy became the one for the implementation of which Menem would use his full political weight. The privatization policy was transformed into a governmental programme, the main objectives of which were not those of increasing economic efficiency and productivity (as would normally have been expected with this policy), but of enhancing fiscal revenues in order to repay the debt, of contributing to stabilization, and improving the quality of public services.

5.1.1. The privatization bills

As explained above, privatization before the convertibility plan was carried out under the pressure of political and economic urgencies. At that time, when attention was being paid to stabilization goals and the construction of a credible image, the government's priority was to sell under the self-imposed constraint of tight deadlines, instead of safeguarding important economic issues, such as the pricing policy of the privatized firms or the establishment of regulatory frameworks. This happened, for instance, with the sale of the telephone company, ENTel, regarded as a leading case by the privatization authorities. The evolution of the privatization process revealed that no previous, detailed, comprehensive, and agreed-upon design of the policy existed, but rather, that any conditions of the deal could be modified as long as the firm was sold.[9] The result was that, in order to keep or secure offers, the government made several concessions to the future owners.[10] However, sooner or later, it would become apparent that the use of discretionary procedures was not the best way to attract bidders. Despite being initially convenient to gain time and awake business interest, these practices in reality did not allow them to predict the future of the process. Thus, the government's tendency to favour future owners with *ad hoc* procedures, not only provoked consumer discontent and protests, but also generated problems with the business sectors interested in the bid. Bell Atlantic, the company assigned to operate telephones in the country's northern area eventually withdrew its bid. Similar problems surfaced in other privatization cases authorized by the State Reform Law, such as that of Aerolíneas Argentinas. As a consequence, although these cases of privatization could serve as evidence of the effectiveness of the government compelled to implement them, they would also be called into question because of the inferior quality of the end product. Moreover, they failed to contribute to the closing of the credibility gap which was precisely what the government was seeking to attain.[11]

The only instance of control over the Executive's activities during this early period was the Bicameral Commission which had been formed in Congress. By using different procedures (written reports, discussion meetings, general directives and suggestions), the Commission's role was especially relevant because all the different aspects of the privatization process during this phase were being approved by decree. Its remit was concerned with prices, the assets to be transferred, bidding bases, users' rights and obligations, market conditions and service availability, bases for the fixing of tariffs, evaluation of offers, adjudication and details of final contracts. However, the Commission's ability to influence the final results was limited. It had to work without the support of proper technical advice, improvise in the process of fulfilling its tasks and, finally, could enact no binding recommendations.[12] In any case, by pointing out the Executive's mistakes, the Commission contributed to publicizing the rapid, careless and highly improvised manner in which privatization was being implemented.[13]

The economic phase inaugurated by the convertibility plan led to a quite different stage in the implementation of the privatization policy. The Ministry of Economy, headed by Domingo Cavallo, made explicit its intention to depart from previous practice by carefully planning the policy and by making improvements in the privatization procedures. Concern for economic productivity and efficiency set aside during the first wave began to be raised in the second.[14] Similarly, in response to accusations of irregularities, the Ministry made explicit its worries about guarantees of legal security for investors, and expressed its wish to give Congress some participation in privatization decisions. The new phase showed that a learning process was being experienced by the policy implementation agencies, but also that the persistence of criticisms of the outcome of the previous phase obliged the government to draw a dividing line in order to recover lost credibility. In brief, during this phase privatization continued to be a priority, but under conditions which forced the government to take more care with the design of the policy.

The implementation of the second phase of privatization required innovation in the legal instruments used. The State Reform Law on which the first phase of privatization was based was not sufficient for the needs of the new period, either because the government was concerned with improving the quality of the instruments used to privatize or because it wanted to extend the privatization policy to other areas.[15] Because of this, the second privatization phase gave a new impulse to legislation and, in fact, inaugurated a wave of new bills. During the six years of his first term as president, Carlos Menem added a total of ten new proposals to the State Reform Law, devoted to taking the reform further. As with the original bill, the others were intended to set the legal basis for the government's policy of privatization, since they affected companies which, because they belonged preponderantly to the state, needed congressional approval in order to be sold.[16] One of them, dealing with the regulation and privatization of the ports, did not originate in the executive branch; it was instead proposed by members of the ruling party in Congress.[17] Considered together, the ten bills provided for either the sale or the concession of a large number of state-owned companies to the private sector. Table 5.1 summarizes this information.

Table 5.1 The parliamentary submission of privatization bills

No.	*Privatization laws*	*Parliamentary submission date*
1	State reform	13 July 1989
2	Ministry of Defence's assets	23 July 1990
3	Altos Hornos Zapla (defence)	27 July 1990
4	Ports	27 September 1990
5	Oil industry, YPF (1st round)	4 April 1991
6	Gas industry	13 June 1991
7	Electricity industry	13 June 1991
8	Mercado de Hacienda (cattle market)	18 September 1991
9	Caja de Ahorro and BANADE (banks)	3 December 1991
10	Pensions	5 June 1992
11	Oil industry (2nd round)	1 March 1995

Source: This table has been prepared on the basis of data obtained from Congressional Reports.[18]

The electricity and gas industries were the prime examples of the second phase of privatization. They were carefully designed with the advice of the World Bank, which monitored the whole process. These privatization cases incorporated the novel element of a regulatory framework and emphasized the regulation of transportation and distribution of the services. They stipulated that production, transportation, and distribution of the services had to be transferred to the private sector. The aim was to encourage free competition whenever possible, and to ensure that those activities with a monopolistic nature would not harm consumers. In this sense, electricity generation and gas production were considered activities that could be freely exploited by private capital, so that the regulation that the bills arranged for would not specifically concern them. Instead, transportation and distribution were naturally monopolistic and, therefore, needed state regulation. In order to secure this goal, regulatory bodies were created by each bill, both possessing powers to determine prices. Thus, regulation characterized the innovative character of these bills, since previously most regulatory features had only been established after the privatization processes were well advanced.

A similar regulatory institution was subsequently established by another privatization bill, although without the power of fixing prices, because of the competitive condition of the markets it affected. It dealt with the pension system. The body was called *Superintendencia de Administradoras de Jubilaciones y Pensiones*, and had the responsibility for regulating and controlling the activities of the wide range of private pension administrators that the approval of the bill would allow for.

Additionally, this bill was another example of a careful design that provided for the reorganization of the whole pension system. The *Ley de Puertos*, or Ports Law, also had a complex design, but that had been fully worked out in Congress.[19] It comprised the federalization, decentralization, debureaucratization and, finally, privatization of all Argentine ports.[20] The law was intended to contribute to state reform both by placing the administration of the ports in private hands (through concessions), and also by providing for their operation on a local basis (decentralization). As in the cases mentioned above, the national government would be in charge of controlling, supervising and defining policies rather than operating and administering directly.

The above-mentioned bills were, however, more the exception than the rule in terms of design. With the remaining cases it became apparent that the Executive's goal was simply to obtain Congress's authorization to initiate the process of privatization. Details on policy design were left to be defined at later stages by the Executive. By asking for an authorizing law or the ratification of a decree, five of the cases (*Altos Hornos Zapla*, Ministry of Defence's assets, *Caja Nacional de Ahorro* and *Banco Nacional de Desarrollo, Mercado Nacional de Hacienda*, the state oil company) were fulfilling the minimal requirements for initiating the process of privatization.

All the bills described briefly in the previous paragraphs required congressional approval of the president's policy. Through them, the Executive kept the legislative initiative, and did not always appear to approve congressional participation in the policy-making process beyond the limits of ratification and control. However, it is important to distinguish the difference between the collective and delegative style of the State Reform Law that was approved during in the middle of the hyperinflationary crisis, with these second-wave bills. Although some of them only sought the simple ratification of privatization plans, the fact is that several bills replaced the delegative character of the State Reform Law giving Congress more information and opportunity to intervene in the policy's general design. Whether Congress used this possibility or not is a topic of analysis in the next two chapters. The next section is dedicated to the consideration of the partisan support that the bills received in Congress.

5.2. Political parties and privatization bills

In view of the favourable distribution of power that Menem's administration faced in Congress, it should not be surprising that the privatization bills obtained legislative approval.[21] However, the government's success in Congress was not completely guaranteed. According to the regulations of the Argentine Congress, 50 per cent plus one member of the Chamber (as a *quorum*) is necessary to begin the consideration of bills.[22] This figure was neither attained by the Peronists in 1989, nor was it achieved by the partial congressional renewals in the Chamber of Deputies, although the party did get quite close to obtaining it, especially in the 1993 elections. The situation was better in the Senate, where the Peronist Party had a *quorum* from the beginning of Menem's mandate. The distribution of power in Congress had two important political consequences: the first one concerned the relationship with opposition parties, since the Peronist Party was obliged to negotiate with other parties to obtain their presence in the Chambers; the second concerned its own party members, and implied that efforts had to be made to discipline most of them, because the more rebellious they became, the more the Executive had to rely on the support of other parties. As a result, it can be assumed that the government was always obliged to establish a dialogue with the legislative branch, either to persuade its own party members or to try to reach an agreement with opposition forces. It appears that the government was able to obtain support for its bills only after a process of negotiation.

In this section, the internal make-up of Congress is explored in order to analyse the composition of the majority that the president was able to construct while seeking support for his privatization policy. As explained above, the constitution of this majority in Congress depended upon the political distribution of seats, the levels of discipline in the presidential party, and the propensity of the opposition to cooperate. Therefore, this section has been divided into three parts, each devoted to studying the posture adopted towards the policy of privatization by the three principal political groups in Congress: the Peronists, the Radicals and 'the third parties'. In order to explore the president's chances of obtaining congressional cooperation, the issue of partisan discipline is addressed in the section dedicated to the Peronist Party. The extent to which the party members remained faithful to Carlos Menem as well as the sort of loyalty that they demonstrated (to the programme, to the leadership) are considered in this section. The manner of opposition that the Radical Party put forward is then analysed and compared to that of the other opposition parties in the Chambers.

To answer these questions, the study undertaken in the following pages is based on several indicators. Firstly, it considers the positions maintained by the parties in the congressional committees and how they voted on the bills. Secondly, it analyses the attitude of the parties in the plenary sessions of the Chambers, that is, the way in which they voted on the privatization bills and their attendance in the Chambers. Thirdly, it explores some aspects of the political discussions in order to determine what the parties understood their role in the state reform programme to be, and whether these discussions matched their actual position in the Chambers.

5.2.1. *The Peronist Party*

If the institutional distribution of power between 1989 and 1995 had granted Menem a large and comfortable majority in the two Chambers of Congress, the question of party discipline would still have arisen. In effect, the presidential turnaround in 1989 left the Peronist Party in Congress in a complicated situation. It was explicitly requested to support a policy that not only went against the political values it had traditionally sustained, but also was in open contradiction to the very recent positions which the party had fervently maintained when the Radicals were in power. Therefore, when seeking cooperation from Congress for the passage of its privatization bills, the Executive faced the double difficulty of dealing with a strict majority in the lower house, and the uncertainty about the attitude that these legislators would eventually assume towards the new economic path. The information presented in this section confirms that dissent existed, but also that it could be handled, so that the government obtained the party's support for the approval of all the privatization bills submitted.[23]

Table 5.2 indicates the voting pattern that allowed the bills to be passed in committee. As can be seen, the ruling party played an important role by participating in the passage through committee of all the privatization bills. However, as the 19 votes by which the committees passed the privatization bills also indicate, the majority rule was only used three times. In contrast, most voting involved the support of two or more political parties, showing that inter-partisan cooperation was an important characteristic of the bills' approval, in the committees of both the upper and lower houses. In the two Chambers, agreements were mainly made with the minor parties ('others' in the table): the Radicals only participated twice.

Table 5.2[24] Voting pattern in the committees

Approval formulae	*Senate*	*Deputies Chamber*	*Total*
PJ–others	5	9	14
PJ	2	1	3
PJ–UCR	1	—	1
PJ–UCR-others	1	—	1
Total	9	9	19

Indeed, the support of these 'others' may mean that other forces, ideologically identified with the political programme, were eager to support the Executive in its privatization policy. But it also suggests that the votes of the other parties could have supplied the margin of support that the government was unable to obtain from its own political force. Nevertheless, this does not seem to be the case with privatization, as can be deduced from the attitude of the Peronists in the committees. Table 5.3 indicates that the Peronist Party was very disciplined since those situations in which the legislators decided to vote against the bills were rather infrequent. From the total of 19 votes taken in committee, there were only five in which members of the Peronist Party expressed any sort of criticism, all of them in the Chamber of Deputies. As the Table indicates, there were four cases of partial dissent; one *dictamen de minoría* (minority report) and not a single total dissent.[25] The minority report represented the only real expression of rejection of a bill, and was championed by deputy Moisés Fontela, who was part of the so-called *Grupo de los Ocho* (the Eight's Group), the only party group openly opposed. The cases of partial dissent meant that the deputies had given their general support to the bill, although they had their reservations and partial objections. The Peronist deputies, Oscar Parilli, Rafael Flores, Humberto Romero, and Ana Kessler were those who acted in this way.

With the exception of the *Grupo de los Ocho*, the Peronist Party appeared to be fairly disciplined when voting for the Executive's proposals in the committees. However, at the time of the formation of this group, the party's internal situation was uncertain and dominated by a general sense of malaise. The group came into existence at the end of 1989, a few months after Menem's arrival in power and after structural reforms (such as the privatizations authorized by the State Reform Law), had begun to be implemented. The group adopted an attitude of opposition to the government's programme, in particular, to privatization.[26]

Table 5.3 Voting pattern in the committees: privatization bills with PJ opposition

Laws	*Voting formulae: Chamber of Deputies*			
	Majority	*Minority*	*Total dissent*	*Partial dissent*
Electricity	PJ–others	UCR	UCR–others	**PJ**–others
Gas	PJ–others	—	UCR–others	**PJ**–others
Defence's assets	PJ–others	1) UCR–others 2) **PJ**	—	—
Pensions	PJ	—	—	**PJ**–others
Oil 2nd round	PJ–others	—	UCR–others	**PJ**–others

It was initially known as 'the eight's group', because it was composed of eight deputies: Moisés Fontela, German Abdala, Carlos 'Chacho' Alvarez, Juan Pablo Cafiero, Luis Brunatti, Darío Alessandro, Franco Caviglia, and José 'Conde' Ramos. Although they were the only ones involved in active and open opposition to Menem's reform plan, for a time they did enjoy the sympathy of many other members of the party. However, in the end they found out that the majority of the party was not disposed to rebel against Menem. Thus, they became isolated and were pushed to the outer fringes of the party.[27]

Committee drafts being approved, congressional discussions continued in the plenary sessions where party discipline seemed to persist. Yet this is difficult to prove, since there is no written evidence as to how given legislators voted on bills. At this point, it is only possible to take into account the information provided by the nominal votes, which took place in the lower house.[28] They show, on the one hand, that the level of attendance of the Peronist legislators in the two Chambers and their contribution to the *quorum* was high. On the right side of Table 5.4, can be seen that the level of absenteeism was variable, oscillating between 32 and 13 deputies. Although the two figures would indicate some lack of discipline, the second is within the margins of the expected absence within a parliamentary bloc of at least 116 members. Among these cases, the Pensions Law is known for being the one where the government faced most difficulty in getting the *quorum*. The consideration of this bill was to commence on 18 March 1993, but was only able to begin during the session of 28/29 April 1993, after five meetings of the Chamber of Deputies had failed to get a *quorum* and so consideration of the bill had to be postponed. As will be explained in Chapter 6, the acceptance of the modifications proposed by the union members of the Peronist Party was one of the main conditions that eventually permitted the beginning of the plenary discussions.

The case of the pensions bill suggests that there was a process of agreement inside the party, which appeared as a necessary condition to obtaining the party's cooperation. If this process was not respected, difficulties and delays would take place when requesting support for a bill. The lack of other similar cases indicates that the pensions bill was particularly difficult and, because of this, followed a path that was more an exception than the rule. However, it was probably an exception because negotiations inside the party turned out to be unsuccessful and this became known outside it. This does not deny the existence of internal negotiations in other cases.

The nominal votes themselves are another indicator of the levels of discipline in the Chambers and an example of what may have happened on other occasions. Table 5.4 lists the information illustrating this point as well as the special case of the pensions bill, when Deputies dealt with a motion to return the bill to the committees.

After comparing voting patterns at the plenary session and in the committees, both differences and similarities can be found. The Peronist Party continued its policy of agreeing with the small parties, but at the same time a few of its members decided to cross the floor to join the opposition. Besides, the total absence of Radical Party votes in the cases of YPF and Gas stands out. The Radicals' refusal to vote, as well as to provide the *quorum* necessary to initiate discussion of the bills, made an agreement with the small parties unavoidable for the majority party. In this way, the meaning of the agreements with the small parties becomes clearer: in a context in which the ruling party has a simple majority, the presence of the small parties contributes to the *quorum* that allows the bills to be dealt with. This statement would remain true if it could be demonstrated that Peronists crossing the floor did not do so in sufficient numbers to enlarge the opposition front enough to represent a challenge.

As the right side of the Table indicates, there was no great challenge to the government's proposal, with the exception of the early case of *Altos Hornos Zapla* (AHZ) in the middle of 1990. In this case, the dissenting votes reached 21.3 per cent of the total Peronists present (38 per cent of

Table 5.4 Cases of nominal votes: Chamber of Deputies

Laws	*Voting formulae*		*Peronist votes*		*N*	*N PJ*
	Majority	*Minority*	*Majority*	*Minority*		*Members*
AHZ	PJ–others	UCR–**PJ**–others	70 (78.3%)	19 (21.3%)	89 (100%)	121
Oil 1st round	PJ–others	Others	102 (100%)	0 (0%)	102 (100%)	116
Gas del Estado	PJ–others	Others–**PJ**	100 (97%)	3 (3%)	103 (100%)	116
Pensions*	PJ–others	UCR–**PJ**–others	105 (99%)	1 (1%)	106 (100%)	116
Oil 2nd round	PJ–others	UCR–**PJ**–others	104 (94%)	3 (3%)**	110 (100%)	126

*In this case, we are not actually considering a nominal vote (because there was not one), but a nominally voted motion to return the bill to discussion in committee. It is understood that these votes also help to explain the political positions.
**Another 3% abstained.

this amount corresponded to the *Movimiento Peronista* or *Grupo de los Ocho*). Furthermore, 32 deputies were absent in this legislative session, so that a total of 51 deputies failed to follow the government's directives. The considerable number of deputies objecting to this bill contrasts with the later cases of oil and gas, which, on the other hand, were economically more crucial. The situation had changed and the percentage of Peronists joining the opposition had gone down 3 per cent and disappeared altogether during the first case of oil privatization. The same pattern was repeated with the absent deputies, whose number had decreased to 14 and 13, respectively. At this moment, the *Movimiento Peronista* deputies had left the party and formed their own bloc (some of them had already left the Chamber), four of the remaining internal dissident voters had finished their four-year periods as legislators, and seven of the remaining eight were now voting affirmatively. This attitude remained in place until the end of the president's term, when another bill furthering the privatization of oil confirmed the higher levels of discipline within the party. In brief, this shows that in times of the discussion of the AHZ privatization, there was considerable reluctance within the party to accept the new economic path. However, with the approval of later bills it can be seen that internal dissent had been overcome and that the government had found a more partisan disposition to comply with its initiatives.

As a consequence, within the general supportive attitude of the Peronist Party in Congress, three more specific postures can be registered between 1989 and 1995: first, support for the emergency bills in 1989; second, a reluctant support during 1990 (the AHZ case) which expressed the general sense of malaise present in the party; third, compliance with the Executive's leadership. What factors explain these attitudes of the ruling party? First, the influence of the context of crisis on the process of approval of the State Reform Law should be stressed. Statements from ruling party legislators during congressional discussions serve to confirm the importance of this factor. Effectively, the economic crisis was a powerful argument in support of those advocating the presidential programme in Congress. It stressed the fact that the economic plan was not the new administration's choice but the policy imposed by circumstances which did not leave any room for alternative courses of action. The Peronist bloc's chief, deputy José Luis Manzano, illustrates this point:

> I repeat that we have received a country in flames. ... This initiative has an emergency component, and I think that it is only the deficit I have just mentioned that justifies the emergency. ... Let me explain

> to you. If one's accounts are in order, one can say: I will keep two, six, eight deficit points in order to foster economic activity.... When the deficit is no longer under one's control and is generated by others, it does not mean that one is becoming liberal. The same happens with a bleeding patient: it is known that he cannot lose more than a certain amount of blood, otherwise he dies. Bleeding must be stopped, and we are now at that stage. Bleeding can only be stopped with economic and administrative emergency laws.[29]

Furthermore, the emergency argument was combined with the idea of responding to popular demand for measures to alleviate the crisis. In this sense, the popular support obtained by Menem after the announcement of the economic measures, contributed to dissipating Peronist doubts about the government's economic direction. Deputy Pepe gave his opinion about this:

> Do you think that many of us like to see the liberals telling us which policies to apply in areas that are fundamental to us? We don't like it. Nevertheless, let me tell you that people who are in politics are products of circumstances, and in the circumstances in which we are living we cannot ask for money from areas of great poverty, where our votes come from.... At the moment, President Menem has what the Radicals could not have, even at the beginning of 1984: the acquiescence of more than 80 per cent of Argentines. This is the moment to make the transformation. If we want an efficient state, we must give the means to facilitate this goal.[30]

Therefore, both the emergency and popular support confirmed that, in supporting the government's new economic policies, the party did not compromise its ideological principles. Emergency bills were the only possible response to an unwanted inherited situation which needed to be dealt with successfully:

> Why are we proposing the state reform? To meet an ideological demand? We are very far from that. Are we doing this because we suddenly became liberal? We are also far from that. We are not like Martinez de Hoz, we are pragmatic.... This is the way in which we act. As Machado says, *making our way as we go*. We did not have it planned, we did not know in advance that we were going to do it in this way.[31]

However, Peronism's actual levels of pragmatism and flexibility were only revealed with the passage of time, since, despite the diffusion of the sense of crisis, the party continued supporting the course of action adopted in 1989. This support, though, did not come either immediately or without hesitation. The formation of the Eight's Group and the internal state of malaise taking place throughout the year 1990 show that, with the end of the hyperinflation crisis, old ideological concerns and demands for economic rectification re-emerged. The fact that the president could lead the party out of this stage and continue obtaining its support was the result of other factors, all of them connected to the central question of the political leadership. Firstly, as explained in the last chapter, Carlos Menem could exert an effective control over the Peronist Party because he was its first real political leader since the death of Perón. With his subsequent electoral victories in the internal party elections in 1988 and in the presidential contest of 1989, Menem had managed to legitimize his leadership within the party, which was crucial in order to gain autonomy in the adoption of governmental decisions. Secondly, Menem's success in channelling the party's internal dissent was due to his adoption of a 'party-accommodating strategy', or, in other words, of an strategy of flattering the party and taking charge of it, which began to take place at the beginning of 1991.[32] This strategy involved considerable leadership efforts to address the party's ideological updating (as Corrales has put it, to 'peronise' the neoliberal programme) and to define new rules for Executive-party relations (based on brokerage and greater inclusion in policy-making processes). Thirdly, electoral victories in the 1991 and 1993 congressional elections renewed the government's popular approval and encouraged the party to continue supporting the presidential leadership. In other words, the sense of party loyalty towards directives coming from the Presidency should not be separated from the subsequent electoral victories and the repeated renewal of the people's support for Menem and his economic programme and team. Thus, given the extraordinary success of the political decision adopted in 1989, the party was not left with much margin to oppose the programmatic turnaround, and had an incentive to follow the course of action ratified by the ballot box.

Having said all this, it would not be surprising that later speeches in Congress contrasted with those pronounced earlier, in the days of the crisis. During the parliamentary discussion of the privatization of *Yacimientos Petrolíferos Fiscales* (the oil company), deputy Parrilli explained that:

> for us, the Justicialist Party, the state's role is not only the fulfilment of specific functions – education, health, security, defence and foreign affairs – but also the obligation to encourage the development of private activity in a framework of competition and transparency. . . . This future law. . . aims to adapt for the current scenario the instruments that the government must have to be sure that the state continues to fulfil its mission. . . . Previously, this instrument was the state-run monopolistic and unique enterprise that handled oil prices throughout the country. Today, we propose that these tools or instruments respond to other mechanisms . . .[33]

Furthermore, at that time, Parilli affirmed:

> when Dr. Menem assumed the Nation's Presidency in 1989, the questions, instruments, and actions that Peronism previously supplied for a national and popular government (as in the 1940s and 1950s) were changed. . . . We now present ourselves here with the firm conviction that we are behaving as the Argentine society and the world are demanding in order to achieve our country's transformation.[34]

As a corollary of all this, I would like to point out that, since Menem was not the natural leader of the movement as Perón used to be (his legitimacy came from electoral support and governmental efficacy), the party's acceptance of his leadership did not always have to mean automatic cooperation and absence of conflict. Thus, it is likely that uncertainty existed about the attitude to be adopted by the members of the ruling party in every negotiation. In this context, agreements with opposition parties enhanced the president's chances of success in Congress.

5.2.2. The Radical Party

In contrast to the style and intensity of the Peronist opposition to privatization during the 1980s, the Radical Party did not totally oppose the privatization policy in Congress during the six years of Menem's first term as president. At the beginning, the party adopted a cooperative posture. As explained in the previous chapter, in accordance with the inter-partisan agreements that surrounded the transfer of the mandate from Alfonsín to Menem in 1989, the Peronists agreed to assume the presidential office before the appointed time, but obtained in return the Radicals' commitment to facilitate the approval of the emergency laws to be sent to Congress between July and December. It was within this framework that the *Unión Cívica Radical* supported the presidential bill for state reform in the two congressional Chambers. After December 1989, relations with Radicalism resumed a normal government– opposition pattern although, in reality, the government continued to benefit from the Radical Party's difficulty in becoming an effective opposition. When the privatization bills were introduced, the Radicals unfolded a strategy of selective opposition: all the bills would be criticized and opposed in the committees, but not all of them would be obstructed at the plenary stage.

Table 5.5 indicates the position maintained by the Radicals towards the privatization bills in the committees. It reveals that the party opposed the presidential initiatives since it neither supported the majority formula (with only the two exceptions of *Mercado Nacional de Hacienda* and the Ports Law), nor did it provide more than two examples of partial dissent (both of them connected to the Ports Law).[35] Instead, it signed almost all of the minority reports and the total dissents (six out of seven, and five out of six, respectively).

However, the Radical Party did try to argue that the rejection of the government's proposals did not necessarily mean the rejection of the policy of privatization. They emphasized that they had had to face the crisis earlier and, while in government, they had learned that the traditional financial resources of the state were in crisis, and so its functions needed to be redefined: 'We are the champions of the necessity to reform the state... and we are the ones who have planted the seed that makes this discussion possible.'[36] However, the Radicals also believed that the sale of state-owned enterprises had to be selective because, as Conrado Storani put it in the Senate: 'We agree with the idea of transforming and modernising the state, but there is no need to throw out the baby with the bath water.'[37]

Therefore, the minority reports signed by the Radical members of Congress did not object to the idea of privatization, but rather to the way in which the government was carrying out this policy. For instance, when the Executive presented the state reform bill in 1989, the Radical Party refused to sign it in the committees and presented its own version

Table 5.5 The Radicals' position towards privatization bills

	Deputy Chamber	*Senate*	*Total*	*Total (N)*
Participation in the majority formula	0	2	2	18
Minority report	4	2	6	7
Total dissent	4	1	5	6
Partial dissent	1	1	2	8

of the bill, which contained the following points neglected by the Executive: 1) it showed a special concern with the employment consequences of privatization, so that it emphasized the importance of consultation with the unions, the necessity of agreement on decisions regarding labour reorganization, as well as the creation of unemployment insurance; 2) it rejected every reference to an emergency not only because it was incompatible with a structural reform but also because it led to the avoidance of the interference of control mechanisms and the use of bidding processes; 3) it expressed the state's obligation to abolish privileges and monopolistic clauses and stressed the role of regulatory laws wherever the concentration of supply and demand was unavoidable; 4) it explicitly excluded external debt capitalization from any privatization case; 5) instead of adding a list of assets that could be privatized to a single bill, every privatization was to be carried out by means of a specific law. However, due to the context of crisis in which this bill was discussed, the Radicals did not pursue the approval of their own report at the plenary sessions. Instead, they used this report to make explicit the items on which they held a different view while, at the same time, they facilitated the passage of the Executive's bill in fulfilment of the pre-established agreements.

When it came to the treatment of the later bills, the Radical Party understood that the transition pact was at an end, and there was no point in continuing to vote for the proposals coming from the Executive. The party opted for rejecting the Executive's bills, but simultaneously trying not to object to the idea of privatization. This led them to oppose the indiscriminate sale of companies. In the case of the privatization of the assets of the Ministry of Defence, it was proposed that only the enterprises not producing war material should be sold; the rest should be maintained under state control for security reasons. Concerning the electricity industry, the Radicals proposed partial rather than total privatization. They totally opposed privatization only in the cases of oil, gas and the two banks (*Caja de Ahorro* and *Banade*), which they did not see any reason to privatize, except to fulfil the macroeconomic objectives of the government.[38] Similarly, while questioning the way in which the government was carrying out the policy, the Radicals said they were not opposed to privatization but only to the concrete procedures adopted by the government. In the case of *Altos Hornos Zapla*, the party claimed Congress's right to control and supervise the actions of the Executive, and demanded as a consequence that the bidding process be approved by the legislative Chambers. Regarding the Ministry of Defence's assets, the party found it unacceptable that the funds to be obtained from their sales were to be used for purposes other than the restructuring of the military forces. Regarding the privatization of the electricity companies, the party emphasized the damage that privatization would cause both to the provinces and to the customers. All these partial objections were not meant to deny the necessity for state reform, but to question the way in which the government was proceeding with it.

In the discussions in the plenary sessions of the Chambers, the Radicals continued with their selective opposition and, as the following table indicates, obstacles to the formation of the *quorum* were presented, but only in a few of the cases.

In the Senate, both Peronists and Radicals were well disposed to seek agreements to disputes, to the extent that there was just one case where there was a problem with the *quorum* constitution (the third reading of the gas privatization bill), and two cases where the Radicals agreed with the majority position. The Senate's behaviour was not new. It had always had the reputation of being the Chamber most inclined to agreement, probably because of its size and homogeneous composition in comparison to the lower Chamber. Menem's government always chose it to initiate the consideration of the bills (with the sole exception of the Pension Law),[39] not only because the Peronist majority was greatest there but also because of the above-mentioned features. As previously stated, the only case in which agreement was not possible was the privatization of *Gas del Estado*: not only did the Radicals deny a *quorum* to begin the treatment of the bill; they also withdrew when the vote was taken.

Behaviour like this was more often adopted in the Chamber of Deputies, where the Radicals imposed obstacles to the passage of the privatization bills on four occasions. The most extreme cases were those of oil and gas, when Radical Deputies were absent at the time of voting, because they were against the whole idea of privatizing those industries.[40] Another difficult case was that of the pensions bill. It had proved to be a difficult matter for the ruling party to support, and so it was for the Radicals, who refused to help to provide a majority which the government was not able to reach on its own. During the five failed

Table 5.6 The Radical Party's presence in the Chambers

Chambers of the Congress	*Sessions with Radical absence*	*Total of sessions (N)*
Senate	1	13
Chamber of Deputies	4	9
Total	5	22

attempts to initiate the legislative session, the Radicals remained 'hidden behind the curtains', as the Peronists said. Finally, the Radicals showed reluctance to provide a *quorum* while privatization of the electricity companies was considered. Although they eventually agreed to participate, the attitude of the Radical bloc delayed the passage of the bill. Their objections were that the Peronists had encouraged the consideration of the bill before it had been discussed in the committees. Having been approved by the committees, the bill could then be considered in the Chamber.

In summary, Radicalism's selective or 'constructive' opposition (as they themselves called it) suggests that this party did not engaged in its role of opposing the government during Menem' first administration with much vigour. In order to understand the reasons for that it is necessary to take into account that, on the one hand, the dramatic end of Alfonsín's government had left the party in a state of internal crisis, with serious disagreements about the party's profile in opposition. This conspired against consistency and unified action in most situations. Concerning the privatizations in particular, the party found itself having to oppose a policy which it had promoted while in government and for which it had then found no political cooperation. On the other hand, Radicalism was viewed by public opinion as being directly responsible for the economic debacle and it could not overcome the memories of the disastrous performance of Alfonsín's last year in power. Thus, the adoption of an strategy of strong opposition to a course of action that had been approved in subsequent elections was thought to increase the negative image of the party, since it imposed obstacles to the reforms that the majority of the people had approved. Moreover, the negative public image of Radicalism was often increased by Menem's declarations to the press. He would often blame the Radicals for being inefficient and statist, and for being directly responsible for the situation of the country. If they refused to provide a *quorum*, they had to suffer from Menem's public accusations of 'laziness and reluctance to work'. It is in this context that the Radicals did not attempt to question the whole economic model, and their role was reduced to criticizing some aspects of its implementation: the concentration of power in the executive branch, the social consequences, and the indiscriminate character of economic decisions guided solely by macroeconomic considerations.

Nevertheless, it cannot be denied that the *quorum* was still a useful instrument in the hands of the opposition. This resource was indeed weak when compared with the amount of institutional resources that the Peronist Party had enjoyed when in opposition during Alfonsín's years in power (for example, it had had the control of the Senate). However, it still introduced an element of uncertainty to every process of law-making that, considered together with the eventual uncertainties within his own party, explain the fact that, during his term in office, President Menem had seriously to consider relying on *ad hoc* agreements with other opposition parties.

5.2.3. The third parties

As has been explained in Chapter 2, the gradual decrease in votes for the two main parties was one of the main features of electoral behaviour from 1983 onwards, especially in elections involving the renewal of congressional members. Those votes abandoning the major parties were distributed among a range of small political forces at least until the formation of Frepaso in the middle 1990s. Numerically irrelevant as individual forces, small parties nonetheless acquired considerable importance as potential allies, particularly if the ruling party held a non-absolute majority. In effect, the third parties played the crucial role of providing the necessary votes to enable bills to be passed when the ruling party was not able to obtain such votes elsewhere for a number of different reasons: an unfavourable distribution of congressional seats (the lack of a *quorum*), uncertainty about discipline in their own ranks, and an adversarial relationship with the other major party, the Radical Party.

Within this arc of small parties, the Democratic Centre Union (UCeDé) stood out. Approaches between this small conservative party and Menem's government exceeded congressional cooperation and led to the appointment of its leading figures to key cabinet positions from the beginning of the administration. These appointments were mainly thought to contribute symbolic support for Menem's ideological turnaround. In fact, UCeDé was called upon by Menem to emphasize the adopted economic strategy, because this party had a long-term tradition of campaigning for an economic course just like the one suddenly chosen in 1989:

> We who have been preaching the necessity for this fundamental change for years, as well as favouring a market social economy cannot do anything different but strongly support a transformation of this nature.... Our support for the change underway will be maintained, as long as the general path outlined by President Menem turns out to be the one anticipated in the declarations and documents that I have been citing. If this path were to be abandoned...we would not hesitate to withdraw. This support does not

imply a pact or a political compromise. It comes from a coincidence on basic ideas.[41]

Thus, UCeDé's contribution to governance was basically symbolic. However, when its congressional seats were added to those belonging to the provincial parties, they formed a wider right-oriented arc of support for Menem's programme, which had great institutional relevance. For example, this support contributed to the unanimous approval of the State Reform Law in the Senate. During discussions preceding the approval of this bill, most provincial parties agreed ideologically on the necessity of the reform (the only exception being the *Partido Bloquista de San Juan*), but preferred to distance themselves from the Peronist programme, either questioning the delegation of power to the Executive (like the *Partido Demócrata Progresista* and *Movimiento Popular Jujeño*), or arguing that they behaved supportively merely on account of the economic crisis (like the *Movimiento Popular Neuquino* and *Partido Federal*). Nevertheless, such objections did not prevent their consent to the discussion of the bill. Neither did they prevent continued agreement with the ruling party throughout the years of Carlos Menem's first administration.

In fact, as the majority voting pattern demonstrated (Table 5.1), they supported the government most of the time. The question of who the parties contributing to the majority were will be addressed in the following tables. These tables reveal the attitude of the small parties during the nominal votes that took place in the Chamber of Deputies. Table 5.7 reveals the parties that can be described as the most loyal allies of the government since they voted on the side of the government on every occasion (with the sole exception of the *Partido Blanco de los Jubilados*, who abstained during the vote on the privatization of gas). They are: *Unión del Centro Democrático* (UCeDé), *Movimiento Popular Neuquino* (MPN), *Partido Renovador de Salta* (PRS), *Partido Blanco de los Jubilados* (P.Bl.Jub.), *Partido Liberal de Corrientes* (PLC), *Alianza Acción Chaqueña* (Acc.Chaqu.), *Partido Demócrata Cristiano Federal* (PDCFed.), and *Partido Conservador Popular* (Cons.Pop.). The last two came from Buenos Aires Province, whilst the geographical origin of most of the others is revealed by their names. On the other hand, the retired people's party (P.B.Jub.) supported its own constituency and together with the UceDé, were the only ones that did not answer primarily to provincial interests. These parties were the government's staunchest allies, because they never cast a negative vote against its privatization bills. This is the main difference between them and those included in

Table 5.8, who supported the government's bills, but on an irregular basis: as can be seen from the table, their vote was either split or wholly in opposition in the two cases of YPF and Pensions. These parties are *Movimiento Popular Jujeño* (MPJ), *Movimiento de Integración y Desarrollo* (MID), *Movimiento Popular Fueguino* (MOPOFU, from Tierra del Fuego Province), *Partido Demócrata Progresista* (PDP, from Santa Fé Province), *Partido Autonomista de Corrientes* (PAC), *Partido Bloquista de San Juan* (PBSJ) and *Fuerza Republicana* (F.Rep., from Tucumán Province).

Finally, the small parties which always voted against the government's policy must be considered. As Table 5.8 exhibits, there are those from the centre-left and the left in the ideological spectrum: *Partido Demócrata Cristiano* (PDC), *Partido Intransigente* (PI), *Humanismo y Liberación-Frente Social* (Hum.y Lib.), *Movimiento al Socialismo* (MAS), *Partido Democrático Popular* (P.D.Pop.), *Partido Socialista Unificado* (P.S.Unif.) and

Table 5.7 Number of votes: the government's most loyal allies at the nominal votings

Bills / *Parties*	*A.H. Zapla*		*Gas del Estado*		*Y P F*		*Pensions*	
	Aye	*Nay*	*Aye*	*Nay*	*Aye*	*Nay*	*Aye*	*Nay*
UCeDé	11	0	8	0	7	0	5	0
MPN	2	0	2	0	2	0	1	0
PRS	2	0	3	0	3	0	3	0
P.Bl.Jubil.	1	0	—	1 Abs.	1	0	1	0
PLC	2	0	2	0	—	—	—	—
Acc.Chaqu.	—	—	1	0	1	0	1	0
PDCFed.	—	—	—	—	—	—	1	0
Cons.Pop.	—	—	—	—	—	—	1	0
Total votes	18	0	16	0	14	0	13	0

Table 5.8 The government's intermittent allies at the nominal votings

Bills / *Parties*	*A.H. Zapla*		*Gas del Estado*		*Y P F*		*Pensions*	
	Aye	*Nay*	*Aye*	*Nay*	*Aye*	*Nay*	*Aye*	*Nay*
MPJ	2	0	1	0	0	1	1	1
MID	1	0	2	0	1	1	1 Abs.	0
MOPOFU	—	—	2	0	2	0	1	1
PDP	3	0	3	0	0	2	0	4
PAC	—	—	1	0	—	—	0	1
PBSJ	—	—	1	0	0	1	1	0
F.Rep.	0	1	4	0	0	3	2	2
Total votes	6	1	14	0	3	8	5	9

Table 5.9 The government's main adversaries at the nominal votings

Bills / *Parties*	*A.H. Zapla*		*Gas del Estado*		*YPF*		*Pensions*	
	Aye	*Nay*	*Aye*	*Nay*	*Aye*	*Nay*	*Aye*	*Nay*
MODIN	—	—	0	2	—	—	0	3
PDC	0	2	0	1	—	—	0	2
PF	0	1	0	1	0	1	0	1
PDM	—	—	0	1	0	1	1 Abs.	0
PI	0	2	0	2	—	—	0	1
Band.Blanc.	0	1	—	—	—	—	—	—
Cruz.Renov.	—	—	0	2	—	—	0	1
Hum.y Lib.	0	1	—	—	—	—	—	—
MAS	—	—	—	—	—	—	0	1
P.D.Pop.	0	1	—	—	—	—	—	—
PSUnif.	0	1	—	—	—	—	—	—
US-HTE	0	1	—	—	—	—	0	3
Total votes	0	10	0	9	0	2	0	12

Unidad Socialista-Honestidad, Trabajo y Eficiencia (US-HTE), and those from the far right having nationalist ideologies, as well as other provincial political forces (*Movimiento por la Dignidad y la Independencia* (MODIN), *Partido Federal* (PF), *Partido Demócrata de Mendoza* (PDM), *Defensa Provincial Bandera Blanca* (Band.Blanc., from Tucumán Province), *Cruzada Renovadora* (Cruz.Renov., from San Juan Province). None of these parties voted affirmatively in any of the studied cases.

A conclusion can be drawn from the above. The small third parties did not form a single legislative bloc (despite being many of them ideologically close) and some did not even maintain a homogenous position within their own ranks. One reason for this could be that their chances of profiting from negotiation were enhanced by individual actions. On the one hand, they could obtain the greater financial resources that the formation of a separate bloc implied according to the congressional budget distribution. On the other, they could make the executive power negotiate individually (rather than through the leader of a single bloc), pushing up 'the price' of their votes. The fact that most of these parties were organized on a provincial basis indicates the strength of provincial interests in legislative processes. Attention to these interests would probably have been a crucial point in defining these parties' proclivity to support the Executive's bills.[42] In brief, this conclusion once more indicates that the approval of the privatization bills demanded a process of negotiation and agreement. In this process, the Executive most probably had to use leadership strategies and grant concessions in order to persuade reluctant legislators either to vote affirmatively or to attend the chambers' meetings. This is a subject of study in the following chapter.

Conclusion

The extent of the economic transformation that Carlos Menem initiated in 1989 involved both the full commitment of the presidential leadership and substantial political and institutional resources. The first part of this chapter explored the motives that led President Menem to implement a far-reaching privatization programme. A combination of political and economic reasons was identified as a source of the profound commitment by the president to initiate the policy and seek the means for its implementation. This part of the chapter also highlighted the markedly institutional character that this policy showed. In effect, after the first stage of privatization authorized by the State Reform Law, another took place in which several bills replaced the collective and delegative character of the first law. Thus, the production of legislation for privatization involved the participation of Congress in the writing and approval of the Executive's proposals.

The second part of this chapter showed that the president benefited from the absence of major institutional obstacles for the approval of his policy. At the beginning, the 1989 crisis contributed to overcome political resistance and, indeed, created an unusual amount of political support which permitted the launch of a vast programme of privatization. Then, since privatization continued being a major concern for the government, it necessarily had to face the accommodation of political strategies to normal times and, so, the uncertainty of reaching the *quorum* to treat its bills. For this, President Menem was favoured, first, with the support of his party. Indeed, Peronism's discipline was a great source of institutional and political power for him, and it was connected both to the party features of pragmatism and flexibility, and to several elements of the presidential leadership, namely, its legitimacy within the party, renewed public support and explicit adulation efforts. Second, the president benefited from Radicalism's limitations to question the whole economic model, which, in practice, meant that its opposition role concentrated in criticizing some aspects of the policy implementation (the indiscriminate sale of state-owned assets, the concentration of power, the social consequences of the reforms) and in the refusal to provide a *quorum* only when the very critical cases were under discussion. Third, the president could always resort to *ad hoc* agreements with the small parties sitting in the two Chambers of Congress.

In brief, President Menem managed to gain the necessary number for the passage of his privatization bills in Congress. However, as will be next shown, the fact of having to deal with the formation of a strict majority gave him no surplus of power, and rather forced him into a negotiation process, through which the contents of his bills had often to be modified in exchange for support.

Appendix 1

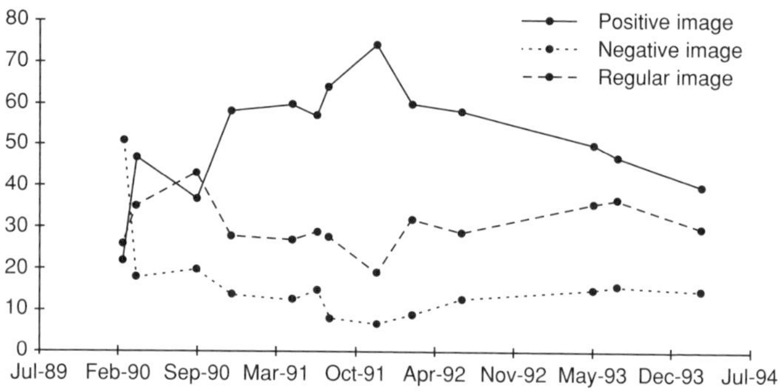

Graph 5.1 Menem: image of the economic programme

Source: Estudio Sociológico y Político Mora y Araujo, Noguera y Asociados. National sample of 800 cases: Argentines older than 18 years. Estimated error: 3.5 per cent.

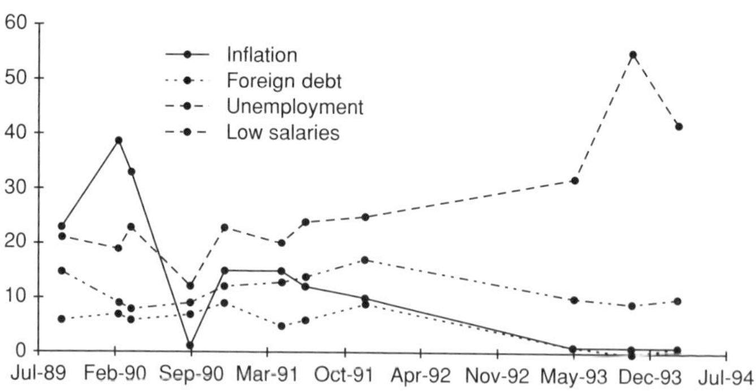

Graph 5.2 Menem: principal problems of the country

Source: Estudio Sociológico y Político Mora y Araujo, Noguera y Asociados. National sample of 800 cases: Argentines older than 18 years. Estimated error: 3.5 per cent.

Appendix 2: Enterprises included in the bill for the privatization of the assets of the defence establishment

No.	Enterprises
1	Astilleros y Fábricas Navales del Estado S.A.
2	Hierro Patagónico de Sierra grande S.A.
3	Astillero Ministro Manuel Domecq S.A.
4	Sidinox S.A.
5	Satecna S.A. para Tecnología Acuática
6	Petroquímica General Mosconi S.A.
7	Sociedad Mixta Siderurgia Argentina
8	Petroquímica Bahía Blanca S.A.
9	Tanque Argentino Mediano Soc. del Estado
10	Empresa de Desarrollos Especiales S.A.
11	Sisteval S.A.
12	Fábrica Militar General San Martín
13	Fábrica Militar de Vainas y Conductores Elec.
14	Fábrica Militar de Acido Sulfúrico
15	Fábrica Militar Pilar
16	Fábrica Militar de Tolueno Sintético
17	Fábrica Militar de Armas Portátiles D.Matheu
18	Fábrica Militar Fray Luis Beltrán
19	Fábrica Militar de Pólvoras y Expl. Villa María
20	Fábrica Militar Río Tercero
21	Fábrica Militar San Francisco
22	Administración Comirsa
23	Complejo Industrial Ramallo-San Nicolás
24	Centro de Exploración Geológico Minero
25	Fábrica Militar de Pólvoras y Explosivos Azul
26	Tecnología Aeroespacial S.A.

Source: C.R.S., 26/27 September 1990, p. 3970

6
The Institutional Dynamics of Privatization

Introduction

By examining the position towards privatization maintained by the political parties sitting in Congress, Chapter 5 described what the political components of the presidential majorities were, and also showed how the president had managed to achieve the necessary number of votes to pass its bills. This conclusion is, therefore, the starting point of this chapter, which aims to explore whether, apart from the final vote of support, it was possible for Congress to affect the contents of the proposals pushed forward by the Executive. Chapter 5 also suggested the existence of a negotiation process, and so the likelihood that compromises had taken place regarding policy contents. This chapter will show that the extent of congressional participation varied over the years and according to the topics under discussion. In effect, two different stages of congressional behaviour can be identified during Menem's first period in office. A first phase took place at the beginning of the period, and represented the greatest imbalance of power between the Presidency and Congress. A second phase, which is the main object of analysis in this chapter, extended throughout the rest of the presidential period, and was characterized by the improvement of the congressional capacities to intervene in the processes of law-making. These phases demonstrate that, within the framework of a fairly stable distribution of power, strategic realignments took place in the relationship between the two branches of government. Furthermore, since the congressional attitude towards the bills varied during the six years of the administration, showing an increasing obstructionist tendency, the Executive was also obliged to modify its approach towards the legislative branch.

The chapter is divided into four parts. The first part presents the general features of the inter-institutional dialogue, that is, the response of Congress to presidential initiatives. The second part presents the indicators that confirm that, during Menem's first Presidency, there was a change in the pattern of relations between president and Congress. Following parts explore in detail the second phase of inter-institutional relations by describing several legislative processes. The last section focuses again on the executive power, although this time describing its final reaction to the intervention of Congress.

6.1. Congress and the privatization bills

The last chapter showed that Congress was not obstructive towards the privatization bills. Most of the bills exhibited the similar pattern of approval in which the Peronist ruling party agreed to cooperate with the Executive while small political parties provided the remaining votes that were necessary to form absolute majorities. Nevertheless, it is worth examining the attitude that Congress adopted towards the privatization policy in addition to the evident non-obstructive behaviour. Table 6.1 provides some illustrative information.

The first column gives the topic of the bills, that is, the sectors, companies or services up for privatization. Remarkably, the first case is the state reform bill which, as was explained in Chapter 4, was the pillar of the entire privatization process and included an extensive number of privatizations contained in the appendices. The remaining cases were meant to take the reform process even further (see Chapter 5) by following the principles established in the first bill. In the second column, the final outcome of the legislative process is shown. As can be seen, this column confirms the high approval levels that privatization bills obtained in Congress. However, this column also indicates that there was a case (number 7) in which the executive resorted to a necessity and urgency decree although the legislative process had already been initiated. Despite this, the privatization of the cattle market by decree was not caused by a situation of institutional conflict. The privatization decision was included in the necessity and urgency megadecree concerning the deregulation of the economy.[1] The decree ordered the decentralization, restructuring, privatization and/or dissolution of organizations in charge of regulating the regional products markets. It not only affected a great number of organizations, but also modified and revoked many laws and other regulations. Congress responded angrily, and although the Executive tried to obtain legislative approval after the enactment, Congress delayed giving an affirmative answer for two

Table 6.1 The parliamentary procedure of the privatization laws

No.	*Privatization bills*	*Approval*	*Congressional procedure duration (month/day/year)*	*Congress's amendment*	*Partial veto*
1	State reform	Yes	1 month (7/13/89 to 8/17/89)	Yes	No
2	Ministry of Defence assets	Yes	17 months (7/23/90 to 12/4/91)	Yes	No
3	AHZ (defence)	Yes	1 month (7/27/90 to 8/23/90)	Yes	No
4	Electricity industry	Yes	6 months (6/13/91 to 12/20/91)	Yes	Yes
5	Gas industry	Yes	11 months (6/13/91 to 5/20/92)	Yes	Yes
6	Oil industry, YPF	Yes	17 months (4/4/91 to 9/24/92)	Yes	Yes
7	Mercado de Hacienda (cattle market)	Decree	(9/18/91)	—	—
8	Ports	Yes	20 months (9/27/90 to 6/3/92)	Yes	Yes
9	Caja de Ahorro and BANADE (banks)	Yes	10 months (12/3/91 to 9/30/92)	Yes	No
10	Pensions	Yes	15 months (6/5/92 to 9/23/93)	Yes	Yes
11	YPF (2nd round)	Yes	1 month (3/1/95 to 3/22/95)	Yes	No

Source: This Table has been prepared on the basis of data obtained from Congressional Reports.

years.[2] The fact is that, as Table 6.1. indicates, the cattle market privatization (which was part deregulation and part privatization), was the only measure adopted unilaterally.

Column three reveals two patterns for the bills' passage through Congress: some were passed speedily, some much more slowly. In spite of the presence of three bills passed without major delay, the majority of the bills needed an average time of ten months to receive congressional approval. Therefore, it should be noted that laws on the same subject required different time periods of approval. This, in turn, suggests that although the Executive was able to obtain quick responses in some instances, it usually faced greater difficulties or, at least, it was obliged to respect the congressional timetable.

Amendment and veto columns add some other related points. As can be seen, all the bills were subject to modifications and, therefore, it can be stated that a positive answer to the Executive's policy did not necessarily imply full acceptance of all its proposals. Exploring the extent of the changes introduced by Congress seems to be a crucial indicator when evaluating the policy's final outcome. Similarly, partial vetoes applied to several bills show the Executive's attempt to correct laws that had been passed by Congress; in other words, its intention to limit a Congress that it felt had gone too far.

Thus, this Table shows that behind what seems to have been Menem's overwhelmingly successful privatization policy there is a hidden and still unexplored role that Congress played whereby it controlled the whole process while not initiating it. Delays and modifications to a policy that was central to the Executive's officers suggest that the final victory was not straightforward. Furthermore, since the policy could not be tied to a single package, the Executive was always at risk of not only being denied approval, but also of facing the inconveniences that delays and modifications would provoke. From this point of view, it is not difficult to imagine that during the six-year period a dialogue was established between the two branches of government. If this is added to the government's change of approach to the policy (which was aimed to improve the conditions of the policy implementation), it all indicates that this process most probably involved advances and reversals, realignments and, finally, changes in the relative positions of power.

The next sections of this chapter illustrate the main features of the relations between Congress and President Menem during his first administration. Two main institutional dynamics characterized the dialogue between the two branches of government during Menem's first presidential term. The first corresponds to the early part of the administration when a *delegative phase* determined the practical subordination of Congress. Chapter 4 described how during this phase Congress lost all its reactive powers, only exercising its capacity for control through a bicameral commission. Delegation was a distinctive feature of Menem's first years in office, and was not repeated later. The subsequent wave of bills inaugurated the *cooperative phase*. As will be seen, this phase was very complex, and although the cases fit into the 'cooperative' pattern, case-study differences are also worth exploring.

6.2. The cooperative phase

President–Congress relations were redefined at the end of the emergency period. The new stage was inaugurated by a number of bills that attempted to take the reform of the state even further. As the delegative stage was over, the Executive found itself in a situation of having to confront Congress on almost every occasion in which privatization was the issue. During this process, it faced a Congress that aspired to alter the position in which the delegation of power had placed it. Two indicators serve to prove this change in Congress's attitude: the first is the legislators' involvement in the writing of the bills, which stresses that, although eventually approving all the Executive's proposals, the congressional majority took its time to make all kind of amendments. The second concerns the Executive's constant displays of leadership efforts to pressure or to persuade reluctant legislators, which means that the Executive could not limit itself to submitting the bills, but rather had to follow their path in Congress in order to secure a successful outcome.

Indeed, the fact that Congress did not obstruct the bills' final approval indicates that strategic realignment did not mean an abrupt change with respect to the previous phase. Thus, it could be argued that Congress was able to recover its 'powers of reaction' (approve, modify, delay, reject) only partially. This is not, however, an insignificant point since this phase of privatization was as important as the previous one. For example, the size and economic centrality of the gas, electricity and oil companies should be considered. Pensions and military assets should also be added to this list. As will be demonstrated, the debate of these cases in Congress shows that inter-institutional relations had entered a different stage. But, first, the next section considers the weapons of presidential power.

6.2.1. Presidential weapons

Congress did not automatically follow the president's legislative orders. Rather, President Menem's undoubted success in terms of policy approvals involved a number of leadership efforts, especially directed towards his own Peronist Party. I have commented in Chapter 5 on the sources of the presidential success in persuading ruling-party legislators in Congress, all of them connected to the central question of the political leadership. In this section I want to emphasize that Menem became an active lobbyist in Congress. Ties were carefully cultivated with the other legislative branch not only to secure support for the final approval of the bills, but also to obtain a satisfactory outcome in terms of the bills' contents. These strategies prove that there was an intense process of negotiation by means of which the Executive could control policy contents, but which also marks the relevance of its interlocutors in the other branch of government. Leadership skills were displayed on several fronts and in different ways. The media was used for public announcements and exhortations. The president's office and private residence hosted innumerable private informal meetings. Further, Menem exercised pressure, applied persuasion, and showed a disposition to negotiate.

Menem frequently used his high profile in the media to make announcements and presentations about imminent plans and bills, to complain about unsatisfactory responses from his party and other actors and to emphasize repeatedly that 'the ongoing economic plan is irreversible'.[3] The most remarkable public strategies were the 'fast moving' and the 'threats'. Menem issued decrees imposing tight timetables and set deadlines for every privatization case. Through them, the president exercised public pressure on the various actors involved in the policy-making process (ministers, secretaries, *interventores*, congressmen) and gave clear signals of his commitment to the economic programme. The best example was a decree enacted in 1991, a few days before a presidential trip to the United States.[4] The decree detailed privatization timetables and established that every single case on the agenda had to be concluded by December 1992. The decree was used to give signals abroad. It was a document of commitment to be submitted to foreign investors in order to inform them that the time for investing in Argentina had arrived. However, the decree was also repeatedly used as a means of forcing policy-makers to move to the rhythm of the president's fixed deadlines. Time pressure strategies were accompanied by public threats. Once terms had been fixed, congressmen would know that the president was ready to use his unilateral legislative resources if they failed to respond accordingly. Threatening with the issuing of a decree was Menem's personal strategy and was repeated many times by his close collaborators. It was imposed with the memory of past measures adopted using this instrument, and the president's words saying that 'We have been regarded as totalitarian. If 86 per cent of the population is endorsing this decree, I prefer to be totalitarian in this way rather than be democratic with 10 or 20 per cent of the population.'[5] The use of this weapon was, however, limited since the president knew that upsetting legislators was counterproductive in the long run. Most likely, he would soon need their votes for another measure so that threats of bypassing Congress had to be used in a selective manner. Something similar happened with threats of sanctions, which they do not seem to have played a great role, although a few remarkable exceptions were widely publicized as illustrations for future cases.

Menem complemented the use of public pressures with other more subtle ways of influencing legislators. Invitations to the presidential residence in Olivos were not exceptional. Deputies and senators attended special meetings in Olivos on several occasions. In the relaxed atmosphere of dinner and tango shows, some improvised words from the president would emphasize achievements, invoke Perón saying that solutions should be found with the help of everyone, thank them for their approval of important laws, and, in the end, ask for action with respect to some delayed legislation.[6] Similar encounters were held with provincial governors where Menem aimed at the source of the congressmen's political power since they normally responded directly to the provincial partisan structure headed by the corresponding provincial governor.[7]

Despite the president's direct involvement, presidential lobbying in Congress was mainly a task of Menem's closest political operators. The General Secretariat of the Presidency, first headed by Alberto Cohan and, from September 1990 by Eduardo Bauzá, directed the political dialogue with legislators from both the Peronist and opposition parties.[8] Bauzá held frequent meetings with the presidents of the Senate and the Chamber of Deputies, and with the heads of the Peronist blocs in both houses. These meetings were designed to coordinate general legislative tasks as well as to discuss particular laws to which objections were being raised by legislators. Approaches did not exclude opposition parties, and meetings were also held with heads of opposition blocs. Bauzá also coordinated activities inside the cabinet, between ministers and legislators, and between politicians and heads of unions and entrepreneurial organizations. Similar activities were occasionally performed by other political sections of the executive branch such as the Ministry of the Interior, and the Legal and Technical Secretariat of the Presidency.

Bridge-building activities developed by the Presidency were accompanied by parallel initiatives from the Ministry of Economy. Probably motivated by separate incentives, the fact is that the president and his economic minister, Domingo Cavallo, boosted the Executive's potential by moving in the same direction. As much as Menem, Cavallo became a media figure, using radio and television to make announcements, put pressure on slow and reluctant legislators and to threaten with decrees. With knowledge as his best resource, Cavallo understood the need to instruct uninformed politicians on economic problems and the necessary solutions. Persuasion tactics resulted in frequent visits to Congress: didactic lectures were given to the Peronist bloc and congressional committees, whilst spontaneous visits to either of the two plenary sessions complemented the informative missions.[9] In the end, however, the energetic manner with which the minister had defended his policies, gave him the reputation of being stubborn and irritable, which hampered his relationship with members of Congress. Irrespective of their political origin, congressmen showed their dislike for the arrogance with which the minister applied technical criteria to political life.[10]

Nevertheless, the minister's lobbying activities were also carried out by secretaries and subsecretaries directly involved in the policy implementation processes. Moreover, these functions began to show an incipient institutionalization as a result of the establishment of congressional liaison offices with permanent staff set up by Cavallo. The staff were in charge of complementing the secretaries' work by documenting respective committee meetings, bills submitted by individual legislators, the progression of presidential bills and the development of plenary sessions. Furthermore, having some people prowling the corridors provided the minister with the informal knowledge that was necessary to enhance his negotiating position or to prevent unwanted legislative developments.[11] Although similar functions were occasionally performed by other ministries, the Ministry of Economy was the only one to use them on a regular basis. Only towards the end of Menem's first term another structure acquired a permanent presence in Congress. As dictated by the constitutional reform, the Head of Cabinet became the main institution in charge of lubricating relations with Congress. However, it did not suppress the already existing structures created by the Ministry of Economy.

Despite difficulties (mostly due to personality clashes and rivalries), lobbying Congress proved to be effective, at least with respect to privatization. The activities simultaneously performed by the president's office and Cavallo's Ministry allowed the Executive to work as machinery of government. It was very important that the president himself stood forthrightly behind the policy, making it clear that this was his programme, the one that people supported. Opposing the programme was, therefore, a challenge to himself and the people's mandate. However, lobbying efforts carried out in coordination with the Ministry of Economy were central in maintaining tight control over the policy-making processes and in achieving the sought results on many policy contents. Section 6.3. provides several examples of the way in which the Executive's strategies were applied.

6.2.2. *The congressional amendments*

Since ten privatization bills were introduced during the cooperative phase, it is to be expected that variations existed owing to the nature and intensity of the demands formulated by congressmen. Nevertheless, it should be highlighted that Congress attempted to modify the bills by aiming for three different objectives. The first objective concerned the policy itself, since changes were proposed not to limit the sale of assets but to improve the conditions of the policy's design. This type of amendment certainly expressed the legislators' concern for the future consequences of the reform. It also revealed that because Congress was not allowed to formulate the policies, importance was given to its participation in the composition of those already selected. Contribution to the design of bills was quite different from a simple ratification of decisions made in the executive arena. The second objective deals with the ability of the legislative power to intervene in the process that puts the policy into practice. In general, Congress sought to extend the supervisory power that had been concentrated in the Bicameral Commission by the State Reform Law in order to gain more active participation in the later stages of the implementation of the policy. Finally, changes made to the bills demonstrated the concessions that had to be granted by the government as part of the negotiations in order to obtain the support of particular interests sitting in Congress. The provinces represented most of these interests and their demands were directed at participation in the control process, guarantees of protection for the inconvenience that privatization would cause in their territories and, in some cases, participation in the profits that were to be obtained from the sales. Other interests, such as the military and unions, also influenced the congressional reforms.

Let us now focus on the distinct legislative paths that individual bills took in Congress. The examples of electricity and gas are used to show the three kinds of modifications that Congress was attempting to introduce to the bills. The oil privatization shows the relevance of provincial demands acting in the Senate as well as their central participation in the redefinition of the bill's design. Privatization of military assets demonstrates not only the involvement of the military lobby, but is also the only case in which differences prevailed inside the executive branch. Finally, the bill with respect to pensions presents an extremely complicated process of negotiation, this time taking place in the lower house.

6.3. Electricity and gas

The bills for the privatization of electricity and gas were those most carefully designed by the executive power. The World Bank provided a close supervision and played an active part in defining these projects. With these bills, Minister Cavallo intended to draw a dividing line from previous privatizations. On the one hand, there was concern with giving signals to credit organizations in order to obtain the financial support required by the convertibility plan. The government submitted the bills amidst intense negotiations with the IMF, which included, among other measures, proposed levels of fiscal surplus to be achieved through privatization.[12] On the other hand, there was also the pressure from future consumers to consider their interests in the course of the sale. Powerful industrial users of gas and electricity were particularly concerned about higher prices, which were crucial for industrial costs. So entrepreneurial organizations (such as the Argentine Industrial Union) monitored the policy-making process closely.[13] From the very beginning it was clear that the proposed bills would be subjected to modifications in Congress. Many of these would be passed.

The manner in which the bills for the privatization of gas and electricity were dealt with by Congress provides plenty of examples demonstrating the three groups of amendments mentioned in the previous section. Beginning with the first group (the design of the policy), the Executive's draft for the privatization of the state gas company stipulated several restrictions on the future participation of the state in the operation of transport and distribution services (Article 4). The state would be in charge of them only in case of a non-satisfactory bid, or in the event that a granted concession had to be later withdrawn for some reason. The article further specified to say that, in those cases, the state's intervention would be strictly limited to the time when there were no private bids made for these services. Once in Congress, the Senate refused to accept such a strong statement and the last sentence was removed. A similar occurrence happened with the electricity bill. The original version included an article whereby the state would provide services if the offers were not satisfactory while another emphasized that the state could intervene in only those cases. Congress disliked this, since senators eliminated the latter article, and deputies altered the former, changing a possibility into an obligation to guarantee electricity services in case of non-satisfactory private offers (Article 3).

To be sure, these modifications did not seriously alter the Executive's original text, nor did they have immediate practical consequences and were too general to be threatening. Instead, they attempted to reflect the spirit that was present in the congressional approach to state reform. They demonstrated that the aversion shown by the Executive towards any involvement of the state in entrepreneurial activities was definitely not shared by Congress. Normally, these initiatives would come from the government's party in Congress, but would also be widely supported by other political forces. Most importantly, these modifications accompanied others which with a similar approach implied further consequences for the reform of the state.

For instance, in the electricity bill, the state was granted a power of veto. This bill created the office of *Despacho Nacional de Cargas* as a public company. The state would initially hold the majority of shares and would be entitled to reduce the holdings to 10 per cent. Congress did not alter this provision but the deputies added that, despite the reduction of shares held by the state, it would maintain its interest and power of veto in the office's directorate (Article 35). Imports and exports were also a matter for discussion when Congress considered electricity services, as well as the transport and distribution of gas. In both cases the Executive's proposal established that export and import activities would not need prior authorization in order to be carried out. Congress, however, established that authorization would be required for both imports and exports regarding electricity (Article 34) and also for the export of gas (Article 3). Following the proposal of the Partido Renovador de Salta, gas export authorization would be granted if internal supply would not be affected. In the particular case of *Gas del Estado*, Congress incorporated further reforms. There was a major debate in relation to how long the periods of concession should be (Articles 5, 6). The Senate arranged 35 years, with possible extensions. Committees in the lower house fixed the extension period to 35 years and left the case open for further renewals. The negative reaction of the Chamber as a whole finally reduced the extension period to ten years withdrawing the possibility of further renewals. Government subsidy provisions were also included. Article 48 challenged the strict subsidy policy that the government was enacting by authorizing the Executive to grant subsidies after receiving congressional authorization. Another article was added in the lower house (Article 92) which allowed for the creation of a subsidy in the event that compensation for tariffs to the provinces would require it. Finally, concern with the workers' situation was also present. The Senate incorporated (Article 80) the provision through which privatization arrangements could include the issue of bonds to allow the workers a share of the company's profits. The deputies confirmed this clause by adding the obligation to issue ten per cent of the company's shares as part of the participated property scheme.[14]

Besides claiming the right to correct the general design of the policy, Congress tried to extend its influence in the implementation stage (second type of amendments). These movements were intended to enlarge its sphere of action, which the State Reform Law had only restricted to some elements of control and supervision. In general, most of the pursued modifications tried to improve the control functions of Congress. However, it was also the case that while seeking supervision Congress was actually trying to become involved in performing executive functions. The electricity bill (Article 93) enlarged the functions of the bicameral commission to include the obligation of issuing reports on three matters: tender basis, assessment of offers and final contracts. The reports were supposed to have a binding nature and, therefore, they could either authorize or stop the privatization process. Besides modifying the existing commission, Congress enlarged its control prerogatives by creating others. It tried to ensure supervision over appointments in the directorate of the regulatory body: before appointing or removing members the Executive would have to defer to a congressional commission (Articles 55 and 59, respectively).

Finally, the gas bill provides many examples of modifications involving particular interests. Most of these modifications were directed to favour the position of the provinces. Article 50 created the regulatory body. The Chamber of Deputies agreed to the decentralization of the body by stipulating the creation of a minimal structure in each distribution area in order to maintain an easy relationship between users and companies. Article 52 specified among the functions of the regulatory body a progressive delegation of functions compatible with the competence of the provinces. Article 54 related to the appointment of members to the regulatory directorate. Although appointments were the Executive's prerogative, the deputies decided that two of the five members would be proposed by provincial governors. Article 82 (amended in the Senate) appropriated 10 per cent of the privatization benefits and distributed them as follows: 50 per cent according to the federal co-participation index, and the remaining 50 per cent using an index that the Ministry of Economy would work out from calculations based on a relationship inversely proportional to the average annual temperature in each province. The deputies then added that the Municipality of Buenos Aires would also share in this 10 per cent. Article 92 created the Natural Gas National Fund. It was to last for five years and the money would come partly from the resources obtained by increasing prices, and partly from the repayments obtained from loans made with the fund's resources. The destiny of the funds would be: 80 per cent to compensate the prices that users had to pay in the colder provinces and 20 per cent for the undertaking of research programmes concerning natural gas. Through Article 95, the state agreed to give a special reimbursement to the provinces in order to compensate them for the projects that had already been undertaken for the distribution of gas to their inhabitants. They would consist of either state shares in privatized companies or some other similar payment.

In summary, this was the way in which Congress contributed to the writing of privatization bills. As can be seen, although some of these amendments might upset the Executive, the fact is that, in general, they did not block the move to privatization. However, it is true that the Executive could maximize its achievements in Congress because the passage of the bills was closely followed by its operators. This meant that some other congressional clauses were not included in the final version. For example, in the case of gas, the Chamber of Deputies attempted to include a provision for the creation of a bicameral commission (Article 94) that was to assist the Executive in the whole privatization process and report regularly to Congress on progress made. The Executive was supposed to consult this commission every time important decisions had to be taken. Eventually, this proposal was withdrawn because the Executive stated that there was a bicameral commission already in operation. In the case of electricity, the Executive was surprised by the modifications worked out by the Energy Committee, where Peronist deputies, in the bill's second reading, excluded the possibility of privatizing a number of hydroelectric dams. Decision on their privatization was, instead, to be undertaken by the provinces in which those dams were located. This amendment provoked an immediate response from the Presidency. The General Secretary, Bauzá, organized an urgent meeting with the head of the committee, Deputy Antonio Cassia, the Secretary of Energy, Carlos Bastos representing the Ministry of Economy, and some senators.[15] Afterwards, the Peronist deputies altered their position on the hydroelectric dams.[16]

Additionally, the Executive was concerned with delays in the process. The bills had been submitted in June, and it was October before the Senate was prepared to begin to consider the electricity privatization at the plenary session. Gas privatization was even more delayed. The Executive would frequently accompany the law-making processes with the public use of its 'time pressure' and 'threat (of using decrees instead of laws)' strategies. Its pressures would even lead the Peronist Party leaders to violate congressional regulations. In effect, the approval of gas privatization bill in the Chamber's plenary session provoked one of the greatest scandals in congressional history. Pressured by Minister Cavallo (who was, in turn, pressured by President Menem), the leader of the Peronist bloc, Deputy Matzkin, knew that he had to obtain the bill's passage on 26 March 1992 in one way or another, and that a *quorum* was almost impossible to attain. Then, immediately after the session commenced, the presence of a spurious deputy sitting in the full assembly was discovered by journalists, and suspicions about the presence of others were also raised.[17] The news spread all over the house and reached the media. Indeed, the session had to be suspended without having previously fulfilled the Executive's desires. But, most importantly, a black stain was left on the public reputation of Congress.

6.4. Privatizing the oil company

Until the end of the 1980s, the oil industry in Argentina was characterized by strong state intervention and the leadership of the state oil company, Yacimientos Petrolíferos Fiscales (YPF). From 1989 onwards, a bold process of privatization and deregulation was initiated with the following objectives: the creation of competitive markets at the different stages of activity, the opening up of transactions to international commerce, the capture of future oil revenue, and the improvement of YPF's productive efficiency.[18] The measures initially adopted to attain these goals worked towards the deregulation of oil exploration, exploitation, industrialization and commercialization activities. As a result of this process, marginal and central oil areas began to be conceded to private companies.[19] The government decided that YPF should resign its control over currently under-exploited and un-exploited areas, which were to be tendered for private exploitation. It also decided that YPF needed to either subcontract or associate itself with private companies in order to optimize the final extraction from central oil areas. In any case, the state would receive a cash payment in return for exploitation and association rights.[20] As a consequence, oil gradually began to be produced by companies other than YPF.

On top of all this, the Executive decided how the restructuring and privatization of the state company would take place. It issued Decree 2778/90 which, in accordance with the State Reform Law's dispositions, needed congressional approval. In April 1991, a bill drawn up on this basis was sent to Congress. It only had a few clauses which set out that YPF's shares could be offered on national and international stock markets, and explicitly indicated that YPF's personnel were entitled to acquire shares as well as to participate in asset-stripping by means of the participated property scheme.[21] However, in the end the government realized that YPF's privatization as proposed would not easily gain approval.

The main problem was that the oil privatization policy revived long-standing unresolved state versus province conflicts concerning the control of the oilfields. Provincial demands dated from 1967 when the *de facto* government approved the hydrocarbons law, according to which oil resources belonged to the national state (Act 17319). The law admitted that provinces where oilfields were located deserved compensation for the exploitation of oilfields within their boundaries: they were to receive between 5 and 12 per cent of the crude oil value (*regalías*). However, from then on all kinds of problems arose. The provinces began to complain that the law was unconstitutional (that the law violated the Constitution's federal system), about the criteria used to calculate oil *regalías* and, finally, about *regalías* debts that the state failed to pay.

Throughout the years, the national governments' reply to these demands had always been mostly rhetoric, and this was how provincial governors regarded the Federal Pact that President Menem signed with them on 24 May 1990. Although the pact was intended to recognize the provinces' control over the renewable and non-renewable natural resources which were found within their territories, the provinces understood that the government's oil policy was undermining these principles in practice. The fact that the government began to concede central and marginal oilfields for exploitation by others was not well received by the provinces. Some of them even took their demands to court. The province of Mendoza went to court when the government put its central oil area 'Vizcacheras' out to tender.[22] It demanded the recognition of its rights in the area as well as a share of the US.$ 97 million that the state had received as payment for exploitation rights.

It was clear that no agreement on YPF's privatization could be reached if the proposed bill did not attempt to solve this conflict between the state and the provinces. The government needed to find a way to respond to provincial demands without threatening the reform process that was taking place in the oil sector. In this context, it was clear that both sides had to make compromises. The state could not guarantee legal security to investors if the provinces were taking their demands to court, and the provinces had to accept that their compensation needed to be in accordance with an economic reform programme that was not to be stopped. Because of this, the Executive decided to withdraw the oil privatization bill and submit another one which combined both the Executive's privatization goals and provincial interests.[23]

This second bill was characterized by its complex structure, through which it attempted to tackle several issues simultaneously. First, it addressed the transference of hydrocarbon resources from the state to the provinces. The federalization of hydrocarbons was established, but in order to protect existing contracts, transference of control to the provinces was going to be implemented after their expiration. Second, the bill attempted to solve the debts that the state owed the provinces. It admitted *regalías* demands, and proposed to pay them with YPF shares or bonds issued for this purpose. Article 19 (then, Article 20) recognized that the provinces were going to share in the benefits obtained from YPF's association with the private companies. Ten per cent of the payment received in return for exploitation rights in central oil areas would be shared with the provinces where those areas were located. Third, the bill established the transformation of YPF and declared it subject to privatization. On this basis, the legislative process began to move ahead in the Senate.

Although the oil privatization bill had been completely redesigned to answer long-term provincial demands, further modifications took place during the legislative process. Senators understood that the bill was only favourable to the provinces in theory, because actually there were many exceptions in the short run. As mentioned previously, Article 1 established that those areas assigned to YPF for exploration and exploitation, those conceded to private companies as well as those whose concession had not yet been decided, were only to be transferred to the provinces after the contracts expired. Senators believed that the position of the provinces could be improved at least in the latter cases, and the provinces were granted the power to analyse, assess, adjudicate and determine the percentage of *regalías* in tenders still in process (Article 2). Representatives from the provinces would also participate in the committee in charge of re-writing the existing hydrocarbons law. The modification of this law, which had been accused of having caused the conflicts between the state and the provinces, was presented as a prerequisite for putting into practice the federalization of hydrocarbons. The drafting committee would be formed from four representatives from the executive branch, four from Congress, and two from the provinces (Article 5).

Besides improving the conditions of the provinces, the Senate incorporated some other important changes that closely affected the policy's design. Probably the most remarkable was the one suggested by the Peronist Senator Pedro Molina. The presidential bill declared YPF subject to privatization and its capital changed to shares, 51 per cent belonging to the national state, 39 per cent to the provinces and 10 per cent to be acquired by the company's personnel. By means of this bill, the state and the provinces were obliged to sell together a percentage of no less than 50 per cent. Molina's modification limited the sale of state shares, as it stated that they could never fall below 20 per cent, unless another law so stipulated (Article 8). The modifications also arranged that the state would be represented in the company's directorate by two persons proposed to the Executive by Congress. Their vote had necessarily to be affirmative in the case of decisions concerning the joining with other companies, total suspension of exploration and exploitation activities and the voluntary dissolution of YPF. Sale limitations and power of veto were among the greatest contributions that Congress made to YPF's privatization arrangements.[24]

Another important modification that helped to unlock the legislative process was a clause specifying the destiny of the money raised by the privatization. During the months between the committees' first report and the final consideration by the Senate, the Executive discovered that a clause on this topic could possibly be used to mobilize popular and political support. Therefore, it proposed to clarify that funds to be obtained from YPF's sale would be used entirely to capitalize the pensions system. The Senate accepted this modification but still found it too vague and general, and Senator Rodríguez Saá (PJ) put forward a proposal to specify that those funds were to be exclusively applied to the increase in pensions (Article 23). Additionally, he proposed the creation of a supervisory commission (consisting of three members from the Executive, four from Congress and two representatives of pensioners) which would be in charge of supervising the bill's implementation.[25] The presence of pensioners on the commission was thought to be a control over the destiny of the money raised from the privatization.

These amendments, which substantially affected the policy's design, were the price paid by the Executive for seeing the bill approved and for achieving by this means the structural transformation of the oil sector within a framework of legality. Once more, this legislative process exemplifies the inter-institutional dialogue that took place to carry out the policy's implementation. Before Congress's intervention, arrangements between the company's directors and the unions were thought to be the only requirements for a successful implementation. After Congress's approval, a wider range of interests involved in the process substantially modified the final text. As Cavallo has written, 'This was how we obtained the legislators' support for this initiative.'[26]

6.5. Privatizing military assets

With respect to the privatization of the Ministry of Defence's assets, the proposal lingered in the congressional offices for 17 months. The bill sought to extend the sale of enterprises belonging to the defence area, the privatization of which had already been initiated with the approval of the State Reform Law. This law had authorized the privatization of eight important state-owned companies administered by the Ministry of Defence, whilst the new bill declared 'subject to privatization' most of the remaining companies in the area.[27] This proposal was the cause of many disagreements inside both the Executive and Congress and, in turn, provoked delays and modifications during the legislative process. The main issues of dispute were concerned with the destination of funds raised from privatization and the strategy for the production of defence material.

The legislative history of this bill began in July 1990 when Erman González was still the Minister of Economy, and Humberto Romero, the Minister of Defence. The times were characterized by the struggle against inflation and by the Ministry of Economy's efforts to bring the state's accounts under control. During those days, decisions regarding the sale of public companies did not come all under the aegis of the Ministry of Economy, but were still shared with the Ministry of Public Works and Services and the Ministry of Defence. In the end, economic officials worked out a plan to centralize decisions in order to avoid the political and social pressures which were arising through the many channels of the Executive's decentralized structure. After several negotiations, a decree transferred responsibility for the state companies' direction, financial management, salary policies and investment programmes from the Ministries of Defence and Public Works and Services to the Ministry of Economy.[28] Those ministries, however, refused to cede jurisdiction on decisions regarding privatization issues.

It was considered a matter of urgency that the adjustment efforts be accompanied by the privatization programme. These goals were explicitly stated when, at the moment of submitting the bill privatizing the

Ministry of Defence's assets to Congress, the Executive explained that it was aimed at 'several enterprises, companies and establishments operating under the Ministry of Defence which, because of their economic situation, should be removed from management by the state in order to help reduce the fiscal deficit'.[29] The Ministry of Economy stressed the need for contributions from all the state's different branches to assist with the fiscal adjustment, and this implied that the use of privatization funds by any body other than the Treasury complicated the achievement of fiscal discipline. By contrast, some voices from the Ministry of Defence simultaneously began to insist on the use of privatization funds to achieve other ends. Military worries about the future of defence production companies leaked out through the Ministry of Defence, which began to proclaim publicly that privatization funds derived from companies under its responsibility should be invested in restructuring and modernizing the Armed Forces.[30] Consequently, disputes between the Ministry of Economy and the Ministry of Defence arose over the destination of funds obtained from privatization. These disagreements continued when Cavallo took over at the Ministry of Economy and Erman González left it to become, ironically, the head of Defence. Cavallo achieved the unification of the Ministries of Economy and Public Works and Services, and managed to exercise control over all the privatization processes except those in the area of defence.

What role did Congress play in this dispute? The two opposing voices – coming from the two ministries – echoed through the halls of Congress during several debates on the subject. In the Senate, where the legislative process was initiated, modifications began to be made to the privatization bill. Remarkably, the Senate included a provision obliging the Ministry of Defence to include clauses for the protection for manufacturing for defence in every tender. This amendment was maintained in the bill's final version (Article 5). However, the destination of funds was still uncertain after the Senate's intervention. It was only after the intervention of the Committee of Defence in the Chamber of Deputies that the bill clearly stipulated that the funds would be applied to the restructuring of the Armed Forces as well as to defence production. They could not be used to meet current expenses (Article 4).[31] Therefore, it could be maintained that the Ministry of Defence managed to impose its point of view, and military demands for the conservation of privatization funds within the area were answered.

The other side of the coin was, however, that the manufacturing of defence goods would be practically eradicated with the bill's approval. In fact, the process of privatizing defence enterprises raised the question whether Argentina needed any capacity for defence production at all. Apart from concerns about the financial problems that such companies were causing the state, Cavallo believed that 'production for defence, so many times proclaimed by Menem during the electoral campaign, was a bad idea, not only because it was unable to contribute to the country's economic reactivation, but also because it was inadequate within the new international framework'.[32] It was clear that Argentina neither had the financial, technical or political capacity to export weapons nor the political will to challenge the United States which controlled the international market. As far as Cavallo was concerned, all companies had to be sold. However, the Ministry of Defence and Congress preferred to discuss which enterprises should and should not be sold. The Radical opposition, for instance, argued that Argentina could not dispense with some capacity to produce war material. They agreed that this sector was too large because it embraced not only the manufacture of armaments, but also, the production of all materials involved in that manufacture. They proposed to sell only the enterprises whose production was not directly related to defence and which could be used for civil purposes.[33] Interestingly, the bill's final wording did not support this position, and included many enterprises that were specifically concerned with the production of war material. In the closing debate at the plenary session, Radical Deputy Bisciotti expressed that, 'I simply want to manifest my sorrow since we are assisting in the decline of Argentina's defence industry.'[34]

As a consequence of its passage through Congress, the law finally included a compromise solution: the approval of a model that was closer to Cavallo's idea of defence production, but with the decisions regarding the privatization process and the funds obtained from the companies' sale being controlled by the Defence Ministry.[35]

6.6. Transforming pensions

'The most negotiated bill among the government's rank and file, the most rejected by opposition, the one that failed more often to obtain a *quorum*, the one that aroused more speeches once the debate commenced, obtained general approval at 2 a.m. this morning in the Chamber of Deputies.'[36] These were the words chosen by the newspaper *Clarín* to report the approval of the pensions bill in the lower house. It was April and the bill had only completed half its journey through the congressional chambers. It had taken eight months to reach this point and the Executive still had to wait until September to see the bill finally passed by the Senate.

The process had been difficult in the lower house. It had taken place in the midst of public debate and mobilization, whilst a significant range of political forces firmly expressed opposition. In fact, opposition was spread throughout the Chamber. The Radical Party opposed the Executive's bill by presenting a bill of its own (by Deputy Juan Manuel Moure). Provincial parties, traditional government allies, were badly divided over this issue. The governmental front in Congress was also fracturing: Peronist Deputy Juan Horacio González Gaviola presented an alternative bill, which had been worked out by the *Consejo Federal de Previsión Social (COFEPRES)* formed by representatives from every provincial government. Moreover, Peronist congressmen from the unions also opposed the Executive's proposal so that González Gaviola soon became the head of about forty rebel deputies, of which 14 had links with the unions.[37]

Opposition was a reaction to the radical changes that the Executive was intending to impose on the existing system. These changes had been condensed in a bill first presented to Congress on 5 June 1992. The bill defined a regime formed by both a public scheme working as a pay-as-you-go system to be financed with a basic contribution from the state, and a capitalization scheme formed with the contributions from affiliated people to be capitalized in their individual accounts. The capitalization scheme was also supposed to be increased with voluntary deposits in the particular accounts. The administration of all the funds so constituted, would be in the hands of *Administradoras de Jubilaciones y Pensiones (AFJP)*, organizations especially created for this purpose. Other important features of the proposal were the compulsory nature of the capitalization scheme for those under the age of 45 and the raising of the retirement age to 65 for both women and men.

This bill did not remain long in the Chamber. It was withdrawn by the Executive once it became obvious that the committees were not going to approve it. They had indeed begun the debate by inviting specialists to comment on the main points. But, as Isuani and San Martino have pointed out,[38] consultations revealed a number of criticisms that dissuaded congressmen from supporting the issue. It became evident that, first, there was a general worry about the proposed privatization of the system, mainly because there were no similar cases to compare it with (except in Chile); second, the probability that contributions to the prevailing system made by people under 45 would not be recognized, provoked all types of negative reactions among legislators and the general public; third, it was not very clear how capable the state would be in controlling and supervising the activity of the administrators (although the bill was supposed to create a legally and financially independent control agency, *Superintendencia*, depending on the Ministry of Labour); finally, there was a general concern for the security and destiny of the pensioners' funds.

Despite the failure of the first attempt, on 27 August 1992 the Executive insisted on going ahead with the pension privatization by sending a new bill to Congress. It encompassed a series of modifications to the original bill and attempted to acknowledge some of the criticisms previously expressed: contributions to the old system were accepted; the age of 45 was eliminated as the age limit between the new and the old system; restrictions were made to the investments that AFJP could undertake with funds obtained from contributions. At this point, it is worth noting that the Executive insisted on the issue, showing its commitment to see the reform implemented despite the obstacles. In the message accompanying the bill, the ministers of Labour and Economy mentioned some of the reasons for their concern. On the one hand, they highlighted the financial crisis of the prevailing pensions system, which did not have the capacity to generate the resources that would guarantee a compatibility between benefits and contributions.[39] On the other hand, they stressed the inequality with which the system in force treated its different members, since it allowed for special privileged pensions, a high level of contribution evasion, and the individual protection of those taking action against the state for non-compliance with the law. These deviations produced considerable inequalities, but they also had severe financial consequences for the system, which, in order to deal with individual claims, was forced to resort to Treasury assistance, indebtedness and the levying of special taxes. Additionally, it should not be ignored that there were some other general reasons why the government was interested in pushing forward with reform, although it did not explicitly reveal them. It has been suggested elsewhere that recurrent deficits explain why state policy-makers needed to reform their social security systems, but they do not explain why policy-makers chose the privatization option. In Latin America as a whole, policy-makers favoured privatization because it promised some macroeconomic benefits: in view of the shortage of investment capital, not only were they another signal of commitment to free-market policies for the financial community, but also the opportunity to attract and retain highly mobile domestic and foreign capital.[40] In the particular case of Argentina, the implementation of the privatization of the pension system was part of its loan agreement with the International Monetary Fund.[41]

The Executive's commitment to the reform suggests that it had no alternative but to face the institutional game that would have to be played in Congress. In order not to compromise its primary goal, the introduction of the system of capitalization, the Executive had to both use ways of persuasion inside and outside Congress and demonstrate its inclination to negotiate by accepting corrections to its version of the bill. Concerning the latter, it is clear that the Executive was only able to obtain the Chamber's approval (and first that of the committees) after profound modifications were incorporated into the bill. According to Isuani and San Marino, the Executive was obliged to keep modifying earlier versions while seeking to remove opposition to the bill.[42] The new versions would include some of the preoccupations that legislators (and the organizations consulted by them) had previously shown during meetings in the committees of *Previsión Social* and *Presupuesto y Hacienda*. The first version to be approved by the committees had already received the main amendments. Peronist Deputy Juan Horacio González Gaviola had worked on them, trying to satisfy the demands of his own party members whose support was conditional on them. Most of the changes, though, had been presented by the *Consejo Nacional Económico para la Producción, la Inversión y el Crecimiento*, the members of which belonged to social organizations. This council had been created by the Ministry of Economy and Public Works as a corporate forum to discuss the parts of the pension system that were generating conflict and, therefore, preventing its approval.[43]

Key modifications involved Article 39 (then Article 40) in which the Executive had established the capitalization system of contributions. According to the Executive's bill, contributions came from three different sources: wage-earners (11 per cent of their wages), employers (16 per cent of the wages) and the self-employed (27 per cent of their income). As mentioned above, these contributions had two different destinations: first, a system of 'pay-as-you-go' to be administered by the state, that would be formed with the employers' contributions as well as 16 per cent of those belonging to self-employed workers; second, a system of personal capitalization which would receive the self-employee's remaining 11 per cent together with the 11 per cent from wage-earners. Article 39 also established that capitalizations would be carried out by *sociedades anónimas* called *Administradoras de Fondos de Jubilaciones y Pensiones* (AFJP). The committees' version accepted this point but extended it, adding some crucial modifications: 1) provincial states as well as any other entity could act as administrators, regardless of their legal status; 2) every rule preventing the participation of workers' and employers' associations, cooperatives, professionals public colleges or any other non-state public entity related to social security, was abolished; 3) it was ordered that *Banco Nación* should act as administrator whilst the state would act as guarantor of contributions granted it, even if those deposits were made in dollars. Lastly, the retirement age was maintained at the age of 65 for both sexes. Indeed, these modifications greatly altered the Executive's version since they not only arranged for the participation of the state bank but also committed the state to be a guarantor, which made this option particularly attractive for the contributors and particularly worrying for the private sector that was prepared to invest but not to offer similar conditions. Private investors complained to the Executive and tried to convince it to hinder the bill's approval and enact the reform by decree.[44] At this point, however, the Executive, could not move backwards without admitting its defeat in Congress. So, it was obliged to accept the amendments as a condition for obtaining the support of its reluctant legislators in the committees.

Besides the amendments, other more obscure procedural strategies were displayed to secure approval in the committees of *Previsión Social* and *Presupuesto y Hacienda*. On 24 February 1993, the committees passed the bill by a very narrow margin of 29 votes against 28 from the opposition, and so faced all sorts of accusations for the lack of transparency of the process. Opposition denounced the manipulation of the committees' composition: two members had to be replaced during the bill's discussion (one of them from the opposition and the other from the government front), but the presidency of the Chamber decided to find a substitute for the latter and maintain vacant the former.[45] Furthermore, a crucial vote was that of Deputy Juan Carlos Sabio, the representative from the *Partido Blanco de los Jubilados* (a party organized to defend pensioners' interests). Even before becoming a member of the Chamber in 1989, he had vigorously campaigned for the rights of pensioners. At the time of the discussion of the pension bill, the national leadership of his party was aligned with the opposition, but Sabio silently opted to sign the Executive's bill (with partial dissent), and later contributed to the *quorum* and voted for the bill in the plenary session. His attitude raised accusations of corruption.[46] Peronists responded to criticisms by saying that there was nothing unlawful about the procedures and that the bill could continue its way through the discussion in the Chamber. However, this step had negative unwanted consequences as the Radicals would refuse to cooperate with the *quorum* in the plenary session: 'Some time ago, we agreed that it was impossible to give way to a report without majority consensus. But now, they want to impose their project on us by compulsion and without debate.'[47] The Peronist Party was condemned to rely on its own discipline.

Consequences were felt immediately. It became apparent that many of the members of the ruling party were still not satisfied with the version of the bill passed by the committees. There were five failed attempts to begin the debate of the bill in the full assembly because the support of the 130 deputies required to form a *quorum* could not be obtained. The Radical Party firmly opposed to contribute to the number, refusing to countenance the irregularities that had taken place in the committees. As a result of this, while arranging the fifth plenary meeting, the authorities of the Peronist bloc had to accept to re-open the discussion on the contents of the bill. As a consequence of this new revision, the Executive's bill was modified even further. An important modification, proposed by the Workers' General Confederation, affected the core of the Executive's proposal: the compulsory nature of the individual system of capitalization was to be transformed into an optional one. Those who preferred to stay in the state system could choose either to pay all their contributions into it or transfer the corresponding percentage to the capitalization system (Article 30). Another important amendment was introduced as a result of pressures exercised by congresswomen: numbers were so tight for achieving a *quorum* that their unanimous threat of absence at the session was enough to persuade the rest of the members to lower the retirement age to 60.

The passage through the full assembly had added further modifications to the original proposal and it was rather difficult to identify how much of the first version was still present in the law. Some authors have even referred to a 'metamorphosis' of the bill.[48] At first, the bill defined a public regime working within a pay-as-you-go system as well as a compulsory capitalization regime for people under 45, both of which would grant retirement benefits to women and men after the age of 65. A second version withdrew the age of 45 as a limit between the new and the old systems since the state would provide a basic benefit, together with a compensatory one that would depend upon the amount of individual contributions to the old system; the capitalization system remained compulsory for everybody, but restrictions were imposed on investments that administrators could undertake. During the committees' stage, it was established that any entity, no matter its legal position, could act as administrator, a disposition which removed obstacles for the participation of the unions in the administration of the pension business; simultaneously, it was established that the *Banco Nación* act as administrator whilst the state as guarantor of the contributions granted it. Finally, the capitalization system lost its compulsory nature in the plenary session. Considered together, the amendments indicated that the original proposal had been substantially altered. The remaining passage through the Senate did not change the terms imposed by the Chamber.

In summary, the process of approval of the pensions privatization bill revealed the following two elements: one, the government's strong commitment to reform, which was demonstrated by its insistence on presenting a second bill after the failure of the first and by its persistence in obtaining the bill's approval; two, a considerable opposition front was formed not only by the Radical Party (normally in opposition) but also by some of the provincial and centre-right parties (the government's traditional allies) and many members of the Peronist Party, remarkably (but not only) the union congressmen. This situation forced the Executive to formulate a strategy that allowed it to breach the opposition front by winning back the support of the party rebels and political allies. Persuasion, negotiation and manipulation of the Chamber's rules were the means adopted to fulfil this goal. The eventual results were favourable to the Executive, but only at some significant cost: considerable delays in the legislative process and a number of important amendments made to the core of the proposal.

6.7. The president's response

In the previous section, we saw several cases of different ways in which Congress was involved in the legislative process of the Executive's privatization bills. This happened after the period of delegation of power so Congress was more capable of deciding upon both the design and the time-tabling of policy. This section returns to the executive power in order to explore its response to congressional intervention and describes how it resisted the idea of losing control of the design of the privatization policy. If the government had initially hoped to continue governing unilaterally, in practice it faced few alternatives to regain its power than by using corrective instruments, such as partial vetoes and the search for corrective decrees and laws.

Regarding partial vetoes, section 6.1 of this chapter has already shown that they were used to suppress specific clauses of several privatization laws: oil, gas, electricity, ports and pensions were the laws affected. The Executive's motives to do so can be summarized in two: first of all, its determination to maintain the policy's direction and implementation within its boundaries, so that restrictions would be imposed on any extension of congressional prerogatives. The Executive tried to ensure that Congress did not enlarge its sphere of influence beyond the powers of control that the first privatization law had granted it through the bicameral commission. Every move that could imply a step forward, especially towards congressional intervention in the implementation stage of the policy, was simply withdrawn. This autocratic attitude was very much related to the second reason for the Executive to use its veto: vetoes were meant to avoid any interference that could divert or delay the privatization reform. The Presidency had set the timetable of reform, had defined its main features, and was totally committed to avoiding any kind of diversion.

However, the partial veto was a weaker instrument than a delegative law. Throughout this chapter, it has been shown that, with variations, Congress's amendments were substantial. They modified laws in a way that could not easily be altered. Indeed, the veto gave the Executive the right to reinforce its view on some issues but never the possibility to return the law to its original format. Thus, the executive power succeeded in keeping Congress away from the implementation stage of the policy and indeed regained some original particulars of the bills.[49] However, it was obliged to compromise other aspects of the policy's design as well as to accept it had to pay compensation to some interests directly affected by the sale of state enterprises. In fact, the Executive's veto did not affect the bulk of the negotiations.[50]

There were two cases in which the president–Congress dialogue did not end with vetoes. They indicate the Executive's dissatisfaction with the laws' final draft and further confirm that the application of vetoes as corrective measures was regarded as insufficient. In these two cases, the Executive decided to return to the legislative arena and seek approval for corrective laws. As explained below, the first case was caused by the Executive's own pressures, and the second, by pressures imposed by the 'Mexican Tequila' crisis.

It has been demonstrated how far Congress was able to go with the amendments it applied to the Pension System Law. Indeed, these changes did not challenge the idea of privatizing the system, although they certainly challenged many of the terms in which privatization was understood by the executive power. The partial veto showed that the Executive disliked many of the congressional modifications, and would have liked to withdraw several others as well. Nevertheless, many of the amendments approved by the lower house could not be removed. The Executive found itself constrained to veto Article 39 (40 in the final version) because negotiations regarding this article's contents were what had precisely led to the bill's approval. In brief, especially in this case in which the bill was subjected to so many modifications, the Executive realized that the partial veto was not enough to remodel the bill to its own liking, and it then decided to fight another battle.

The Executive's principal concern with this article was not that a wide range of organizations could act as *AFJP*. Nor was it that the *Banco Nación* was one of them. Instead, it was concerned with the special guarantees offered by the bank to those opting for its administration, which could (as interpreted by the Economy Ministry) discourage private capital investment in the system. For this reason, another bill was introduced by the Executive at the beginning of 1994, aimed at modifying this aspect of the bill before putting the system into practice.[51] However, Congress did not show any interest in debating it. Therefore, a few days before the implementation of the new pensions system, the Ministry of Economy issued a necessity and urgency decree. This decree objected to the dollar guarantee offered by *AFJP Banco Nación*. The guarantee was considered technically unfeasible since it established special advantages for the administration, while it considerably affected 'responsibility, transparency, equality and free market competition'.[52] According to the Ministry of Economy, the necessity and urgency decree was justified by its urgency at a time when contributors had to choose either to stay in the old system or to begin their individual capitalization. Since the submitted bill had not received approval, the government understood that people choosing *AFJP Banco Nación* were going to make their choice with the expectation of obtaining Article 40's guarantees in full. Since it would be impossible to pass a law in time, it then became a matter of urgency to issue a decree in order to modify the article. Congress was left with no alternative but to accept and approve the Executive's corrective bill.

Another interesting case concerned YPF's privatization. As explained above, one of Congress's victories over the executive power had been Article 8 of the oil privatization law, which ensured that 20 per cent of YPF's shares would remain state property, unless another law ordered their sale. This congressional arrangement had prevented the government from selling all YPF's shares. However, the country would soon be shaken by another crisis: the Mexican financial crisis of December 1994 which forced the government to prepare the groundwork for privatizing the state's remaining YPF shares.

The impact of the Mexican peso devaluation was very acute in all Latin American emerging economies, because, by raising the risk factor in these countries, it provoked capital flight and the withdrawal of deposits from the banking system.[53] In Argentina, the consequence was an increase in interest rates, which put an end to the period of economic growth which had begun with the convertibility plan, and initiated a period of severe recession.[54] According to Minister Cavallo, the Mexican financial crisis triggered one that had been latent in Argentina.[55] The crisis affected the financial institutions which, enjoying the 'bonanza' generated by the convertibility plan, had failed to undertake the necessary adjustments in order to become efficient and reach higher levels of productivity. When the value of Argentine bonds and shares began to fall in international markets, and financial aid from private foreign banks was being cancelled, many Argentine banks faced severe problems. Then, the Central Bank and the Ministry of Economy, with the support of the IMF, actively attempted to avoid the collapse of the economic programme, and resorted to the submission of several bills to Congress.[56]

Among the various measures taken, the government sought to finance the privatization or abolition of provincial banks and to restructure other private financial institutions affected by the crisis. In so doing, it created a Provincial Development Fund, 'with the objective of assisting provincial banks which were subject to privatisation and promoting the privatization of provincial public service companies'.[57] Simultaneously, Congress had to deal with a bill authorizing the Executive to reduce the number of YPF shares held by the state. The revenues obtained from the sale of these shares were, together with other means such as international loans, to be used to boost the fund in support of the provincial structural reforms. Thus, the second oil privatization was approved by Congress within the context of the Mexican crisis. Congress acted rapidly. The Mexican crisis had burst in December 1994, five months before Argentina's presidential elections. Although the pre-electoral climate was favourable to adversary politics, the severity of this crisis annulled this and facilitated the approval of the bill in accordance with the Executive's desires.[58]

In brief, the Executive succeeded in getting the final version of these two privatization bills closer to its original goals. By invoking the situation of urgency in both cases, it forced Congress to respond immediately in favour of the Executive's demands. However, it is remarkable that the approval of these bills also involved the renewal of legislative discussions, the re-creation of a presidential majority, and, again, modifications before approval was granted. Despite limitations on the exercise of its role, Congress's intervention was not suppressed in the new context of emergency.

Conclusion

This chapter was concerned with the study of the institutional relations that Presidency and Congress established during the second stage of the privatization policy formulation. Differences from the first phase are clear. With the difficulties characterizing the beginning of Menem's administration, a strong executive power was gained by means of the delegation of legislative powers. Thus, the Executive was granted leadership of the economic restructuring process, which involved the design of the general policy and of the particular privatization cases as well as control over everything concerning the policy's implementation. The only function reserved to Congress was that of controlling the implementation process. Once the emergency was over, however, it became apparent that the Executive had to choose other means if it wanted to continue implementing the policy. At this point, there were two alternatives; first, to ignore Congress by using necessity and urgency decrees, second, to seek approval of bills in the congressional arena.

For a government showing a disposition to issue decrees, the choice of the latter might be surprising. However, as seen in Chapter 5, during the initiation of the second wave of privatization, the government was suffering from the bad reputation it had gained during the previous phase. The closure of the credibility gap was necessary for future economic reforms, and the use of decrees for the sale or concession of state companies might hamper the process by deepening the existing malaise on issues of legal security and other social demands. Similarly, outside the period of crisis, it became difficult for the government to implement some of the economic reforms in a totally unilateral way. Being political and social forces realigned, the government realized that it could not avoid taking their opinions into account. With no other alternative but to comply with the letter of the State Reform Law, the government had to face Congress whenever privatization was the issue.

This chapter has also shown that the beginning of a more integrated policy-making did not mean that the executive power was inclined to cede political power. Despite congressional intervention, the policy had to be designed and implemented according to its particular view, without further modification. However, in this second stage of inter-institutional relations, the Executive discovered that it could not reproduce the previous dynamics of dominance and subordination. Congress adopted a general approval attitude although not without complaints and criticisms. Its non-subordinated reaction made a difference to the policy's final results. At the same time, it managed to impose controls and to reduce the Executive's margin for unilateral action. Having recovered from the initial shock, Congress (as well as the parties and other players) attempted to enlarge the narrow margin of participation they had been given in the previous phase in order to contribute to the policy's design, to have a say in its implementation and, finally, either to look after particular interests or to have a share of foreseeable profits. Facing this situation, the Executive had to make a great effort in order to persuade Congress for a rapid and satisfactory response. It used a number of weapons to lobby different parts of the legislative process, and also some institutional instruments, such as vetoes, decrees and corrective laws, to reconstruct political power after Congress's intervention. In any case, the final result was far from what the delegative policy-making phase had been, since, although these resources were powerful means of maintaining and reconstructing political power, they could not annul the influence of Congress on the policy's design.

It has been suggested here that, throughout the years of Menem's first presidential period, president and Congress entered into a dynamic and changeable process of communication which shifted from a first stage of executive dominance and congressional subordination to another in which Congress became more powerful. This recovery of legislative powers was significant, but it was still only partial because Congress did not refuse to supply support for the final approval of the presidential bills. This chapter showed how Congress could influence policy by delaying and modifying the Executive's drafts. In the following chapter the description of the course of president–Congress relations is related to Congress's recovery of its legislative powers in full and its refusal to consent to the Executive's bills.

7

President, Congress, and Privatizations after Re-election

Introduction

In July 1995, Carlos Menem began his second presidential term. His re-election was possible by virtue of the Constitution of 1994, which stipulates, in Article 90, that 'the President and the Vice-President hold office for four years and can be re-elected... for only one consecutive period.'[1] Electoral results – Menem won the elections with 45 per cent of the vote – gave him the opportunity to enjoy the constitutional provision for which he had fought during his first administration. Re-election would, however, inaugurate a second four-year administration where the institutional and political resources available to the president had changed. On the one hand, the president was favoured with an absolute majority in the Chamber of Deputies for the first time since his arrival in power in 1989. As a consequence, Menem could initiate his second mandate with a majority in the two Chambers of Congress.[2]

On the other hand, in accordance with the new Constitution, Menem ordered the creation of the office of the chief of the ministers cabinet, the functions of which were 'to perform the general administration of the country' and 'the functions delegated by the President of the Nation...' (Article 100, subsections 1 and 4). The chief of cabinet was to be appointed and removed by the president (Article 99, subsection 7) and was politically responsible to Congress (Article 100). The latter meant that it could also be dismissed by Congress, although only with the vote of the absolute majority of members of both houses (Article 101). Since Menem was supported by a favourable majority in Congress, the chief of cabinet office would be entirely under his control and, therefore, he was able to add this new institution to the already powerful political structure of the government. Eduardo Bauzá – general secretary of the Presidency and one of Menem's closest collaborators – was the first person to be appointed as chief of cabinet. In brief, after re-election, Menem had apparently increased the political resources with which he could deal with the business of government.

However, other changes in the political scenario indicated that during his second term, Menem was going to face some political difficulties that had not previously existed. Firstly, the dual leadership exercised by both the president and the minister of economy in the economic policy-making process began to reveal problems. Rivalries between the technocrat and the political sectors of the government, which had been latent since Cavallo's appointment, began to surface towards the end of Menem's first administration. These rivalries had not seriously affected the development of the economic policy-making processes in the past, but from then onwards, the path followed by some of the economic reforms would be strewn with obstacles. For many Peronists, it became evident that Cavallo not only had the interests of an economist, but more importantly, he was working for his own political aspirations. Cavallo was transforming into another political competitor, rather than merely remaining as a technocrat. Secondly, Menem began to face problems from within the Peronist Party. During his first mandate, president–party relationships had been characterized by a skilful leader and a fairly disciplined party with incentives to follow the leader's directions. After re-election, leadership efforts to control the party failed on many occasions. The party began to consider the presidential succession, and alternative leaderships began to emerge, aiming at the next presidential prize in 1999. Thus, the president had to face incipient competition from some of his party factions, the consolidation of which would result in the progressive decline of his power.

Menem, therefore, began his second four-year term faced with the challenges to his authority over the rank and file of his party. This chapter will show the manner in which the internal situation of the Peronist Party affected the functioning of governmental institutions and, in turn, the policy-making processes during the first two years of Menem's second administration. Once more, the privatization policy, which remained central for economic reasons, was used as an instrument to test the relative capacity of the different sectors trying to either preserve or to gain political power. The chapter mainly describes the feeling of dissent or even opposition prevailing in the Peronist Party which resulted in, it has been said, this party tending to act as though it was a political system in itself – a system in which the same party played the role of both government and opposition.[3] This chapter will then demonstrate the emergence of another leadership challenge when, towards the end of the first two years of the administration, the recovery of the opposition parties added normal government–opposition rivalry to the existing problems within the Peronist rank and file.

To summarize, the aim of this chapter is to show the institutional and political reorganization of resources taking place after Menem's re-election by concentrating on the privatization policy-making process. It begins by describing the external conditions, that is, the environment in which policy-making processes had to take place. The chapter then explores the formulation processes of privatization cases which turned out to be markedly different from other cases previously described. These case studies summarize the elements of the new political scenario which acted as a constraint to the fulfilment of the policy aims of the president. Finally, the chapter concentrates on the Executive, its strategies and the resources it used to maintain power, and its degree of success.

7.1. The contextual conditions for privatization

The government began its second administration with renewed incentives for privatization along with other austerity reforms. Although the fiscal accounts had significantly improved and the deficit had disappeared in the years 1992 and 1993, fiscal problems reappeared again in 1994. The government began to be accused of not being able to remain true to the austerity programme,[4] and of supporting economic reforms that produced more costs than benefits.[5] Furthermore, with the severe recession of 1995 resulting from the effects of the Mexican peso devaluation, the government had to face additional problems with tax collection.[6] Thus, as in the previous presidential period, privatization appeared at the top of the presidential agenda. However, the conditions surrounding the policy implementation did not remain as favourable as they had previously been. Graphs 7.1 and 7.2 summarize the public mood as captured by the opinion polls.

This graph contrasts the popularity of the president, the economic policy and privatization from 1986 to 1997 throughout three presidential periods: the second half of Alfonsín's administration (1986–89), Menem's first administration (1989–95), and the first half of Menem's second administration (1995–97).[7] It is remarkable that the privatization policy maintained a positive image around 30 per cent after 1986 – and well above that between 1989 and 1992, but, in 1995 it began to fall under this figure. The economic policy curve shows that the highest

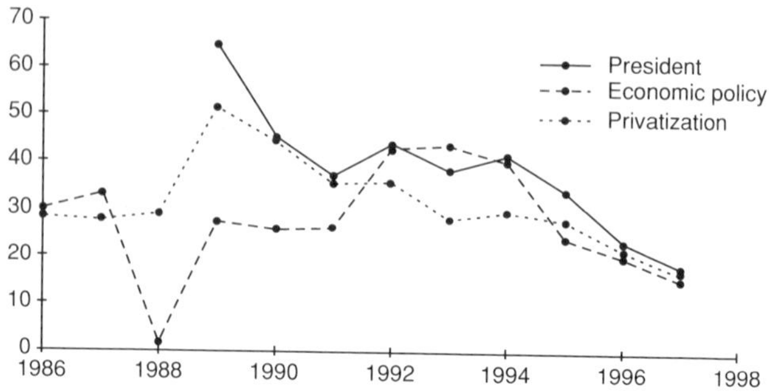

Graph 7.1 Positive image of... (year's average)
Source: Centro de Estudios Unión para la Nueva Mayoría.

popularity levels for the economic plan began with the introduction of convertibility in 1991, reaching its peak between 1992 and 1994. Meanwhile, President Menem enjoyed the greatest popularity at the beginning of his mandate, and managed to keep it above 35 per cent until the beginning of his second mandate. In brief, after 1995 the three curves coincide in a similar descending path.

As regards privatization, it has already been explained that the policy implementation had been accompanied by the public awareness of the consequences that the public enterprises' financial deficit had for the constantly deteriorating services that they provided. Therefore, the privatization programme had counted on popular support. From this point of view, people were not disappointed: the programme had managed to generate major investment in infrastructure and to improve the quality of the public services.[8] However, the urgent pursuit of private capital for the purposes of securing investment and contributing to macroeconomic stability had also favoured the maximization of rents over market competitiveness. The privatization programme had then resulted in a bolstering of the privileges of the existing establishment (in cooperation with foreign companies) through the concentration of power in hard cores of investors in newly privatized firms. These private groups were empowered with the possibility of buying in the favourable conditions of protected product and capital markets. Thus, high tariffs and inadequate regulatory frameworks came with the early privatization of the national airline and the telephone company. It is true that in the second stage of the privatization plan juridical and administrative regulatory frameworks were established, but their rule was always subject to considerable limitations.[9] Because of this, it is possible to state that the government did not aim at

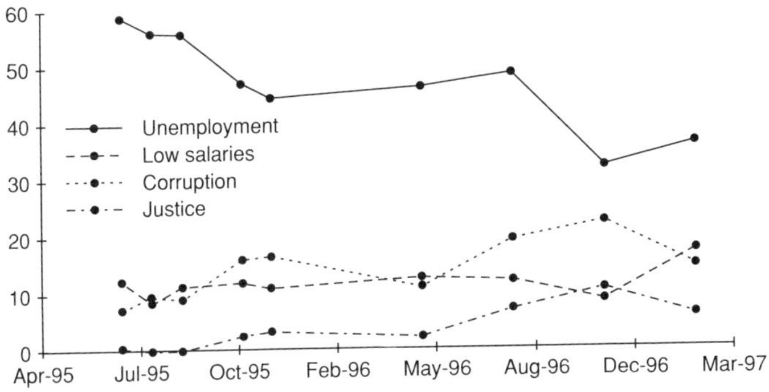

Graph 7.2 Evolution of problem priority

Source: Centro de Estudios Unión para la Nueva Mayoría.

creating a compensating network of protection for public service users. Moved by other motivations, it underestimated the fact that unprotected users could become a source of future social discontent. Graph 7.2 suggests other reasons for the government's declining levels of popularity also related to both the negative effects of economic reforms and the method chosen for their adoption.

On the one hand, the unemployment curve confirms the high public priority acquired by this problem and mirrored in the opinion polls since 1991 (see also Graph 4.3). It is remarkable that in May 1995, when Menem was about to begin his second mandate, unemployment reached a peak of 18.6 per cent of the economically active population. Similarly, the problem of low salaries also maintained its position among the priorities. On the other hand, a new feature of problem priority was the increasing public concern with corruption and the operation of the judicial system. Demands for a more transparent administration and the reform of the judicial system grew, connected with the careless and sometimes obscure manner with which the government normally carried out its administrative business. This concern related to many governmental actions, including privatization. Specifically, the lack of transparency in the first wave of privatizations had aroused concern, but this was also the case in other later privatizations, some of which are being discussed in this chapter. The fact is that these problems served to reactivate the political life of the opposition. Immediately, opposition parties took up the fight against corruption, unfurling the flag of an honest administration with a socially sensitive economic plan.

7.2. Privatization bills after re-election

As in 1989, the economic situation at the beginning of Menem's second presidential term determined that economic adjustment was one of the government's top priorities. However, the political conditions for the implementation of economic reforms had changed somewhat. In 1989, taking office in the context of a weekly inflation rate of 50 per cent, Menem enjoyed an outburst of state–society cooperation. Almost every social and political sector approved the president's economic decisions, and therefore he could exploit this honeymoon period to obtain significant powers from Congress. In 1995, taking office whilst experiencing the consequences of the 'tequila effect', Menem also attempted to increase his legislative powers, only to discover that the favourable situation for power delegation that he had enjoyed in 1989 no longer existed. Public opinion faced the prospect of further adjustment with reluctance rather than enthusiasm. It had only been a year since a protest march from the northern provinces to Buenos Aires had taken place (6 July 1994) as well as a national strike (2 August 1994) organized by the opposition unions. Moreover, the provinces were experiencing frequent strikes and other protest demonstrations led by public employees. At the institutional level, Congress was reluctant to grant special powers and delegate legislative functions.

A delegative law granting the Executive special faculties to undertake institutional reorganizations and to create a system of personnel administration turned out to be very weak. The period and objects of delegation were limited, clearly specified, and subjected to parliamentary supervision. The Executive, using its constitutional power of control over public administration, could centralize, merge, reorganize or suppress decentralized organizations. It could also suppress resources assigned to the public administration nationally and set it aside for specific purposes, excepting those involving expenses of the provinces and the social security system. Finally, it could proceed to privatize or concede some peripheral services and projects dependent on the central administration, but 'the present delegation excludes the total or partial privatisation or concession of public enterprises, universities, public financial entities, public services regulatory bodies, and shares belonging to the national state, which will continue under the regulation of the corresponding legislation'.[10]

Therefore, the inauguration of the second presidential term did not provide any honeymoon period for the president. In adopting decisions regarding privatization, he had to follow the ordinary legislative path, that is, the submission and discussion of several bills in Congress. Five privatization bills were debated in Congress during the first two years of Menem's second administration. The legislative procedure for the post-office privatization bill had already been initiated during the previous period, and had even obtained the approval of the committees in the Senate in October 1994. The privatization of the 'Yacyretá' hydroelectric dam which was under construction was put forward during the period of extraordinary sessions, at the beginning of 1995, after the signing of an international agreement with Paraguay, which shares ownership with Argentina. The remainder of the bills – the privatization of nuclear plants, airports and the National Mortgage Bank – were all submitted and debated during Menem's second administration. Table 7.1 summarizes the main features of the congressional procedure of these bills.

This table indicates the presence of an institutional conflict for the first time since 1989. The conflict was precisely located in the Chamber of Deputies where the post-office, airports and Yacyretá privatization bills were delayed after having received approval in the Senate. This is a new feature of presidential–congressional relations because approval of privatization bills had not been denied by Congress during the first six years of Menem's administration. Table 7.2 confirms this information.

This table compares Congress's attitude towards the privatization bills in Menem's first and second terms. As they have extensively been considered in previous chapters, privatization bills received overwhelming congressional approval during his first period in office.[11] In contrast, the fact that the number of non-approvals surpassed the number of approved bills appears as a new feature of the period initiated by Menem's re-election. As will be explained, the proportion of privatization

Table 7.1 Congressional procedure of privatization bills (1995–97)

Privatization bills	*Approved*	*Congressional procedure duration*	*Modifications*	*Vetoes*
Post-office	No (decree)	Detained in the lower chamber	—	—
Nuclear plants	Yes	From 1/18/95 to 4/2/97 26 months	Yes	Yes
Airports	No (decree)	Detained in the lower chamber	—	—
Hydroelectric dam	No	Detained in the lower chamber	—	—
Mortgage bank	Yes	From 10/10/96 to 7/2/97 9 months	Yes	Yes

Table 7.2 Privatization bills: congressional results (1989–97)

Privatization bills	*First Menem Presidency*	*Second Presidency – 1st half*	*Total of bills*
Approved bills	10	2	12
Non-approved bills	0	1	1
Non-approved/ decrees	1	2	3
Total of bills	11	5	16

decrees is also significant in this period. The distinctive feature of this stage of the privatization policy was the beginning of a conflict between the Executive and the lower chamber.

In reality, conflict was not the only feature of president–Congress relationships during this period. Table 7.1 shows that, together with the contentious cases, there were another two which tended to continue the pattern set by the second phase of privatization. The legislative procedures of the bills privatizing the nuclear plants and the Mortgage Bank showed features of the law-making processes of the second phase: first, Congress passed them; second, the passage introduced amendments to the original version; third, the duration of the procedures was close to the average for the second phase. In other words, these cases corresponded to the main features of the legislative process that led to the approval of earlier bills, such as the oil, electricity and gas privatizations. The conclusion is that two patterns of congressional procedure coexisted during Menem's second Presidency. The first pattern includes 'the cooperative cases', as they repeated the earlier behaviour of Congress when the bills became law; the second encompasses 'the contentious cases' and is defined by the bills that were stopped in the lower chamber.

Characterized by these two simultaneous patterns of institutional relationships, the discussion of privatization bills in Menem's second period in office gave place to a third phase of president–Congress relations, which was characterized by a balance between the powers. In effect, the first phase, which took place in 1989, was named 'the delegative phase' because Congress had resigned all its legislative powers and was practically subordinate to the Executive. The second phase occurred afterwards and was described as 'cooperative' since Congress had partially recovered its legislative powers, and was able to delay and modify the Executive's initiatives. During the third phase, beginning in 1995, Congress not only maintained its 'reactive powers' of delaying and modifying, but also added the power to deny the approval of some bills. Thus, during this stage, Congress recovered its powers of reaction in full. Furthermore, it exhibited some 'preventive' ability by discouraging the government from continuing with its plans to privatize the National Bank (*Banco Nación*)[12], and later on, when it decided to modify the terms of the already privatized pension system.[13]

In order to discover the reasons for the political conflict, the following pages concentrate particularly on the cases that failed to receive congressional approval. However, those where it was still possible to have cooperation are briefly described first.

7.2.1. The cases of cooperation

This section intends to explore the nature of the criticisms and discontent inside the Peronist bloc. The two bills for the privatization of the nuclear plants and the National Mortgage Bank were greatly modified in the Chamber of Deputies, mostly by the Peronists. This party was demanding participation in two clear ways: first, to influence the design of the policy and, second, to look after the provincial interests which it represented. In pursuit of these objectives, the party managed to influence the wording of the bills.

The parliamentary discussion of the National Law of Nuclear Activity began after the bill was submitted by the executive power at the beginning of 1995. However, disagreements about its contents prevented its final approval. Instead, some Peronist deputies belonging to the Energy and Fuel Committee of the Chamber of Deputies worked out another initiative arguing:

> Differing opinions were the result of meetings and edicts taking place in this committee, which led us to discuss again with the Secretary of Energy the terms of the bill that the executive power had initially submitted. As a result, a bill was produced . . . which includes valuable rights that contribute to enriching the original bill. We must take into account that the spirit originally put forward by the executive power is nonetheless maintained.[14]

Thus, the second version established a regulatory framework for nuclear activities as well as a Nuclear Regulatory Authority. It also declared 'subject to privatization' the generating activity of *Nucleoeléctrica Argentina* (maintaining 20 per cent of its capital in the hands of the state), and the direction and execution of the nuclear projects carried out by *Empresa Nuclear Argentina de Centrales Eléctricas*. In the two privatization cases, a veto power was reserved for the state in decisions concerning any extension of the companies' capacity, the abandonment of services, and the construction of new nuclear plants. Committee members having agreed on this wording, the bill was passed and prepared for debate at the plenary session.

However, discussions at the plenary session demonstrated that resistance inside the Peronist bloc had not been completely overcome. It was at this point that deputies from Patagonia exhibited an ability to act together in order to defend the interests of their provinces. They were opposed to supporting a bill that was being debated while there were rumours circulating about the choice of some areas in the south of the country as being suitable for depositing nuclear residues. Their opposition, based on ecology, economics, tourism and respect for federal sovereignty, was effective in provoking the failure of the first plenary session. As a consequence, the passage of the bill was only possible after a modification was introduced in Article 12. This amendment ordered that the affected province had to consent in advance and unequivocally by law. Additionally, a report had to be submitted by the Nuclear Regulatory Authority in relation to the nuclear and radiological security of the area.[15]

The privatization of the National Mortgage Bank resembled the case of nuclear plants because of the close involvement of provincial interests. In reality, the legislative process was much more complicated due to the magnitude of the financial operation implied by this bank's privatization. Differing from many other privatization laws, the law concerning the bank's sale clearly specified the destination of the funds to be generated. The Executive's bill set out the creation of a Federal Fiduciary Fund for Regional Infrastructure, whose objective was to finance a programme of public investment in economic, social and regional development infrastructure. The beneficiaries would be the national state, the provinces and municipalities. The fund was to be financed from the sale of the bank's shares, which would mainly be offered to home and foreign investors and, a smaller proportion, to the bank's personnel (using the participated property programme). The conservation of the historical goals of the bank – financing the construction of popular housing – was guaranteed by means of the state's holding of shares and the state's power of veto on future key decisions.

Although the fund was thought to favour provincial and local situations, the Executive's bill did not clarify the mechanism for the distribution of resources. The provinces remained cautious and suspected that the national administration could divert the funds if these mechanisms were not agreed to before the passage of the law. This was the main point queried by the legislators, who expressed their reluctance to accept a law that did not clearly specify the system for the distribution of benefits. Important modifications would have to be incorporated in order to please the provinces. The most remarkable modification affected Article 8: a hundred million pesos would be deducted from the fund to meet the needs of the most underdeveloped provinces. The rest would be equally shared by the nation and the provinces, the latter distributing their 50 per cent according to the federal co-participation index.

This article was the product of intense negotiations between the national and provincial governments. In these negotiations, the Peronist governor of Buenos Aires province, Eduardo Duhalde, played a crucial role. His support was essential because, representing the most populated province in Argentina, Peronist legislators from Buenos Aires province formed the largest proportion of the Peronist bloc in the lower house. Additionally, Duhalde did not hide his aspiration to be a presidential candidate. His efforts were directed to disassociating himself from the party's national leadership. To do this, he used the opportunity given by discussions on issues about the government's agenda in order to demonstrate a different stance. The National Mortgage Bank's privatization provided an opportunity for this strategy. In the middle of legislative discussions, one of Duhalde's deputies, Alberto Pierri (who was the president of the Chamber of Deputies) submitted a bill that disagreed with the Executive's by laying down that all funds generated by this privatization were only to be distributed to the provinces (and not to the nation). The possible rebelliousness of the deputies from Buenos Aires caused the negotiations that resulted in the writing of Article 8, as commented upon in the previous paragraph. The final agreement was sealed at a dinner that Menem held with the Peronist governors.[16]

7.2.2. The cases of conflict

Unlike the previous privatization cases, the bills to be considered in this section did not receive congressional approval. These three privatizations – the post-office, the airports, the hydroelectric dam – reveal the type of institutional and political constraints that President Menem had to face during his second administration: the reluctance of party members to accept the Executive's proposals and the increasing tensions between the president and the minister of economy.

7.2.2.1. The post-office privatization: The privatization of the post-office had already been put forward in 1989 by the State Reform Law, which had included the concession of the state company (Encotel) in the list attached to the main text. Although other companies in the same appendix were soon privatized, the post-office followed a rather different course. It underwent a restructuring process whereby Encotel was transformed into a limited company (Encotesa) with the goal of improving the company's efficiency before its sale. Additionally, different administrative decisions were made in order to redefine the conditions of a highly regulated market. They were intended to lift restrictions regarding market prices, the supply of goods and services, limitations to consumers' information about prices and qualities, and the difficult conditions then existing for the entrance of new participants (foreign and local) in the market. This process had led to the complete restructuring of both the state company and its market, paving the way for a privatization that had not yet taken place.

It was only five years after the passage of the State Reform Law that the post-office privatization again appeared in the legislative scene. This time the initiative originated from the Peronist bloc in the Senate. Senator Juan Carlos Romero, accompanied by his colleagues Eduardo Vaca, Oraldo Britos and José O. Figueroa, were the presenters of a law that consisted of two main parts: the first established a regulatory framework for the development of postal activities, the second stipulated the concession of Encotesa. In general terms, the bill seemed to agree with the tenor of other privatization initiatives submitted by the Executive. The specific contents, however, would promptly arouse the Ministry of Economy's concern. In fact, with regard to the first part, Article 2 put forward the objectives of the law. Its aim was to guarantee a speedy, efficient and updated postal service for all citizens, together with free and equal competition among the companies in charge of providing it. Nevertheless, from this article onwards, the law established a series of regulations that, in many senses, seemed to contradict and hamper the fulfilment of the objectives put forward at the outset. First of all, the law provided definitions and classifications of different postal terms and products which, in practice, were hindering the creation and improvement of new services that an open market would naturally allow. It also constrained the right of postal companies to choose what kind of services they were willing to provide. Secondly, the law established a set of strict registration requirements (for example, the availability of goods, amount of human and material resources) that, in practice, would act as restrictions in an open market and turn a free-access system into a concessionary one. Thirdly, the law divided the market into seven areas, with the idea of assigning each area to different companies. This clause allowed companies to avoid competition because it was distributing the market among them. Besides limiting the access to the national market, through these requirements, this clause was also limiting the number of companies authorized to participate. Finally, the law recognized the National Commission of Mail and Telegraphs, which had already been created, as an autonomous entity, and confirmed its functions of regulating, disciplining and imposing penalties on postal activities when necessary.

The second part of the proposal concerned the issue of privatization (Article 50). This part also established that the bidding procedure would not impose access restrictions, although senior and experienced bidders would be given preference and the participation of foreign capital would not be allowed to exceed 30 per cent.

The bill was rapidly passed in the Senate. Radicals and Peronists voted together so that only five senators remained opposed.[17] Likewise, it was expected that the bill's passage would be just as smooth in the lower house and it would become law without major obstacles and delays. In this context, a conflict between the Ministry of Economy and the Senate began to surface. The starting point was the fact that the Ministry interpreted the bill as going against the economic policies advocated by the government since 1989. The bill appeared to oppose the principles of free market and deregulation that the Executive had decreed. In the Ministry's view, 'the bill embraces almost all of the regulation criteria in force before decree 1187/93, which the government modified because of their incompatibility with the economic policy implemented since 1989'.[18] The bill had astonished Minister Domingo Cavallo. It represented a challenge to his policies and demonstrated that the government's decisions on economic policy, although clear to him and the economic team, were not always shared by the political branch of the government. Even more, unless energetic measures were immediately taken, the latter's intentions would likely succeed.[19]

As a matter of fact, the argument went even farther than these disagreements on economic policy. The public dispute involved a coalition of interests that went beyond the two confronting institutions. Minister Cavallo stated that 'In this case we see powerful enemies which are the enemies of the economic transformation that Argentina has put forward, and could end up being enemies of a fully participatory democracy in which decisions are made by the people and not by *mafia* groups.'[20] The groups he was referring to were connected with an accusation made by himself about the Senate proposing a law that perfectly met the monopolistic interests of a particular post-office entrepreneur. Cavallo was denouncing the close links between Peronist senators and

Alfredo Yabrán, who was suspected of owning the majority of the private companies active in the market, and who had amassed an enormous amount of capital under the protection of years of state regulation. When Cavallo's deregulation policy was launched, Yabrán initiated legal actions against the state. Minister Cavallo's concerns with the bill for Encotesa's privatization were the potential prejudicial effects for post-office users and the risk that monopolistic practices would have for security, considering the fact that the law, besides facilitating the formation of a monopoly, also restricted police control over postal vehicles.[21]

The Peronist senators responded with irritation. They expressed the view that the minister had condemned the Senate to surrendering its legislative prerogatives. The president of the Peronist bloc declared to the press that 'the Minister cannot demand that laws be made to suit himself, nor can he get upset when laws do not conform to his view'.[22] Even the president of the Senate, Eduardo Menem, defended the right of the Senate to preserve the initiative; he explained that 'acceptable or not, the proposal had been drafted by exercising a legitimate right granted to them by the Constitution.... Besides, we have a bicameral system in which one of the Chambers can correct the other.... In any case, if the government does not agree with the contents of the bill, it has the institutional means to either modify or reject it.'[23]

The legislative process continued in the Chamber of Deputies, where the bill was subjected to many modifications. Almost a year later, the bill had been unanimously passed by the committees and had begun to be considered in the plenary assembly. Cavallo, still unsatisfied with the bill after the amendments, decided to participate in one of the Chamber's meeting, in order to speak openly (to legislators and television), about the consequences of this bill for the consolidation of existing *mafias* in the postal market.[24] His long and well-documented speech explained the ministry's policy and gave plenty of details about the *mafia*'s operation. For instance, when decisions began to be adopted to allow the participation of new companies in the market, the results were as follows:

> I advised Abel Cucchietti (Encotel's *interventor*) that he open the Registration of Licensees again and manage it directly.... Since Cucchietti took the decision to eliminate the standard charge of fourteen pesos for the entry into international correspondence and began to grant permits to postal companies, he began to receive daily threats to his life and his family's. At the beginning, as they were anonymous

phone threats, he did not take them seriously. But later two simultaneous events took place. First, the threats became real. The day the Israeli Bank of Córdoba had decided to award the company Cargo a contract that was previously in the hands of the company OCA or OCASA – I do not remember which, but it surely belonged to the cartel group – two bombs exploded: one in the house of Mr. Abel Cucchietti, head of Encotel, and ten minutes later, another in the headquarters of the company Cargo. Of course, accusations were made, and the police verified that the explosive elements were of the same type and clearly had the same origin.

On the other hand, judicial problems began for Abel Cucchietti and the subadministrator, Hugo Ramos.... That is to say that here we have the first case of two members of the economic team that were dealt with by a judge, although... President Menem and I had signed an ordinance confirming Abel Cucchietti's actions, since these had been his duties, because the only thing that he had done was to repeal a resolution that another holder of Encotel had previously signed.[25]

The Ministry of Economy discovered other mafioso activities and acted thus:

From experiences of other countries we know that when there are groups that act as mafias they usually need to finance themselves. They can be financed with white utilities, but the declared utilities, those that figure in the financial statements, have to be presented very meticulously. Then, they need to generate black utilities, that is to say 'black money', if they want to finance activities that cannot be documented.

Therefore, it occurred to me that it was important to order a wide investigation of this group of companies through the *DGI* (the Tax General Direction) in order to see if we detected the financing sources. The *DGI* sent inspectors to the companies OCA, OCASA, to others that appear linked, as Edcadassa, or those that lease services in the airport, like Interbaires or Intercargo, to Zapram Anonymous Society, Zapram S.R.L. and to others that appear linked as service providers.

We discovered the most treacherous fiscal fraud mechanism of recent times. It was the first time that we had detected it. The mechanism... consists of a company sending 'Losses' expenditures documented with false invoices, of people that do not exist, that have disappeared... In all these cases, with very eloquent proofs,

> the *DGI* presented itself in different penal economic tribunals to put forward the corresponding accusations.[26]

The impact of the minister's intervention in the Chamber was such that this bill could never again be considered in the plenary assembly. The legislative process was returned to the committee level where further modifications were proposed in order to ease the suspicions that the minister had raised about the bill's contents. However, a year later when President Menem urged the Peronist bloc to approve another modified version of the bill, newspapers reported that the post-office privatization was no longer to be discussed in Congress.[27] The Radical opposition refused to make up the *quorum*, and the Peronist Party was deeply divided on the issue. Once more, this privatization was used to reveal the differences that some Peronist sectors had with Menem's leadership. For instance, in a public declaration, the Peronist group 'Project Ortega '99' affirmed that it continued to hold 'deep differences with the committee's report', since its suggestions, 'which were juridical and practical, had not been accepted.'[28]

The case of the post-office privatization indicates several issues for analysis. Firstly, it is different from other privatization cases, since no previous privatization had exhibited such a denunciation of mafioso activity. Cavallo himself was the one who drew a dividing line between this and other cases. In doing so, he earned the enmity of the entrepreneur he had attacked and suffered several judicial proceedings. Despite this, he maintained his view and determination to fight against this evil.[29]

Secondly, the case illuminates the issue of the ruling party and its relationship to the Executive. This case shows a legislative process that was eluding the control of the Ministry of Economy. The lack of subordination led the Ministry to adopt all the measures it considered necessary to prevent the bill's approval: the Ministry spared no efforts to defend its economic policy from interference, and showed inflexibility when considering any modifications to its plan. This stubborn position upset the legislators who defended their power to initiate legislation. However, the Minister's denounciations were so serious and had been so widely publicized through the media that many legislators refused to become involved in the debate. On the one hand, the Radical Party, whose members had initially signed the majority report at the committee stage, eventually withdrew their support for the formation of a quorum and demanded the creation of a committee of investigation. On the other hand, some Peronist deputies also refused to become involved in what seemed to be the protection of *mafia* interests. More importantly, party members with presidential ambitions had reasons to avoid completely a privatization proposal that had become unpopular and politically dangerous.

Thirdly, this case also clarifies some internal aspects of the Executive which are important when evaluating the presidential leadership. This privatization provoked one of the most serious cabinet crises in Menem's administrations. Cavallo had gone too far with his denunciation. Although not explicitly, his words implied possible connections between the 'mafioso' groups and governmental sectors, that is, the senators who had passed the bill without major objections, and the president, who had not given any clear indication to stop the process. Rather, the case showed the president's reluctance to explicitly support the position of the minister, which had initiated an unstoppable wave of speculation about corruption. This marked the beginning of the end of Cavallo as the head of the Ministry of Economy.[30] A year later, another cabinet crisis – this time involving Cavallo's attempt to reduce some social benefits – ended with his dismissal. Roque Fernández, who was at that time the president of the Central Bank, and also a technocrat trained at the University of Chicago, took over the office.

7.2.2.2. The airports privatization: The outcome of the airports privatization was closely linked to that of the post-office, since Cavallo's denunciations also involved a company, Edcadassa, which was suspected of belonging to the Yabrán group. This company was operating in the area of the international airport, and had been granted the concession of services connected to fiscal deposits by means of an ordinance signed by former President Alfonsín and his minister of defence, Horacio Jaunarena. The concession also involved the Air Force, which was associated with the private company in this business. According to Cavallo, the error was that Edcadassa held exclusivity rights for 20 years renewable for ten more:

> This was an error of former President Alfonsín's government . . . since the services for the fiscal deposit left a monopoly which is very expensive and everybody complains about it. Regrettably, we are not able to deregulate them unless we buy shares in the company Edcadassa, but this will cost us a lot of money . . .[31]

The problem was made worse by other concessions involving other airport services, such as the duty-free shop. The companies Edcadassa,

Intercargo and Interbaires, which were accused of supporting mafioso activities and were thoroughly investigated for tax evasion, had to be 'paid off' to give up the business. Before this situation, 'it is very difficult to think of privatising the airports in a way that would provide a good infrastructure and good services . . . This would require the concession of everything, but with these partial concessions or bad privatisations, such as that of Edcadassa, it is not possible.'[32] Therefore, Cavallo supported the idea of privatizing the airports once a solution was found for the existing concessions. However, President Menem decided that this privatization was to be directed by the Chief of Ministers Cabinet, who submitted the corresponding bill to the Senate in the beginning of 1996. It is remarkable that the Senate's approval of this privatization had such a symbolic effect. It was obtained while under pressure from the Executive which demanded signals of support after Cavallo's removal from the Ministry of Economy. In order to diminish the political impact that Cavallo's dismissal would provoke, Menem required a demonstration of political commitment to the reforms. Once more, the privatization policy served this function: Congress could show commitment by furthering an issue that it had reluctantly considered during the last years of Cavallo's term in office. In this sense, Congress responded positively. In August 1996, two bills were passed by the Senate – the airports and the hydroelectric dam privatization bills – as well as the nuclear plants bill in the lower house. Later on, as we have already demonstrated, the nuclear plants bill went all the way through Congress and became law, whilst the other two bills remained in the Chamber of Deputies without receiving final consideration.

It was the process in the lower house that raised most concern. The airports privatization bill was approved by the Transport, Defence and Budget committees, but these committees' report was impugned by the opposition deputies, who alleged irregularities in the legislative procedures. After this, the bill did not receive any further consideration. The Executive resorted to some of the persuasion and pressure mechanisms that it had used in other similar cases – directors of the Peronist bloc were invited by the president to discuss the issue and deadlines were agreed to put an end to the debates – but the chamber did not respond accordingly.[33]

Before beginning to analyse the Executive's response, the third and final area of conflict in the legislative passage should be discussed. The privatization of the hydroelectric dam, Yacyretá, was another failure of the Executive in Congress. Located on the border with Paraguay, this dam was a binational Argentine–Paraguayan project: the largest infrastructure project that Argentina had ever undertaken. Its construction had lasted for decades and remained unfinished in the 1990s, when it began to be regarded as a drain on public funds.[34] Menem coined the expression 'a monument to corruption' to refer to the uncertain destination of public money assigned to the binational body in charge of the construction projects. To resolve the situation, the president intended to put forward the dam's concession for public debate and the government began to work out the details. Privatization was proposed to Paraguay, with which country a protocol was eventually signed authorizing it. This agreement required congressional approval in both countries. In Argentina, opposition was initially led by legislators representing the border provinces directly affected by the dam (Misiones, Corrientes and Entre Ríos). The opposition increased even further because it became obvious that the government was going through with the privatization simply for fiscal reasons.[35] Despite succeeding in the Senate, the executive power could not overcome political opposition in the lower house, and the protocol finally expired.[36]

7.3. The Executive's response

Would the Executive have to accept the unfavourable outcome of the institutional game? What, if any, were the mechanisms utilized by the Executive to reconstruct its political power? These are the main topics addressed in this section.

As a matter of fact, the Executive had to respond to two different policy outcomes. On the one hand, there were cases in which cooperation had succeeded so they had eventually been passed by Congress. The Executive reacted as it had in other similar cases: it used the partial veto to apply corrections to the final drafting of the laws. Table 7.1 showed that the two cases of cooperation during this privatization phase were subjected to this kind of correction. On the other hand, the Executive had to respond, for the first time, to Congress's unwillingness to pass the other three cases. These cases gave rise to an institutional conflict that had not happened before.

President Menem had good reasons for not giving up the privatization policy: he still had some three years in office and could not afford to see his political power dissolve at the hands of his own party. If he was forced to accept congressional results on privatization, this would be a clear indicator that he had to take a back seat to Congress, allowing for the growth of alternative party leaderships. This was obviously an unacceptable solution for an extremely ambitious and skilful leader, who had not only presided over one of the greatest economic transformations in the country's history, but also forced the opposition political parties to agree to constitutional reform. Furthermore, this solution seemed to be unacceptable within the new Constitution's institutional framework, which allowed outgoing presidents to return to power after a four-year interval. The president now had added incentives to exert control over the presidential succession by encouraging the nomination of a presidential candidate from within his inner circle. Because of this, it could be foreseen that he would continue overseeing political operations in order to maintain control over the policy-making process. In so doing, he counted on the plethora of resources that his institutional position gave him.

We have already shown the use of one of these resources in the previous section. It was related to the unipersonal nature of the presidential office and its power to appoint and dismiss the members of his cabinet. This was the resource used by Menem when disagreements with Cavallo threatened the integrity of the presidential institution and his own leadership. It became apparent that the dual leadership regarding the economic process could no longer be maintained so that Menem needed to show that he had the last word. The dismissal of Cavallo turned out to be less traumatic than initially thought, and Menem regained the direction of the policy processes. The appointment of a low-profile technocrat to the Ministry guaranteed the continuation of the economic plan and served Menem's political ambitions.

When he came to deal with inter-institutional relationships, President Menem had other resources to call on. If the legislative branch did not give consent to his policy, he could still find a way to bypass its intervention. Several categories of decrees and other administrative resolutions were alternative means for the adoption of decisions, only involving the participation of executive officers. In fact, the three privatization cases where there was conflict exemplify different uses of these resources with the sole objective of reversing unfavourable legislative decisions.

Firstly, in the case of the hydroelectric dam, the Executive sought a solution that implied 'neither decrees nor laws'.[37] If the dam could not be sold or a concession arranged, its current administration (the Binational Entity Yacyretá) would resort to contracting out management tasks and projects pending. Once the Argentine–Paraguayan protocol expired in Congress, the government began to move in this direction while simultaneously seeking to reach a new agreement with Paraguay.[38] Almost a year later, it became clear that the private sector participation would only take place in two ways: one, by private management, which would be encouraged to increase efficiency through a punishment and reward payment system; second, a private investor would be put in charge of completing the pending construction projects, receiving as payment the right to commercialize a percentage of the additional energy obtained from these projects over a fixed period of time.[39] Finally, some other complementary projects would be financed with loans from the World Bank and the Inter-American Development Bank. As can be seen, the Executive could now move forward after its failure in Congress. However, it had to give up its initial goal of privatizing the dam and adopt a solution that was closer to what the legislators had been suggesting.[40]

Secondly, concerning the post-office privatization, the Executive considered that since there were problems with the bill being debated in Congress, it needed to resort to the alternative method proposed in the State Reform Law. As a matter of fact, this law had delegated to the Executive the power to privatize the post-office by concession (consult Chapter 4, appendix). The president of Encotesa, Arturo Puricelli, explained that 'a law was only necessary if the post-office shares were going to be sold. But, a concession has had a legislative permit since 1990.'[41] This was the justification used to undertake the privatization of the post-office by decree. The Executive abandoned the law and enacted a decree.[42] A few months later, the concession had been granted to a private group, which was not the one accused by Cavallo.[43] However, the validity and constitutionality of this decree was a subject of legal controversy. The Executive could not avoid this privatization being questioned and new actors intervening to have a say in the process: the opposition parties and the judicial power. The Radical opposition argued that the ruling party had itself prevented the use of the decree by previously submitting in Congress a privatization bill which, moreover, was still under consideration. Because of this, the party took the case to court to stop the process.[44] Although this case did not proceed, it anticipated a technique that the opposition would later on be able to use more successfully.

Thirdly, the airports privatization was approved by a necessity and urgency decree. However, contrary to the Executive's expectations, the process leading to the adoption of this measure was not straightforward. If the privatization had remained in Congress for a year, taking the case outside this arena would not prevent the fact that almost one more year would be necessary to see the privatization implemented. During the first stage, the Executive had confronted the ruling party in the legislative arena. In the later stages, the Executive was challenged by opposition legislators in the judicial branch. In effect, the first solution that the Executive found to congressional deadlock was the enactment of a regular decree whereby the airport privatization was approved in accordance, it was argued, with some old laws still in force.[45] This solution did not satisfy the legislators, and a group of opposition deputies took the case to court in order to stop the process. The judge supported their arguments: the decree was unconstitutional (and, therefore, nullified) because the State Reform Law established that privatizations had to be authorized by Congress, and because the 1994 Constitution (Article 42) stated that public service regulatory frameworks had to be approved by law.[46] The decision was upheld by the chamber to which the Executive eventually appealed. This tribunal ruled that the Executive was invading the jurisdiction of Congress, especially because there was a bill still under debate.[47]

In response, the Executive enacted a necessity and urgency decree arguing that 'the government considers it essential to undertake urgent repairs in airport infrastructure and connected services', since they were provoking 'serious problems in aeronautical security with imminent risks for persons and goods...'[48] However, what was really important to the Executive was that 'the courts have argued that this privatisation requires a law, and this requirement can be satisfied by this decree'.[49] Once more, opposition legislators took the case to court (later on accompanied by the People's Defender) and, again, the decree was declared unconstitutional. The judge ordered the Executive to stop the ongoing privatization process.[50]

However, the Executive continued moving further. After successive failures in both the legislative and the judicial branches, the Executive played its last card: the Supreme Court. All the participants knew that this was likely to be successful, although highly costly from a political point of view since 1997 was an election year. The election was for the partial renewal of the lower house and survey polls showed, for the first time in ten years, that opposition parties had a chance to win. Radical and Frepaso candidates had united to form an alliance (known as the Alliance) campaigning against the evils of Menem's administration: corruption, lack of justice, and the social costs of the economic model. Newspapers reported that 'the government is no longer sure about the decisions coming from the Supreme Court'.[51] Finally, in October, the Executive presented the case before the Supreme Court using the *per saltum* mechanism.[52] A few days later, the elections resulted in Peronism losing its absolute majority in the lower chamber of Congress.

For two months the airports privatization occupied the front pages in all newspapers, which continued to describe this case as the most controversial privatization. It was the main political dispute after the elections. President Menem sought a gesture of political affirmation in the Supreme Court. The Alliance, although certain about the Court's final decision, intended to make the government pay the political cost of exhibiting its control over the judicial system in public. When the Court made a decision favourable to the Executive in December, the privatization process was eventually unlocked, and the highest court was faced with the impossible task 'of mending inch for inch its diminished moral position'.[53]

Conclusion

In this conclusion, I would like to underscore the ambivalent nature of the institutional processes that completed the privatization policy after 1995. On the one hand, there is the final policy outcome. It was undoubtedly favourable to the Executive: four of the five proposed privatizations were approved and implemented. As in previous privatization phases, results were very close to what the president was seeking. Moreover, a distinctive feature of this phase is the Executive's proclivity to make privatization decisions unilaterally. Whilst in previous years this had been avoided in decisions concerning privatization, its appearance in the third phase confirms the autocratic style of the Peronist president. On the other hand, a simple glance at the final results overlooks the complexity of the processes leading to them. These privatization decrees are far from being symbols of a president with absolute powers, but rather the proof that the president was weak in terms of political resources. These decrees do not compare to those enacted at the beginning of Menem's first administration, when the president enjoyed popular consent and had the authorization thanks to the conditions of hyperinflation. Rather, these decrees were the solution for a president facing a blocked legislative process, which impeded him from reproducing previously successful strategies, such as negotiating some contents of the bills in exchange for their final approval. The other aspect of these decrees is a Congress that recovered its legislative powers in full, by adding to its existing powers to modify and delay legislative processes the ability to reject bills and prevent the submission of other initiatives. Decrees were the 'weapons of the weak', of a president that could no longer control either the Peronist Party or the opposition.[54]

The ambivalent nature of these policy-making processes involves not only a negative consequence for the consolidation of democratic institutions. Although it is certain that President Menem ought to be blamed for acting on the edge of constitutionality, his weak political leverage, the rebirth of opposition, and the public discredit of the Supreme Court appeared as fairly auspicious features.

8
Conclusion

When evaluating the first two decades of the democratic regime inaugurated in 1983 in Argentina, the specialist literature has been in almost complete agreement in pointing out the concentration of political power in the executive branch of government as one of its distinctive features. This has often been interpreted as a result of a combination of constitutional and historical factors, as well as of the critical circumstances in which the holders of the Presidency had to operate, especially towards the end of the 1980s. Most concerns on the institutional development of the regime have been raised by Carlos Menem's experience in government, since terms such as *uniteralismo, decisionismo, decretismo*, presidential cesarism, hobbesian style, personalist style, among others, have been coined to express the strong propensity of his Presidency to centralize the adoption of decisions.[1] Likewise, it has been highlighted that the other side of this process of concentration of power has been the loss of autonomy and the pronounced reduction in the capacities of the other institutions of government, Congress and the judiciary. Therefore, the predominance of the executive office, the misfunctioning of political institutions, and a version of democracy which was far from being based on participation, deliberation and the search for consensus, seem to have been the salient features of Argentina's first two decades of democracy.

This book has focused on the interactions between the Presidency and Congress, that is, on one of the aspects of the regime which has been most subject to criticism. It has done so by showing the institutions at work, specifically, while dealing with the rule-making process of privatization on which Argentina, like many other countries, embarked at the end of the 1980s. Its aim has been to contribute empirical evidence for a better understanding of the functioning of political institutions in

Argentina. This conclusion tries to summarize the results of this research. First, there is a description of how president–Congress relations evolved around the policy of privatization, emphasizing its dynamic and complex character and showing how they affected the making of the policy. Secondly, the outcome of the case-study of privatization is compared to those of other policy-making studies and conclusions are drawn on the achievements of the political regime.

8.1. President, Congress, and the policy of privatization

As has been explained in Chapter 2, the institutional resources that Argentine presidents have to participate in the legislative process are many and broad, and this gives the presidential institution a central position in the political system. However, it has also been stated that the centrality of the Presidency coexists with the system of checks and balances that characterizes the separation of power set out in the Constitution. Within this institutional framework, the adoption of decisions can well be the result of a process of inter-institutional negotiation and consultation, or a product of the unilateral action of the Executive. The selection of the model to solve political conflicts depends on several factors, but two acquire particular relevance: both the type of leadership and the situation in which it has to operate.[2] In this sense, the moderate centralizing tendency evinced by Alfonsín's government contrasts with the pronounced concentration of unilateral resources in the Executive taking place throughout the years of Menem's first administration, which has been connected both to the opportunity for discretion presented by the crisis that accompanied Menem into office in 1989, as well as to his autocratic style of leadership. This powerful combination of leadership and opportunity seemed to put aside the cooperative practices that had been expected to consolidate the democratic regime. Evidence for this appeared conclusive: first, the delegation of power; second, the extensive use of necessity and urgency decrees; third, the formation of a favourable majority in the Supreme Court; fourth, an increased centralization of power within the confines of the executive branch, and last but not least, other subtle ways of controlling the political process, such as the manipulation of legislative procedures and the practice of corruption.

As a consequence, the president's use of discretionary means to make political decisions was taken as indicative, for instance, of 'the absence of autonomy and independence of important democratic institutional powers (in this case, the Legislative); the pervasive delegitimisation of democratic mechanisms; and the *de facto* institutionalisation of rules that were not agreed upon by common consent (the internalisation and acceptance of these regularised patterns of interaction and decision-making by all actors).'[3] In particular, it seems that the privatization case studied in this book partially contradicts these kinds of statements. It would appear, on the one hand, to confirm that discretion was undoubtedly a dominant feature of Menem's leadership whilst, on the other hand, to show that this political style was on many occasions subject to constraints and, in fact, did not block the simultaneous development of other cooperative practices contributing to the legitimization of the regime. The remainder of this section summarizes these developments.

In studying the prerogatives of Congress in the privatization case, Jean Blondel's analytical distinction of the roles played by legislatures has been used (see Chapter 1). Besides the power of controlling the implementation stage of a policy, Blondel distinguishes three other roles played by legislatures, connected with their major prerogative of participating in the rule-making process of government: the powers of initiation, prevention and reaction (the latter includes the sub-powers of approving, rejecting, amending and delaying legislation). Considering these legislative prerogatives, it has to be taken into account that the formulation process of the privatization policy did not grant much power of initiation to Congress, because this policy was the president's initiative. Thus, the starting point of an assessment of president–Congress relative positions must admit this power imbalance in the president's favour. However, within this framework of relative imbalance, the remaining legislative powers (reactive and preventive) were found at different stages of this analysis. By applying a diachronic approach to the study of president–Congress relations, it has been found that the exercise of Congress's legislative prerogatives varied over time, as did Congress's position *vis-à-vis* the Presidency. In this sense, the mere possession of control powers (and the practical absence of legislative ones) indicated a subordinated position with respect to the Executive. Conversely, the total recovery of reactive and preventive powers resembled a situation close to a balance of power. As the process of formulating the privatization policy has shown since the late 1980s, some other positions can be found between these two extremes, which meant that four different phases can be distinguished:

1. Alfonsín's years in office illustrate the deadlock situation. During his rule, no policy outcome was possible because Congress exercised its most powerful reactive prerogative of blocking the legislative process. It is also the clearest case of balance between the powers.

2. The first period of Menem's administration represents the opposite situation. Congress virtually gave Menem a blank cheque to deal with the crisis as he saw fit. The delegation of power in the Executive provoked Congress's subordination for a fixed period of time. After having delegated its legislative prerogatives, Congress only retained the power to control the implementation process of the policy.
3. Two remaining phases began after this delegative period, both of them exhibiting Congress's recovery from the previous situation. Immediately after the delegation, and for the rest of Menem's first presidential period, Congress ceased to subordinate itself. Instead, it manifested the cooperative attitude of approving the Executive's bills, but only after exercising its reactive powers of modifying and delaying. During this phase, although power was still considerably tilted in favour of the Executive, there was no delegation and, therefore, no subordination.
4. Finally, the phase initiated after Menem's re- election showed the most equilibrated institutional situation during his whole tenure in office. It was due to Congress's use of its preventive power and the totality of its reactive powers. Despite being fairly equilibrated, power in this phase did not reach the balance of Alfonsín's years (when the inter-institutional relations were characterized by a stalemate). Congress continued cooperating (approving, modifying and delaying) as in the third phase, but at the same time some bills did not find their way through. There was a reluctance to pass certain bills, instead of the total rejection that had characterized Alfonsín's last years in office.

The variation in the powers of Congress is closely related to the attitude adopted by the political parties sitting in it. Indeed, the clearest situation of a balance of power (Phase 1) took place when Congress was controlled by the opposition. In this case, it was the Peronist Party in the Senate that exercised its power of impeding the approval of the Executive's initiatives.[4] Phase 2 depicts the paradoxical picture of a similarly constituted Congress behaving quite differently. In accordance with inter-partisan agreements and high levels of discipline, parties agreed on the delegation of congressional powers to the Executive. Phase 3 combines the existence of a governmental majority (absolute in the Senate, simple in the Chamber) with a high level of discipline in the Peronist Party and the cooperation of minor parties. The Radicals' return to opposition stands out. Finally, Phase 4 describes the situation of a government backed by an absolute majority in the two houses, but constrained by relatively lower levels of discipline in its own party, especially in the lower house.

The above description of political support for the presidential initiatives could also be presented as a variable formed basically by three components: the partisan composition of the congressional chambers, the levels of discipline displayed by the governmental party and the propensity to cooperate by the opposition parties. This variable could be called *the size of the president's majority in Congress* and defined as the amount of party support that the presidential policy can raise. This majority can be greater or smaller than the majority (total number of seats) held by the president's own party since the high and low levels of the variable are produced by different combinations of its three components. The higher position in this range is represented by a *large majority*, in other words, a majority that comfortably exceeds the *quorum* barrier. In this case, the president is practically independent of Congress, even if he wishes to propose an ambitious legislative agenda. However, this is normally the case for relatively brief periods of the president's term in office. The medium-high position is represented by a *strict majority*. As such, this majority precisely reaches the *quorum* level, thus leaving no surplus resource. The presidential policy is approved, although only in exchange for concessions requested by the members of the majority. The lowest position in the range is the *simple or no majority*, which implies that the majority supporting the president in Congress is not enough to obtain the passage of his bills. Indeed, since Congress is formed by two chambers with equal prerogatives for passing legislation, these categories are defined after considering the presidential support in both of them. Thus, the absence of a majority in one of the chambers places the case in the 'simple-no majority' category, because this fact will block a positive final approval. Following this characterization, Graph 8.1 synthesizes the features of the evolution of party support for privatization bills over time. Different type faces distinguish the successive phases that characterized president–Congress relations during Menem's Presidencies.

As can be seen, the graph illustrates that the result of the variations in the presidential majority in Congress was that the position of Congress towards the privatization policy changed over the years of Menem's administrations. This happened in spite of the Executive's invariable interest in seeing its policy fully implemented. In effect, either for political (credibility and reputation) or economic reasons, the Executive pursued a thorough implementation of the policy. The characteristics of *presidential leadership* that maintained the policy initiative can also be expressed as a variable consisting of two components. The first one would measure the degree of the president's identification

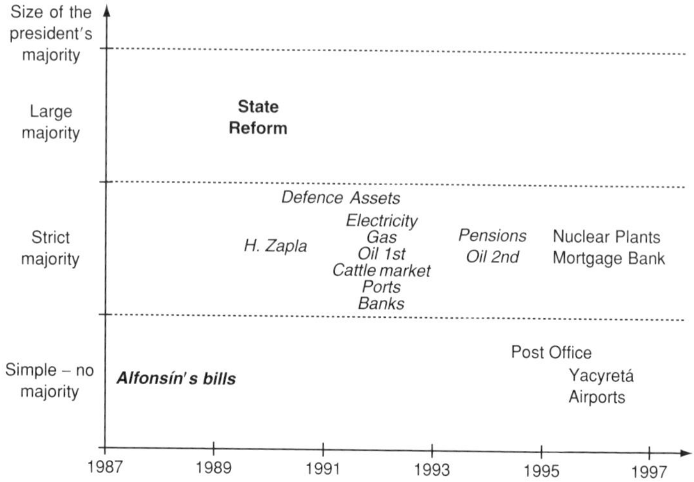

Graph 8.1 Congressional support of privatization bills over time

with and commitment to the policy. The second variable would be defined on more institutional grounds to show the Presidency's institutional capacity to speak with a unified voice. This refers to policy coherence within the confines of the executive power, that is, unity of purpose between the president and the minister in charge of the process, as well as among ministries dealing with different aspects of the same proposal. These two components can vary along a continuum, in which the highest position is characterized by positive levels in both of them. In other words, the situation in which the political leadership becomes the *chief legislator* is found in the category resulting from the president's commitment to the policy and the Presidency's unified policy command. Intermediate situations exhibit either lower ratings in the two components or a negative sign in either of them. These produce the *moderate political leadership* category. The other extreme exhibits negative points in the two components and represents a situation of *soft leadership*.

As most of the cases discussed in the chapters of this book have shown, the presidential leadership became a 'chief legislator' in the Menem years with regard to privatization. Indeed, this had consequences for the political viability of the policy. As the first component of the variable political leadership suggests, policy outcomes are benefited or hindered according to how forthrightly the president stands behind his legislative proposals, because the extent of presidential vacillation (or determination) has important effects, not only for the immediate bill under discussion. In effect, vacillation affects the long-term prospects of the policy, since the legislators' disposition to continue going out on a limb in support of a presidential programme will be reduced if they cannot count on the president to stay out there with them. Similarly, the underlying idea in the second component is that the strength and power of persuasion of a Presidency speaking unanimously has a greater positive impact on the other branch in terms of policy results. To take the lead consistently through a process of policy innovation requires the maximum reduction of divergences or, at least, of external perception of internal disagreement. Going back to the privatization case-study, Graph 8.2 organizes the privatization bills studied in this book in accordance with both the type of political leadership and the size of the congressional majority that was constructed in support of the bills. Time is symbolized by the arrows within the graph.

The most successful privatization cases are located in the upper right and centre rectangles, where the combination of ample majorities and firm command of the economic reforms by the Presidency facilitated the approvals of the bills. The unsuccessful cases are on the bottom left of the graph. In this sense, Alfonsín's failures in privatizing are a product of both soft leadership and lack of a majority. As explained in Chapter 3, the government's privatization goals were weakened by the many overlapping

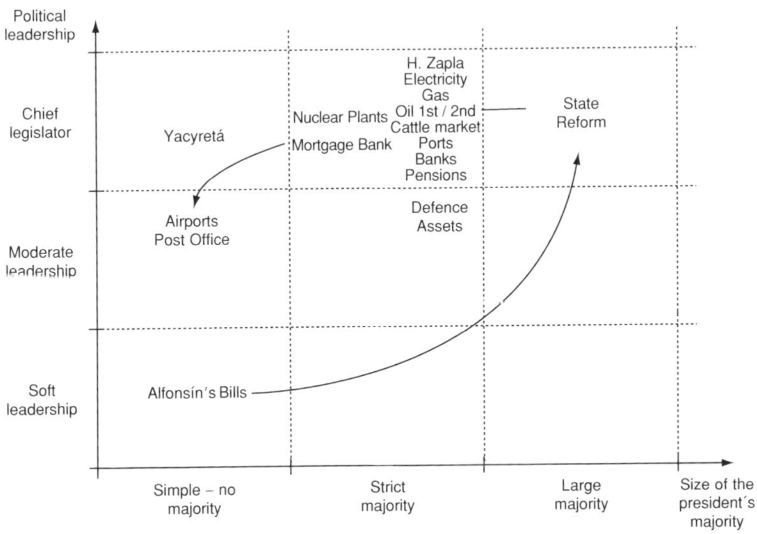

Graph 8.2 Congressional support and political leadership: the privatization cases

areas of concern which hampered the president's commitment to tackling economic problems. Similarly, when dealing with privatization, the government failed to create an image of internal agreement behind the policy. Indeed, this is just one part of the story, since only the hostility that Alfonsín's proposals faced in Congress can explain the completely negative outcome of his policy. The cases in the middle rectangles share the condition of a moderate leadership in charge of the policy process. It therefore seems that these cases reveal a weakness in the second component of the leadership variable: the government's inability to speak with one voice. Various disagreements at the heart of government reduced, in one way or another, the potential for command. However, the policy's persistence at the top of the president's programmatic preferences (as a result of the aspirations and motives that have been explained extensively in Chapters 4 and 5) prevented the leadership from descending to lower levels of effectiveness. Thus, a key to the policy success of Menem's administration was the construction of a forthright leadership.

Nevertheless, it should be kept in mind that moderate command of the policy by the leadership in 1990–91 (the case of defence assets) did not eventually prevent congressional support, as would later happen to bills proposed under similar moderate leadership conditions after 1995 (Yacyretá, the airports and the post-office). It can therefore be concluded that there is a point at which leadership skills in controlling a particular policy are insufficient to understand this policy's outcome. It is the process of gradual weakening of the presidential leadership as a whole that matters here. It should be noted that Menem began to lose his consensus-building capacity after he was re-elected, so that the timing of the reform seems to have an important explanatory value. Both public support and party support decreased, the first, after starting to experience the negative consequences of penetrating reform and recent recession (the Tequila crisis); and the second, once re-election ensured that the ruling president had lost control over the next presidential succession, and this was again in the Peronist Party's hands.

As a corollary, the study of privatization policy-making helps to clarify important aspects of the question of how able democracies are, compared with other types of regime, to address economic reforms with appropriate strategies. From the empirical evidence gathered in these pages it can be confirmed that a centralized pattern of decision-making is a necessary condition for far-reaching policy reform. However, a successful centralized style is far from being only unilateral action, *decretismo*, delegation and state technocratic elite isolation. Although these conditions could be considered sufficient for the initiation of structural reform, the implementation of a piecemeal long-term reform, such as privatization, demands the construction of relatively stable coalitions of political support. It was the ability of Menem's government to construct such coalitions at institutional, political and social levels that was the key to policy success over time. Likewise, the privatization case-study demonstrates that there is a limited time in which the leadership can maintain high levels of acceptance. If a president is re-elected, constraints will probably begin with the presidential party's concern for succession. If economic reforms have had a radical character, sooner or later the time will come when people seek to redefine their links to the leader. As has been stated, 'Presidents who have maximally achieved early are likely to be on a downward spiral, especially through a second term when they must face up to the problems their achievements have caused.'[5]

8.2. A role for Congress?

The policy-making process in the case of privatization had the special characteristic of being markedly institutional, which does not exactly agree with the widespread conception of structural reforms implemented unilaterally. In addition, the four different phases identified in this book in the relations between president and Congress do not exactly correspond to the features usually indicated by the literature as characteristic of these inter-institutional relations, that is, a dominant president and a quiescent Congress. On the contrary, only one of these phases, when delegation of power took place, seems to accurately meet the idea of congressional subservience. Even in this case, it could be argued, delegation was the product of a legislative act in which political forces agreed to vote to reduce their legislative powers merely to those of control exercised by a bicameral commission. As a consequence, concepts such as that of 'delegative democracy' seem to be better equipped to characterize the institutional features of a critical conjuncture than to describe the permanent attributes of the political regime. Nevertheless, to set out what the actual role of Congress has been in the past decades, I would like to relate the conclusions of the case-study of privatization to the results obtained by other studies of the Argentine Congress during the same period of time.

Some recent works have drawn attention to the existence of two subsequent political styles in the implementation of economic reforms during the 1990s in Argentina.[6] The first style corresponded to the hyperinflation crisis and favoured the concentration of authority in the Executive.

The second was characterized by a reorganization of the relationships between the government and the social and political actors and took place once the stabilization of the economy was achieved. Although these works are general interpretations and have not been particularly concerned with Congress, they agree to maintain that the role of this institution improved in the later stages of reform. Other works have especially concentrated on Congress and the production of legislation. They suggest, first, that the use of autocratic resources to adopt political decisions did not suppress the normal production of legislation during Menem's years in power. Both urgency decrees and laws were the instruments used by the government to adopt legislative decisions. If at least 336 necessity and urgency decrees were enacted during Menem's first Presidency, 835 laws were also approved during the same period, 46 per cent of them having been initiated by the Executive and the remaining 54 per cent being submitted by the legislators.[7] The first percentage indicates that Congress cooperated with the Executive by approving its initiatives, the second, that Congress took care of the legislators' bills and so exercised its legislative powers of initiation (a similar tendency can already be observed during Alfonsín's term in office, when 645 laws were approved, 47.6 per cent of them having been submitted by legislators). Besides asserting its powers of initiation, Congress used most of its legislative prerogatives in the treatment of the Executive's initiatives. In effect, not all the Executive's bills were passed (40 per cent of the bills submitted by the Executive between 1989 and 1995 were not approved), and those which were, had first been modified (50 per cent of Menem's bills were modified before being approved).[8]

Secondly, for the topics of the laws considered and approved by Congress during Menem's years, several works underscore that Congress passed legislation that was crucial for the implementation of the programme of economic reforms. The most notable case was probably the Convertibility Law, which set the basis for monetary stability in Argentina and which ruled the macroeconomic policy of the country for at least a decade. Most other economic legislation concerned structural reforms, of which privatization was not the only one to be dealt with in Congress. In fact, a study of the reform of the labour market shows how unevenly the government progressed in the implementation of different structural reforms.[9] This work points out that, in contrast to the presidential success with privatization in Congress, the Executive's labour policy suffered from considerable congressional obstruction. In this policy, the government faced the constraints imposed by the old members of its own coalition, the unions. They were supportive with the privatizations, but with the labour policy they forced the government to the negotiation table and were prepared to use their representatives in the Committee of Labour of the Chamber to stop everything concerning it which had not previously been agreed upon. Moreover, the Executive also felt constrained to implement this reform by decree since trying to carry out the reform unilaterally put further tension on the coalition and so endangered the passing of other crucial economic legislation. As a result, the government's goals in this policy field were only partially achieved.

In contrast with this policy, the Executive made extensive use of necessity and urgency decrees to legislate on the tax reform, a reform that was especially relevant for Menem's administration by being closely linked to the state's capacity for delivering macroeconomic stability. Nevertheless, Eaton has shown that many of the most important and controversial fiscal reforms were passed by the legislature.[10] Furthermore, their passage involved the introduction of important amendments in the president's proposals by Peronist legislators, particularly in response to their provincial concerns. Thus, the approval of tax legislation shows, once more, the existence of a process of inter-institutional negotiation, by means of which legislators this time exchanged their supportive vote for improvements in the provincial share in tax revenues or for lessening the impact of harmful measures on their own provinces. The extent of congressional amendments resulted in the president using his power of partial veto to undercut the deals made in the legislature, but in fact most of the modifications designed to defend provincial finances were not vetoed. In the same way, in his study of the formation and execution of the national budget, Jones has shown that the smooth passage of the budget through Congress since 1992 was not due to ineffectual congressional checks on the Executive.[11] Rather, it was so because in most instances the interests of the Peronists legislators had already been satisfied during the draft stages, prior to the submission of the bill to Congress. The author concludes that Menem could not have been able to achieve the timely passage of the budget if he had not taken into account the legislators demands of benefits for their provinces.

Therefore, as these case-studies reveal, the government faced considerable tensions within its own coalition of support, which were expressed at an institutional level, both in the refusal of the members of the ruling party to comply to the government's directives, and in their disposition to modify the contents of the Executive's proposed legislation. These conclusions coincide with those resulting from the study unfolded in this book and other works on the privatization topic. In effect, in his study of the reform of the pension system, Alonso stresses the difficulties the Executive faced to attain the support of the ruling party congressmen. Their reluctance to support the law opened a process of bargaining with important consequences for the contents of the reform. Once more, the unions were the main actor engaged in the introduction of amendments to the Executive's bill either through negotiations taking place in the corporate rounds of consultation or though their representatives in the lower house. However, they were not the only ones. Differing from other cases of reform, for the pensions reform, congressional opposition (ruling party members, Radicalism) managed to articulate a technically solid alternative project so that Congress was better equipped to challenge the Executive's view on the matter. As a consequence, the Executive had to make important concessions to the members of Congress, which deeply affected the contents of its original proposal, and which could not be suppressed by using the partial veto.

At this point it is probably important to draw attention to the substance of congressional intervention during the past decade. As the above studies suggest, many congressional amendments were directed to satisfy the demands of the interests sitting in Congress. The provinces represented most of them, being their main concerns those of exercising control of the policy process, of obtaining guarantees of protection for the inconvenience that reforms could cause in their territories, and of participating in the profits expected from the market reforms. Similarly, other interests, among which the unions stood out, also influenced the congressional amendments. However, as suggested by the above studies and highlighted in Chapter 6, when modifying the Executive's bills, Congress aimed at other objectives as well. Congress was concerned with the policies themselves, and changes were proposed not to alter the direction of the reforms but to modify the terms of their design. This type of amendment certainly expressed that legislators were not only worried for the effects of these policies on their districts and constituencies, but also for their general consequences for the Argentine state and society. This also revealed that because Congress was not allowed to choose the policies, importance was given to its participation in the formulation of those already selected. Finally, Congress sought to have a say in the implementation stage of the policies by creating new commissions of control or other similar mechanisms that allowed it to write binding recommendations. As this book has shown, Congress was not very successful with this later type of amendments (which were often vetoed), but it did have a great deal of success with the other two.

Having said all this, it is probably clearer why I have been inclined to sustain that political developments in Argentina in the past decades were both complex and diverse, and by no means only negative. It is also probably clearer why I understand that those arguments supporting the existence of congressional subservience, hyperpresidentialism, Congress's inability to impose checks to the Executive, and the absence of a consultative manner of adopting decisions, must be tempered. Indeed, it is certain that Congress's capacities to intervene in the processes of law-making continue being reactive. However, there are some political, technical and constitutional reasons why one should not expect them to be another. The political reasons are mainly connected to the logic of loyalties between the president, leader of the government and the party, and the ruling party sitting in the two Chambers of Congress. According to this logic, the president cannot expect the party's subordination or its unconditional support, but he can, indeed, count on the fact that open challenges to his leadership will be rather rare. This is so because no party wants to be defeated, and a presidential defeat in Congress is often in fact interpreted as a defeat of the ruling party. Therefore, since president–Congress relations also involve the relation between the president and the ruling party, a logic of cooperation will prevail or, as Mustapic has put it, a parliamentary logic, according to which, like in the parliamentary systems, the president (or prime minister) exercises the leadership of the party and the political process.[12]

The technical reasons leave Congress in a situation of technical inferiority in comparison to the high levels of expertise and specialization exhibited by the Executive branch, especially by the Ministry of Economy. Indeed, this is a point where improvements can be made (or could have been made) to favour Congress's relative position in the political system. In any case, however valuable they were, an increase in the technical instruments available to congressmen would always coexist with the decentralized structure of Congress, the multiplicity of interests to which its members feel responsive, and the various and disparate tasks and topics with which they have to deal.

Finally, there are reasons connected to the constitutional resources of the Executive to act unilaterally. In this sense, congressional actual capacities are not independent of the political style displayed by those occupying the presidential office and their proclivity to use unilateral resources. Congress's degree of intervention in the adoption of decisions will always depend to a great extent on the margin of participation that it is left by the president. Indeed, this is the most severe restriction to Congress's legislative powers and the cause of the greatest concerns with democratic institutionalization. They have led some authors to qualify the Presidency in Argentina as 'potentially dominant' since Argentine presidents are practically granted, with these resources, the permanent ability to get their agendas enacted.[13] Despite this apparent institutionalization of discretion, this privatization study has illuminated several aspects of the usage of necessity and urgency decrees which suggest that presidents are not simply powerful by virtue of the office they hold.

Undoubtedly, necessity and urgency decrees were a powerful weapon in the hands of Menem and an unquestionable indicator of his propensity to govern in an autocratic manner. However, if individually analysed, many of these decrees would be better described as powerful weapons in the hands of a weak president. A president who can decree, is always institutionally powerful, but not always politically strong. Paradoxically, a president who uses decrees is only politically as strong as he can manage not to have his decree repealed by a law, but also is weak because he has to opt to govern by decree and not by means of a law approved by Congress. The privatization case-study offers some examples of the president depending on the use of decrees because of his weak political leverage. During Menem's second term in office, the phase of greatest conflict in the relations between president and Congress took place, and the president resorted to his unilateral powers to adopt decisions that were being refused by Congress. However, at that time, the effectiveness of these unilateral resources had markedly weakened (compare, for example, the regulatory megadecree enacted in 1991 with the problematic decree for the privatization of airports), and the Executive could not avoid the political erosion provoked by harsh criticisms which were aroused because of their use (again, as happened in the case of airports), and the Supreme Court's popular discredit (as the institution complying with it). In addition, it is not clear that presidents holding proactive powers, that is, those who are allowed to issue necessity and urgency decrees, have the permanent ability to get their agendas enacted. In Menem's second term, when inter-institutional relations became so conflictive, the use of necessity and urgency decrees actually declined. Ferreira Rubio and Goretti have verified that 'The rate at which the administration issues NUDs has declined by more than 50 percent relative to the period before the (1994 constitutional) reform. In the first twenty-seven months under the new 1994 Constitution, the administration issued sixty-two NUDs – less than its yearly average over the 1989–94 period.'[14] This suggests that presidents can not always maximize the opportunities they are given by the institution they occupy, and so that if they are politically weak in their ability to obtain the passage of laws, they also do not seem to be strong enough to govern solely by decree.

Indeed, necessity and urgency decrees are the clearest restriction to the legislative role of the Argentine Congress. It is, though, likely that Menem's excessive use of them had already marked the accepted limits on their use, and that both government and Congress had learned by the risks to be faced with their use. As with the other factors affecting the powers of Congress, much depends on the future evolutions in civil and political societies.

In conclusion, although probably reactive, there is still a role for Congress in Argentine democracy. As the privatization study developed in these pages intended to show, this role has already been played, with advances and reversals and not without difficulty, in the first two decades of the new Argentine democratic regime.

Notes

1 Introduction

1 Huntington, S. (1993).
2 For the minimal procedural conditions for democracy, consult Dahl (1989). Also Schmitter and Karl (1996: 42–3) for an extended procedural definition of democracy that includes control over non-elected officials, and O'Donnell (2000: 529) who similarly explains that elections must be decisive, in other words, that the winners should be allowed to occupy their posts and to adopt decisions without the veto of non-elected organizations (such as the military). For a meticulous review of current definitions of democracy and the convenience of adopting one 'without adjectives', see Collier and Levitsky (1997).
3 Diamond, L. (1996*a*: 23).
4 O'Donnell, G. (1998: 113). As the author explains in another work (O'Donnell 2000: 535), these characteristics (horizontal accountability, equality before the law and an independent judiciary) are not components of the definition of democracy. Instead, they serve to describe differences among the cases qualified as democratic by the restrictive definition.
5 Levitsky, S. (2000: 57).
6 Stallings, B. (1992: 82).
7 Considering the introductory purposes of this chapter, this section only presents a concise account of the existing broad literature on democratization. Nonetheless, many of the points raised here are considerably expanded in the appropriate parts of later chapters.
8 This literature has highlighted a number of weaknesses present, in different degrees, in most Latin American countries. Palermo (1998), from a critical perspective, has summarized them as follows: a weak state which is unable to become a centre of public authority; a structure of institutional incentives which hinders political cooperation and governmental capacities; either party systems which are too fragmented or parties with heavy hegemonic traditions; corporate actors, which both depend on the state and penetrate it, and so have great defensive capacity; a weak civil society linked to the political sphere mainly through *clientelismo* and *particularismo*; a political sphere dominated by autocratic legacies.
9 See O'Donnell (1997: 42).
10 O'Donnell, G. (1997: 50).
11 O'Donnell, G. (1998).
12 O'Donnell, G. (1994*a*).
13 Huntington, S. (1997: 9).
14 Linz, J. and Stepan, A. (1997: 19).
15 Haggard, S. and Kaufman, R. (1994: 12–13).
16 Nelson, J. (1994: 61); Ducatenzeiler, G. and Oxhorn, P. (1994: 42); Domínguez, J. (1998: 89).

17 Przeworski, A. (1995: 84).
18 See, for instance, Haggard and Kaufman (1995); O'Donnell (1994*b*); Smith, Acuña and Gamarra (1994); Torre, J. (1994).
19 The expression belongs to Keeler (1993a).
20 Bates, R. and Krueger, A. (1993); Haggard, S. and Kaufman, R. (1995); Haggard, S. and Kaufman, R. (1992); O'Donnell, G. (1994*b*); Teichman, J. (1997); Williamson, J. (1993).
21 Rossiter, C. (1963).
22 Keeler, J. and Schain, M. (1996: 28).
23 See Diamond (1996*b*: 60).
24 Gibson, E. (1997); Knight, A. (1998); Roberts, K. (1995); Weyland, K. (1996).
25 See Nino, C. (1996) and other works by the same author.
26 Nino, C. (1996: 165).
27 According to Nino (1996: 165–7), some prerogatives of this strong Presidency are: Argentine Presidents do not need to seek legislative confirmation when appointing members of their cabinet or other executive offices; they have broad regulatory powers by means of decree; they can independently declare a stage of siege when the Congress is not meeting; they have the power to intervene in provincial governments, and have important veto powers as well as power to control important agencies, such as the Central Bank. These features were reinforced by historical developments (political instability, periods of military rule) which enhanced the position of the Presidency by adding to the already important constitutional powers other *de facto* or para-constitutional powers, such as necessity and urgency decrees.
28 For instance Linz, J. and Valenzuela, A. (1994).
29 For a critical assessment of the perils of presidentialism identified by this literature, consult Mainwaring and Shugart (1998).
30 Corrales, J. (1998); Eaton (1998); Etchemendy, S. and Palermo, V. (1998); Gibson, E. and Calvo, G. (2000); Jones, M. (2001).
31 See Etchemendy (2001).
32 Mustapic, A. (2000).
33 Lowenthal, A. (2000: 52). The author also includes the other countries of the Southern Cone – Chile and Uruguay – as parts of the same tendency.
34 The World Bank (1993: ix).
35 Gerchunoff, P. and Cánovas, G. (1994: 11).
36 Gerchunoff, P. and Cánovas, G. (1994: 11).
37 See, for instance, Margheritis (1999).
38 Other studies have proceeded in a similar way with other structural reforms of the Argentine economy. Chapter 8 analyses them and evaluates their contribution.
39 Ikenberry, J. (1990: 90).
40 Nelson, J. (1994: 53–4).
41 The same can be said for the processes of other structural measures, such as financial-sector reforms, rationalization of the public sector, liberalization of labour markets, and restructuring of social services and social security systems.
42 See Vickers and Wright (1988: 3) for a list of elements in a wide definition of privatization.
43 See McBeth (1996: 8).

44 Roberto Dromi (1991: 34, 75, 76), Menem's first Minister of Public Works and Services, and an specialist in administrative law, wrote: 'From the 1930's onwards, genuine public enterprises are created to develop commercial and productive activities under different juridical formulae and models: for instance, autonomous and autarkic entities, state enterprises (Act 20705), mixed enterprises (Act 19550 and Decree-law 23549/46), private enterprises controlled and/or administered by the State (Acts 17507, 18832, 22229, 22334, and so on), enterprises and public corporations.... Our constitutional order, our own republican system's government and control executive and legislative inter-relation, the necessary participation of the Legislature as expression of the popular will, and the circumstance that decentralised entities, whatever their juridical type were created by law, determined the need to enact a specific state reform law.' See also Dromi (1997: 15–21).

45 Note that modern Argentine Presidents, for reasons that will be explained later, rely on necessity and urgency decrees to take legislative decisions in a unilateral way. The use of these resources will also be taken into account in this study.

46 See Chapter 2 for greater details on the Argentine constitutional design.

47 The analytical distinction belongs to Blondel (1973), who has identified these as resources shared by most legislatures of the world.

48 It should be noted here that the question of whether contemporary legislatures generally possess real initiative powers or not is a matter of contention, even in established democracies where policy direction and initiative normally seems to be a prerogative of executive powers. This is the case in disparate political systems such as the United States and Great Britain.

49 The imbalance existing between Alfonsín's and Menem's administrations in terms of privatization initiatives prevents us from undertaking a two-presidency comparative approach. The different specific weight of this policy in the two presidencies is the reason for that, but also there is the fact that we are dealing with two consecutive presidencies and, so, that Menem was building on the basis of a policy that had begun to be discussed before his arrival.

50 Vickers, J. and Wright, V. (1988: 19).

51 Tsebelis, G. (1995).

2 The Argentine Presidential System

1 Nino, C. (1991).

2 For further information on the features of a presidential system, consult Linz (1994).

3 It is important to point out that some of these characteristics were modified by the constitutional reform of 1994. The most important modifications are described in section 2.2.3.

4 See Nino (1996: 165) and Serrafero (1993: 27–44).

5 Alberdi, J. B. (1981: 183).

6 Nino, C. (1996: 165–167).

7 Shugart, M. and Mainwaring, S. (1997: 40–52).

8 Jones, M. (1997: 285).

9 Shugart, M. and Mainwaring, S. (1997: 49).
10 Molinelli, G. (1996: 70).
11 Mustapic, A. (1995: 64–5).
12 Molinelli, G. (1996: 75).
13 I explain in Section 2.2.3. that these two political practices – necessity and urgency decrees and partial vetoes – were included in the Constitution after the constitutional reform of 1994.
14 Mustapic, A. (2000).
15 See Mustapic (1997: 5) and Portantiero (1987: 277).
16 The Radical candidate, Hipólito Yrigoyen, became president following the approval of President Sáenz Peña's electoral law in 1912, which led to the democratization of the political regime. This law established the universal obligatory secret male vote, and incorporated the legislative representation of the second minority (which would obtain a third of the Chamber of Deputies' seats). These clauses involved guarantees of participation and representation, thus permitting, for the first time, the institutionalization of the political opposition. The reform sought the gradual incorporation of the opposition in the political arena, opening a participatory process that would be led by the established elites. The idea was that opposition would first have access to legislative seats, while forming the Executive was only a future possibility. The 1916 electoral results, however, transformed what was going to be a gradual process into an abrupt change, and the Presidency came to be in the hands of the political force that had acted until then as an anti-systemic organization.
17 See Mustapic, A. (1984).
18 See Mustapic, A. (1984: 105–06).
19 Actions against the opposition went beyond the institutional framework and involved clear authoritarian decisions, such as restrictions to the freedom of expression (closure of newspapers, control over the distribution of press paper, monopoly of the means of communication).
20 De Riz, L. and Smulovitz, C. (1991: 130–1).
21 Consult Manzetti, L. (1993); McGuire, J. (1995); Snow, P. and Manzetti, L. (1993).
22 Giovanni Sartori cited in McGuire (1995: 200).
23 Gibson, E. (1997: 342–7).
24 Edwards, S. (1995: 44).
25 Gerchunoff, P. and Torre, J. C. (1989: 7–10).
26 Cavarozzi, M. (1994: 131). Cavarozzi has referred to the development model as 'the state-centric matrix'.
27 Cavarozzi, M. (1994: 133).
28 Botana, N. and Mustapic, A. (1988: 19).
29 Senators were elected by the legislatures from their provinces using the plurality formula. Each of the provinces as well as the Federal Capital were represented by two senators.
30 Because of the broad basis of his electoral support (52 per cent of the vote), Alfonsín was regarded as the natural heir to the great popular movements that had shaped the nation's history: Yrigoyenism and Peronism.
31 See more information about Frepaso in Section 2.2.2.
32 Catterberg cited by Manzetti (1993: 122).

33 Zuleta Puceiro cited by Manzetti (1993: 122).
34 Adrogué (1995: 27) has written about 'a tension between the fragmentation of political life at a regional level, where new and more actors join and concentrate decision making power at the local level, and bipartism at a national level, where Radicals and Peronists maintain their predominance'.
35 Aldo Rico headed the military uprisings of *Semana Santa* (Easter) during Alfons!n's administration.
36 Novaro, M. (1994).
37 Novaro, M. and Palermo, V. (1998: 29–44).
38 Novaro, M. and Palermo, V. (1998: 88).
39 Mustapic, A. and Goretti, M. (1991: 30–2).
40 Interview with Federico Storani, November 1996. Note that Radicalism reached two agreements. The first one was this pact between Menem and Alfonsín facilitating the constitutional reform and Menem's re-election. The second, in 1997, led to the formation of a credible opposition alternative (the Alliance, agreed upon with Frepaso) for the first time since 1989.
41 See Smulovitz, C. (1995: 81–2) for further information.
42 Despite the introduction of the figure of Chief of Cabinet, the system clearly continues being presidentialist. Ferreira and Goretti have stated that 'The incorporation of the chief of cabinet, in any case and depending on a series of factors that are beyond constitutional-juridical aspects, will not be able to attenuate presidentialism, but rather weaken some of the negative consequences or effects of the presidential system.' See Ferreira Rubio, D. and Goretti, M. (1995: 83).
43 Jones, M. (1997: 292).
44 It should be taken into account that constitutional provisions for limiting the president's emergency powers have still not been codified and, therefore, that no bicameral commission exists up to now to control the enactment of urgency decrees.
45 Molinelli, G. (1996: 75–8). Molinelli is referring in particular to necessity and urgency decrees.
46 The *Peralta and others case* was an *acción de amparo* (extraordinary resource) against the state and the central bank. It demanded that decree 36/90 be declared unconstitutional. By means of this decree, and in the midst of a second hyperinflation phase, the government had ordered the seizure of depositors' bank deposits. About the Supreme Court's attitude on this case, Molinelli (1996: 77) has written that while facing this case: 'the Supreme Court accepted, for the first time in history... the validity of DNUs (necessity and urgency decrees). But, instead of explaining this result as the consequence of a Court inappropriately subordinated to the presidential wishes ... it must be noticed that the decision was unanimous... and that two of the judges (Fayt, Belluscio) had been appointed during Alfons!n's period, and had (and have) not had any political relations with Menem's administration.'

3 Privatizations in Alfonsín's Agenda

1 Margheritis, A. (1999: 123).
2 Margheritis, A. (1999: 124).

3 González Fraga, J. (1991: 76–7).
4 CEPAL (1994: 15).
5 H. Schamis (1992: 57) states: 'In the Southern Cone, as the crisis of the import-substitution strategy worsened during the 1970s, the policy debate was reopened, and the developmentalist economic culture was displaced by the re-emergence of laissez-faire doctrines, this time under the combined sponsorship of cruel generals and monetarist economists.'
6 Haggard, S. and Kaufman, R. (1992: 12–13).
7 Message to the Legislative Assembly by President Raúl Alfonsín in *Síntesis Periodística* (1985: 199–200).
8 The framework of the new political regime was to be provided by the 1853 Constitution 'which guarantees all rights, liberties, and the modern world's social and cultural advances, at the same time that it assures the responsibilities of those who govern before the people by means of the juridical and political mechanisms of control that the same Constitution has foreseen, and the periodical renovation of power through the exercise of voting'. President Raúl Alfonsín in *Síntesis Periodística* (1985: 199).
9 *Clarín*, 13 September 1983. By democratization of the unions, Alfonsín meant to reverse the unions' historical practice of a single candidacy and give full participation to minorities.
10 See, for example, Canitrot (1992: 130–1), and Acuña and Smulovitz (1995: 188).
11 This is true not only of the Radicals, but also of the Peronists. For further details, consult Palermo and Novaro (1996: 50–60).
12 *Clarín*, 11 September 1983.
13 Raúl Alfonsín, *Clarín*, 11 September 1983.
14 *La Nación*, 1 August 1983.
15 Alfonsín criticized the consequences of the excessive protection of private interests provided by the military, stating that 'from 1976 onwards, the champions of liberalism had allowed inefficient companies to survive'. *La Nación*, 5 August 1983.
16 For further information, see Canitrot and Sigal (1994: 114–16), Palermo (1990), Canitrot (1994: 81).
17 Interestingly as regards the foreign debt, Alfonsín was convinced that the debt problem had to have a 'political solution', which implied, in practice, a reduction of payments. He also thought that the favourable attitude demonstrated towards democracy by the United States, could also be extendible to the debt negotiations. However, the United States interpreted the debt problem in strictly economic terms. In September 1984, when inflation started to get out of control, the government had to accept a first agreement with the IMF.
18 Juan Sourrouille had been the Secretary of Planning since December 1983, and most of the members of the new economic team had worked with him there. Machinea (1990: 14) states: 'With only a few exceptions, the team members were not part of the Radical Party (the President's party). This proved to have some disadvantages, at least at the beginning. We were considered "intruders" and it was necessary to prove that we were trustworthy. Moreover, the President himself had to convince the party that it could trust us.'

19 Damill, M. and Frenkel, R. (1993: 51–2).
20 In a television speech, the Minister of Economy, Juan Sourrouille, explained that this decision mainly included *SOMISA*, in the steel sector, as well as *Petroquímica Bahía Blanca* and *Petroquímica General Mosconi* in the petrochemical field. The minister's speech was published in *La Nación* on 7 February 1986.
21 Adolfo Canitrot, the Economic Coordinating Secretary. *Clarín*, 23 February 1986.
22 In the government's view, the existing legislation – Act 22177 dating from the last military regime – constituted a very rigid framework because it limited the process of privatization to the bidding procedure. Thus, the proposal was to incorporate some other legal instruments, such as public auction sales and direct contracting.
23 According to previous legislation (Act 20705), the executive power was meant to be in charge of initiating any eventual process of privatization. Therefore, the proposed law was intended to 'confirm' the path opened by legislation already in force.
24 Message from the executive power accompanying the privatization bill, from 9 October 1986. C.R.D., 22 October 1986, p. 6613.
25 These enterprises were the following: 'Empresa Nacional de Telecomunicaciones; Empresa Nacional de Correos y Telégrafos; Aerolíneas Argentinas; Agua y Energía Eléctrica; Ferrocarriles Argentinos; Gas del Estado; Yacimientos Petrolíferos Fiscales; Servicios Eléctricos del Gran Buenos Aires; Hidroeléctrica Norpatagónica; Obras Sanitarias de la Nación; Yacimientos Carboníferos Fiscales; Canal 7 ATC; LRAI Radio Nacional Buenos Aires and the broadcasting stations that comprised the official network; Empresa Líneas Marítimas Argentinas S.A.; Administración General de Puertos Empresa del Estado.' See C.R.D., 22 October 1986, p. 6618.
26 Another important section of the bill was dedicated to encouraging the participation of workers, users and service buyers as shareholders.
27 Press declarations by Marcelo Kiguel, the Secretary of Control of Public Enterprises, and Emérito González, director of *Agua y Energía* and member of the Energy Commission in UCR's National Convention. *Clarín*, 22 February 1986.
28 Canitrot, A. (1992: 220).
29 Machinea, J. (1990: 32).
30 For the causes of the failure of the Austral plan consult, for instance, Canitrot (1992), Damill and Frenkel (1993), and Palermo (1990).
31 Speech by the Minister of Economy published in *La Nación*, 21 July 1987.
32 According to Damill and Frenkel (1993: 60), the measures for structural reform included: a new law of tax participation between the nation and provinces, deregulation of public services, reform of industrial promotion regimes, oil deregulation, reduction of import restrictions, commercial deregulation of basic industries and, finally, privatization.
33 In the case of ENTel, the government tried to clarify that 'there is no sale here, neither of shares nor assets, but the incorporation of goods for the constitution of a new society. The difference is decisive, and it is acknowledged by the law and the economic reality that would never equate sale to contribution, as they are autonomous and distinct concepts.' See C.R.S., 2 March, 1989, p. 4524.

34 I refer here to the letters of intent signed by the Argentine government and SAS in February 1988 on one hand, and, on the other, by the government and Telefónica de España in March 1988.

35 *Clarín*, 5 February 1986; *La Nación*, 16 February 1986. The declarations were made at the same time as another member of the government, the Minister of Economy, announced the latest views of the government on the issue.

36 Document by a sector of the Radical Youth, *Tiempo Argentino*, February 1986.

37 *Solicitada* by the National Committee, *Clarín*, 11 March 1986.

38 *Clarín*, 20 July 1986.

39 *Clarín*, 20 July 1986.

40 Message accompanying the bill, C.R.D., October 1986, p. 6675.

41 In an interview with the author (July 1993), Socchi maintained that his proposal 'had never been understood by his fellow party members'.

42 *La Nación* reported, concerning one of Terragno's visits to the Radical National Committee, that 'One of the main questions that the partisan audience asked concerned the secrecy in which the negotiations (with SAS and Telefónica) had been held and the absence of prior debate. On this matter, (Terragno) justified the secrecy of the agreements by stating that it was a strategy founded on the necessity to stop the lobby interests and the typical scepticism of a society discouraged by too many years of stagnation.' *La Nación*, 30 March 1988.

43 In an interview, Deputy Hugo Socchi explained how unwelcome to the party had been the government's decision to put aside all previous efforts at cooperation with the opposition party and to disregard the bills negotiated in 1986. On the other hand, Minister Rodolfo Terragno affirmed in another interview that he had avoided resorting to the 1986 bill because 'it prohibited any privatisation'.

44 *Tiempo Argentino*, February 1986.

45 Deputy José Luis Manzano, *Clarín*, 20 July 1986.

46 Eduardo Menem was Carlos Menem's brother, who was concurrently campaigning for the Presidency. Interpellation to the Minister of Works and Services, C.R.S., 27 April, p. 3219.

47 'How does (Terragno) think that the state will maintain control of the enterprise (Aerolíneas) if it will not hold either the necessary majority in the directorate nor administration of the enterprises?' Senator Jiménez Montilla, C.R.S., 27 April, p. 3244.

48 Senator Menem during the interpellation to the Minister of Defence, José Horacio Jaunarena, C.R.S., 8 September 1988: pp. 2665–6.

49 Corrales, J. (1998: 36).

50 Corrales, J. (1998: 27–32).

51 One very effective tactic was to refuse to buy companies for sale. For instance, when discussing SOMISA, Norberto Bertaina, the Secretary of Promotion for Growth, publicly stated: 'Although its privatisation is an interesting goal, it is possible to say that it is not yet an opportune moment. We say this because society still has not demonstrated an interest in buying this company. We have to fit the offer to the receptivity of a private sector that is still growing.' *La Nación*, 12 October 1986.

52 Machinea (1990: 98–9), a member of the government's economic team, recounts a story that illustrates this point: 'After the announcement of the

intention to privatise the largest steel plant in Argentina (SOMISA), the board of directors of the enterprise "showed" evidence to everyone that its "market price" was around $4 billion US Dollars. During a meeting with President Alfonsín and the economic team, the president of SOMISA tried to demonstrate that "a fair price" was around $4 billion US, while in fact, given the market conditions at that time, it was difficult to justify a price of more than $1 billion US. Therefore, on this issue, the government had to face not only some opposition from inside the Radical Party – and the total opposition of the Peronist Party – and the General Confederation of Labour – but it also had to prove that a reasonable price was not more than 25 percent of the one "the experts" had estimated as being a good price. That was too much, and the idea was given up within the next six months.'

53 It should be noted, though, that in the particular case of the military and human rights policy, an initial confrontational attitude could be evaluated as negative in terms of the governability resources with which the President was left, but as positive in the long run for the subordination of the military to the civil government. Acuña and Smulovitz (1995: 193, 194) have concluded that 'the threat of trial and its consequences . . . was such for the Armed Forces as an institution, that any military calculation on an eventual political intervention would not be able to avoid taking into consideration the new costs and unacceptable institutional risks that this option raises.'

54 Indeed, the 1980s were particularly characterized by the military problem, that is, by how the military's influence could be neutralized in order to achieve the consolidation of democratic institutions. Alfonsín's government aimed at finding a balance between social demands for justice and punishment for human rights' violations during the authoritarian regime, and military vindication for their actions against terrorism. Further, Alfonsín suffered from the state of malaise reigning in the military forces which was eventually expressed in the uprisings. The solution was to retreat, and alter the direction of the human rights policy in order to meet military demands.

55 Machinea (1990: 127) states that 'stability was just another of the government's priorities, the most relevant of them being to minimize tensions that might otherwise interfere with the process of democratic transition. This implied the enactment of a policy which would avoid confrontations that could conspire against taking some tough economic measures which were nevertheless extremely necessary.'

56 In 1989, privatization's average positive image rose to 51.7 percent. This aggregated information also probably indicates the boost of popularity that Menem's arrival in power imposed on the policy. Privatization data was provided by the Centre of Studies '*Unión para la Nueva Mayoría*.'

57 Juan Carlos Torre (1994: 10) explains the relationship between the main Argentine political parties in the following way: 'The victory of Raúl Alfonsín in 1983 did away with almost forty years of Peronism's unchallenged electoral hegemony, opening up room for a redistribution of political power. Since then, the dispute that began in an attempt to seek either the consolidation or rectification of this new scenario, dictated the attitudes of both Radicals and Peronists, hardly favourable to cooperation.'

58 Mustapic, A. and Goretti, M. (1991: 30).

59 Mustapic, A. and Goretti, M. (1991: 30–1).

60 Palermo, V. and Novaro, M. (1996: 77).
61 After the military uprisings, Alfonsín did manage to get congressional support for the approval of the due obedience law (which sought to restrict the punishment for human rights violations by distinguishing different levels of responsibility) and the *punto final* law (the objective of which was to put an end to military trials by means of a deadline for starting court enquiries).

4 Privatizations in Menem's Agenda

1 See, for instance, Haggard and Kaufman (1995); Nelson (1994); O'Donnell (1994*b*); Przeworski (1995); Smith, Acuña and Gamarra (1994); Teichman, J. (1997); Williamson (1993).
2 The explanatory value of the variable economic crisis has recently been questioned by Corrales (1999), especially in relation to this second point. The author argues that economic crises do not provoke any cooperation among economic actors. Rather, economic crises complicate governability. In the particular case of Argentina, the author finds that state–society cooperation after the hyperinflation crisis was very short and fragile. With the exception of the first three months, Menem's first two years in power were chaotic, with all interest groups assuming non-cooperative behaviours. Although I share Corrales' view that the crisis alone is insufficient to explain the sustainability of an economic plan, I still prefer to maintain that its role in the creation of governmental capacities was far from being insignificant. This section explains why.
3 Consult Palermo and Novaro (1996: 85–94) and O'Donnell (1994*b*: 175).
4 Gerchunoff, P. and Torre, J. (1996: 4).
5 Canitrot, A. (1994: 86).
6 Consult Canitrot (1994: 85, 86).
7 Cerruti, G. (1993: 193–98).
8 Mustapic, A. (1988: 25).
9 Cerruti (1993: 277, 278) has written that 'every (campaign) meeting was transformed into a religious act. He concealed his lack of oratory with appeals to hope and prayers: "For the hunger of poor children, the sadness of rich children, for the young, the elderly, with the flag of God, which is Faith, and the flag of the people, which is the flag of the *Patria*, for God I ask you. Follow me, I shall not deceive you."'
10 'For two months Menem travelled tirelessly throughout the country, to cities, towns, hamlets. In every place, a multitude was waiting for him... The "*menemóvil*" ("Menemobile") sometimes went to villages with less than ten thousand inhabitants, and Menem spent hours talking to people, listening to their problems. He tried to adopt the typical habits of every place in order not to seem impolite: he would ride in rural areas, drink *mate* when he was offered it, wear a hat in Formosa, dance *chamamé* in Corrientes. Five, six, ten acts per day. He kissed all the children and women who approached him, received party leaders in hotels until dawn, spent countless hours climbing into the *menemóvil* with the arms opened in a papal gesture. He repeated plain, meaningless phrases in his speeches.' Again, Cerruti (1993: 277).

11 Novaro (1994: 65) has spoken about a 'crisis of representation' that began to be manifested in a general distrust of parties and 'party politicians'. By positioning himself as an outsider of the whole political class, Menem managed to overcome the discredit that most democratic political leaders were facing. See also Chapter 2, Section 2.2.2.

12 *Salariazo* consisted of a massive increase in salaries that was thought to boost popular consumption and, as a consequence, reactivate production.

13 Smith (1991: 40) states that prices had started to explode 'in April (when wholesale prices soared 58.0 per cent, and consumer prices jumped 33.4 per cent).' In May, 'wholesale prices jumped a fantastic 104.5 per cent while wages and salaries lagged far behind.' They would increase even more in the following months: 'consumer prices sky-rocketed 114.5 per cent in June and 196.6 per cent in July.'

14 The agreement was sealed in a Compromise Act signed by the presidents of the two major political parties, Edison Otero (UCR) and Antonio Cafiero (PJ), and the heads of the Peronist and Radical blocs in both the Senate, Alberto Rodríguez Saá (PJ) and Antonio Nápoli (UCR), and the lower house, José Luis Manzano (PJ) and César Jaroslavsky (UCR). *Clarín*, 16 June 1989.

15 In his resignation message to the country, Alfonsín acknowledged his weakness: 'At this moment, it is a clear reality for everybody, especially for those who have less, that the current government's room for action is too small. The depth of the socio-economic crisis demands measures not only energetic but also permanent. That is just the opposite of what, beyond its will and dedication, a government whose mandate is expiring can offer. Any delay, then, will cause greater suffering.' *Clarín*, 13 June 1989.

16 Interviews of the author with deputies César Jaroslavsky and Federico Storani. See also statements by Deputy César Jaroslavsky, C.R.D., 9/10 August 1989, p. 2187; 10/11 August 1989, p. 2303. The number seventy-five was not arbitrary, as it was the total number of members that the Radical bloc would have in the Chamber after the congressional renewal (from December 1989 to December 1991). Therefore, if the transition had not shortened the congressional period as it had done with the presidential one, the inter-partisan agreements would provide the majority that the new president had obtained in votes, but could not yet see translated into congressional seats.

17 *Clarín*, 25 June 1989.

18 Canitrot, A. (1994).

19 For Menem's credibility problem consult Gerchunoff and Torre (1996); Palermo and Novaro (1996); Torre and Palermo (1992).

20 Decisions taken in respect to foreign affairs can be cited as an example of this. Menem's foreign policy not only mirrored the turnaround that had taken place in the economic sphere, but also its spectacular nature. The new policy cast off the traditional Justicialist 'Third Position', instead accepting North American leadership in the Western Hemisphere. Escudé (1992: 31–6) has explained that many measures were directed towards demonstrating alignment with the United States and the disposition to avoid confrontation with it and the other Great Powers, like, for instance, the reestablishment of diplomatic relations with the United Kingdom (under a formula characterized as an 'umbrella for sovereignty' in the case of the Malvinas/Falklands), and the disposition to avoid anything that might raise suspicions that the

aims of Argentine nuclear policy were anything other than peaceful. But the participation in the Persian Gulf crisis can probably be regarded as the ultimate example of this. The decision to contribute two naval units to the multinational force led by the United States was seen as the opportunity to show the First World that Argentina sided with it. This decision circumvented legislative procedures as well as any consultation with Argentina's neighbours, as if the government was not disposed to allow any kind of institutional interference. Paradiso (1993: 196) has highlighted this episode not just because of the issue itself, which could have had some reasonable justification, but because of the way the decision was adopted, as an unexpected and spectacular turnaround that showed the disposition to cede more than could be demanded, and disregarded formal procedures. Indeed, it is in the context of the 1989 economic emergency that urgent signals to the world powers can be understood, but the exaggerated character of the signals could only have originated in a government that was facing a credibility problem.

21 Torre, J. and Palermo, V. (1992).

22 Later on, María Julia, Alsogaray's daughter and also a known member of UCeDé, was put in charge of dealing with all the issues of the telephone company's privatization.

23 See Palermo and Novaro (1996: 169) and Margheritis (1999: 101).

24 Corrales, J. (1998: 39).

25 Palermo, V. and Novaro, M. (1996: 215).

26 The party's acceptance of Menem's leadership was an important source of political and institutional power. However, it did not always mean automatic cooperation and absence of conflict. As on other fronts, the president also needed to display considerable leadership efforts which gave way to a mutual interchange of favours and political pressures. This a matter to be considered in Chapter 6.

27 Murillo, V. (1997: 82–8). Once more, privatization provided business opportunities, this time for labour unions. They could, for instance, purchase firms in their sectors, establish firms to provide services to privatize companies, or manage the employee-owned stock of privatized state enterprises.

28 It was then that a minority of unions of the opposing confederation abandoned the CGT, and joined together under the CTA (Argentine Congress of Labour). The CTA was the union organization which maintained a confrontational attitude towards Menem's government, although without the power to modify the ongoing process of reform.

29 Palermo, V. and Novaro, M. (1996: 235).

30 Peruzzotti, E. (1997: 138).

31 For a further description of the emergency law clauses, see Bonifacio (pp. 4–6).

32 Both the Ministry of Economy and the Ministry of Public Works and Services were the leading structures of the economic reforms. The latter was headed by Roberto Dromi, a specialist in administrative law, who had spent most of his career as a lawyer in his native province of Mendoza. Dromi had been a member of the Peronist Party since 1983, and was working as an adviser of Senator Eduardo Menem (Carlos Menem's brother) at the time of his appointment. He, together with the vice-minister Rodolfo Barra and the Director of Juridical Issues, Juan Carlos Cassagne, worked out the details of the state reform bill. See Verbitsky (1991: 41–44).

33 Declaration issued by the executive power, C.R.D., 19 July 1989, pp. 1088–90.
34 These companies have been listed in an appendix at the end of this chapter.
35 Although the large number of enterprises to be privatized *per se* shows the sense of urgency that was driving the government's proposal, this urgency is also present in other provisions of the bill, such as those dealing with the cancellation of all public works, *locación de servicios* and consultancy contracts as well as the suspension of all judicial sentences that would require any of the state entities to pay out money. In the context of a general public financial crisis, the state would not have to fulfil its monetary obligations.
36 Alonso (1997: 9) explains that 'unions involved in public enterprises managed it so that the shares, although owned by individual workers, remained unionised. Union leaders attained the approval of this criterion faced with the opposition of the Minister of the Economy, who preferred that the shares remained dispersed. For unions, this mechanism . . . would facilitate their access to information about the enterprises, besides avoiding the fragmentation of the workers' interests. Participated property programmes would be the launching base for so-called business unionism.'
37 See Margheritis (1999: 100).
38 Ekmedjian (1990) states that Articles 2 and 3 of the State Reform Law (Act 23696) delegated to the Executive the ability to intervene in state companies. Articles 3 and 4 granted the *interventores* and respective ministers and secretaries the power to disregard a wide range of legal dispositions concerning the internal organization of those entities. Article 6 allowed the Executive to modify the legal framework of the existing entities. Similarly, Articles 15, 18, 61 and 65 contained a delegation of legislative functions to the executive power. Moreover, Article 67 empowered the Executive to sub-delegate to ministers powers that had been given to it by this law. Ministers could also delegate their own powers to the secretariats of their ministries.
39 Ekmedjian (1990) establishes that the Economic Emergency Law (Act 23697) delegated to the Executive the following functions: Articles 24 and 25 delegated to the Executive certain powers relating to changes in the execution of the national budget; Article 28 authorized the Executive to alter the destination of funds; Articles 30 and 31 delegated to the executive power the setting of official fuel prices; Article 41 delegated the legislative power to regulate the functioning of the capital market; Article 63 delegated to the *Superintendencia de Seguros de la Nación* not only legislative powers, but also the possibility of modifying insurance contracts already in force. These retroactive effects are not allowed by law.
40 Only a short reference to this matter here because the process of the approval of the state reform bill is fully discussed in Chapter 5.
41 Other clauses suggested by Congress (particularly, by the Peronist Party) and rejected by the Executive were that the state would secure the supply of public services in non-profitable areas, that the government would be obliged to abolish all those clauses that were obstructing the de-monopolization of the services being privatized, that previous agreements among government, unions and purchasers had to remain in place in order to avoid negative effects on employment, and that clauses which authorized the state to use private consultancy firms as well as emergency contracts would be cancelled.

42 Keeler, J. (1993a: 442).
43 Ferreira Rubio, D. and Goretti, M. (1996: 451).
44 From a total of 336 decrees issued between 1989 and 1994, 30 were adopted during the period from July to December 1989, 63 in 1990, 85 in 1991, 69 in 1992, 62 in 1993, and 27 from January to August 1994. However, their use decreased after the constitutional reform of 1994. Consult Ferreira Rubio and Goretti (1996: 454).
45 Verbitsky (1993: 33–46) has maintained that, besides the government's preoccupation with the constitutionality of the emergency norms, the reform of the Supreme Court was also meant to obtain the Court's endorsement of the solution to the military problem. The pardon (*indulto*) granted by Menem during the first year of his administration covered more than two hundred of the military who had participated in the 'dirty war' in the 1970s, the Malvinas war, and the 1987 and 1988 uprisings.
46 The legislative process in the Chamber of Deputies was criticized for its irregularities. First, it has been noted that, thanks to an irregular procedure, the Chamber managed to prolong the bill's discussion for several hours in the middle of the night. Although a vote was arranged to approve the discussion's postponement until the following day, a 'non-clear' majority decided on the continuation of the session. In effect, it was alleged that the majority was achieved by the presence of people other than legislators sitting in the legislative seats. Second, the bill was approved 'in general', which is the first step in the approval process, but never 'in particular' (articles considered separately) simply because the meeting was considered over after general approval had been given. For further details, consult, for instance, Vidal (1995: 73–104) and Verbitsky (1993: 47–51).
47 Menem also influenced the composition of other officials in the judiciary. He appointed the *Procurador General de la Corte* (in charge of supervising the investigative and trial functions of the judiciary), without fulfilling the constitutional requirement of obtaining the Senate's agreement. He also secured the resignation of four of the five members of the *Tribunal de Cuentas* (the body in charge of overseeing the legality of government expenditures). See Larkins (1998: 430–1).
48 The Supreme Court's voting, in this case, consisted of six positive votes, two abstentions, and one vote of dissent. Carlos Fayt, the only minister voting against wrote in support of his position: 'Congress's legislation is very clear when it states that cases such as this one must be solved by a National Appeal Chamber before the intervention of the Supreme Court. In this sense, the rule concerning the federal justice procedure regime is expressed in Act 4055, Article 6: "the Supreme Court will rule, on appeal, on the definitive sentences pronounced by the National Appeal Chambers…"' Dromi, R. (1991: 794).
49 Ferreira Rubio, D. and Goretti, M. (1996: 466–9).
50 Torre, J. and Palermo, V. (1992).
51 Margheritis, A. (1999: 137).
52 The merger was the product of a bill presented to Congress on 6 February 1991, which modified the Law of Ministries. Because the Constitution of 1853 stipulated that there had to be eight Ministries, the merger of two of them was accompanied by the division of the Ministry of Education and Justice into two.

53 Weyland (1996: 16, 17) has highlighted these similarities in political strategy as one of the 'unexpected affinities' between neopopulism and neoliberalism.

54 'Without the necessity and urgency decrees no more than a twenty percent of the economic reform would have been implemented', Minister Cavallo to *La Nación*, cited in Palermo (1995: 98) and in Ferreira Rubio and Goretti (1996: 446).

5 Privatization and Political Parties

1 The World Bank, cited in Llach (1997: 213–14).

2 Damill, M. and Frenkel, R. (1993); Gerchunoff, P. and Torre, J. (1996); Gerchunoff, P. and Cánovas, G. (1995); Torre, J. and Palermo, V. (1992).

3 Alonso, G. (1997: 8).

4 Rausch (1994: 147) has explained that the privatization programme 'was backed by a World Bank Sectoral Public Enterprise Reform Adjustment Loan and a technical assistance PE Reform Execution Loan. These provided the necessary funding for both sectoral adjustment (layoffs, early retirement and others) and tailor-made privatisation plans.'

5 Gerchunoff, P. and Torre, J. (1996: 739).

6 The concept of self-ties has been developed by Palermo and Novaro (1996: 288–92) and Gerchunoff and Torre (1996: 745–46).

7 See Graphs 5.1 and 5.2 in the Appendix at the end of the chapter. Graph 5.1 shows how the image of the economic plan evolved. Graph 5.2 demonstrates that public concerns about inflation only began to decrease permanently after the launching of the convertibility plan. Similarly, inflation, which had dominated public concerns since the 1980s, was replaced by a slow but gradually increasing public preoccupation with unemployment.

8 Frenkel and Rozenwurzel (1996: 230) have pointed out that 'more than one-third of the private capital account surplus in the period 1991–1993 can be attributed directly or indirectly to privatization.'

9 Margheritis, A. (1997: 212–34).

10 Margheritis (1997: 212–34) has also explained that, despite claims of deregulation and liberalization, privatization conditions granted future owners: monopoly of the market for a minimum of seven years with an option to extend it for another three years; a free rate (which was already substantially increased before the transfer), adjustable by a combined index, with a guaranteed rate of return of 16 per cent; the possibility that the state would subsidize them if profits dropped, and exclusion of the tax of 25 per cent that had previously been used to provide pensions; the state would still be responsible for liabilities; some requirements for future investment were eliminated.

11 Note that Menem's government decided to begin by selling the companies that the previous Radical administration had fruitlessly attempted to privatize, and whose privatization the Peronist Party had fervently opposed. Besides, it is noticeable that this phase favoured the transfer of public service enterprises, many of which were natural monopolies, instead of giving priority to the sale of industries that were operating competitively.

12 Soria, D. (1994: 31).

13 Deputy Alberto Natale (1993: 33), a member of the Commission for four years, has written that 'its functioning significantly surpassed what previous similar committees had ever done'.

14 Gerchunoff and Canovas (1995: 485) identify two periods within this second phase. The first one commences at the beginning of the convertibility plan, when privatizations were used to balance the fiscal accounts. The second period started when the fiscal accounts were in a better state, and other non-macroeconomic goals, such as those of efficiency, could be pursued.

15 As already stated in Chapter 4, subsection 4.4.3.1., the State Reform Law laid down that for all enterprises not included in the appendix accompanying this law, new laws had to be passed declaring them 'subject of privatization' (Article 9).

16 One of them also affected the pension system, not a company but a service that had traditionally been carried out by the state and, for that reason, needed a complete legislative reformulation.

17 This proposal was based on previous bills presented to Congress by opposition senators (Juan Trilla, from UCR, Romero Feris, and Aguirre Lanari, members of PAC and PLC, respectively). The ruling party drafted a text that was approved by consensus in the committees of *Asuntos Administrativos y Municipales, Obras Públicas, Transporte, Presupuesto y Hacienda* and *Economías Regionales*. However, the initial proponents expressed their 'partial dissent' to the final version. See C.R.S., 28/29 September 1990, pp. 4381–385.

18 All the tables presented in this chapter have been prepared for this research with data obtained from *Diario de Sesiones* and *Boletín Oficial*.

19 The ports bill is an example of how, outside the period of emergency, the Executive opted for accepting the approval of a new law, instead of resorting to the authorization on privatization that it had already received under the State Reform Law (see Appendix to Chapter 4). This fact not only indicates that the Executive had changed its view on the legal requirements for privatization. It also confirms that privatization was a political process and that, in order to see the policy implemented, the Executive needed to involve other actors in the definition of its details.

20 C.R.S., 28/29 September 1990, p. 4395.

21 See Chapter 2, subsection 2.2.1. for the distribution of congressional seats.

22 Article 14 of the *Reglamento* of the Chamber of Deputies.

23 The case of the Cattle Market privatization is an exception since the legislative process was interrupted once the Executive included this privatization in a necessity and urgency decree. This point will be expanded in the next chapter.

24 It must be remembered here that the composition of the committees is determined by the distribution of power resulting from the elections and its translation into congressional seats in the Chamber.

25 When approving a bill in the committees, legislators can adopt any of the following positions: they can sign the majority report, that is, the bill's successful version that becomes the committee's report to be later on considered at the plenary; they can sign a minority report (normally, written by opposition parties), which consists of another version of the same bill; they can approve the majority report while simultaneously objecting it totally or partially (dissent).

26 Novaro, M. and Palermo, V. (1998: 81–8).

27 Towards the end of 1990, they had formed a separate legislative bloc, *Movimiento Peronista*. Later on, some of them (remarkably, 'Chacho' Alvarez) would have a central role in the formation of the opposition alliance, *Frente Grande*.

28 In plenary sessions, bills are normally approved by the consent of a given majority, – names of those voting for and against are not registered. Nominal votes are occasionally required to register explicitly the position maintained by every legislator or legislative bloc. For a thorough empirical study of nominal votes (roll call votes) in the Chamber of Deputies (1989–91), consult Jones (1998).

29 C.R.D., 9/10 August 1989, p. 2177.

30 C.R.D., 16/17 August 1989, p. 2468.

31 Deputy José Luis Manzano, C.R.D., 9/10 August 1989, pp. 2178–80.

32 Corrales, J. (2000: 136–7) and Corrales, J. (1998: 20–3).

33 C.R.D., 23/24 September 1992, p. 3164.

34 C.R.D., 23/24 September 1992, p. 3163.

35 It is interesting to see that the Ports Law was an agreed-upon initiative of the legislators (not an Executive bill) that gained the approval of both Radicals and Peronists. It is also interesting to note that, although the agreed-upon final draft had the support of the two parties, the Radicals maintained the position of expressing disagreement with specific points (partial dissent).

36 Deputy Jesús Rodríguez, C.R.D., 8/9 August 1989, p. 1864.

37 C.R.S., 14 November 1991, p. 4107.

38 While considering YPF's privatization, the Radical senators justified their minority report saying that they accepted the sale of Dock Sud, San Lorenzo and Campo Durán refineries, the reduction of the oil fleet, some concessions to the company's personnel, as well as the privatization of the oil-drilling sector. However, they would never accept the sale of the main central areas. See C.R.S., 24 June 1992, p. 1261.

39 The treatment of this bill had to begin in the lower house for constitutional reasons: it is in this Chamber where all the bills containing tax matters must be introduced. The pensions bill was so long that it included over one hundred articles, some of them tax-related.

40 It is striking that the privatization of the oil company did not provoke obstacles in the Senate (as *Gas del Estado* did); the most likely reason is that several issues that concerned the provinces were included in the same bill.

41 Deputy Alvaro Alsogaray, C.R.D., 8/9 August 1989, p. 1878.

42 In fact, it has been stated that provincial parties were responsible for many of the amendments made to approved bills. They also obtained the approval for some of their own bills, probably as part of the same negotiations. Palanza, V. and Sin, G. (1997).

6 The Institutional Dynamics of Privatization

1 Necessity and urgency decree 2284/91, *Boletín Oficial*, 1 November 1991. Article 12 declared 'subject to privatization' the National Cattle Market.

2 Ferreira Rubio and Goretti (1996: 463) explain that the Executive sent the decree and a ratifying bill to the lower house, but this house did not debate them until December 1993. Eventually, 'Ratification did not concern that bill, but the 1994 budget bill which also included the approval of nineteen necessity and urgency decrees enacted between 1990 and 1993.'

3 *Clarín*, 2 August 1990.

4 *Ambito Financiero*, 13 November 1991.

5 Words used in response to criticisms of the enactment of the economic deregulation megadecree. *Ambito Financiero*, 8 November 1991.

6 For instance, on 17 October 1990, *Clarín* commented that some eighty deputies had been invited for a dinner with the president. In his speech Menem asked for the approval of the employment bill, and confessed that he envied the power that Pinochet had had in Chile to implement his economic plans without obstacles.

7 Mustapic (2000: 578–81) has explained that, due to the federal features of the regime, the major Argentine political parties have a decentralized organization which consists of two major structures of authority: national and provincial. This system generates multiple political loyalties, since the national leadership (the president, if the party is in government) relies on the support of a coalition of provincial leaders who, in turn, rely on coalitions of local leaders. This multiplicity of loyalties is also represented in Congress.

8 On the occasion of his appointment to the General Secretariat of the Presidency, Bauzá said that the essence of his office was to cooperate with the president and to improve relations with legislators by facilitating their dialogue with the executive power. He also affirmed that his task was inspired in the firm conviction that 'there is no other alternative to the fulfilment of this programme'. *La Nación*, 25 September 1990.

9 An example is the presentation made by Cavallo and the Subsecretary of Fuel, Raúl García, when the bill for the privatization of gas was submitted. On that occasion, he addressed the Peronist bloc in the Chamber of Deputies. *Ambito Financiero*, 17 June 1991.

10 In an interview, the Peronist Deputy Juan Carlos Maqueda described Cavallo: 'His character has an authoritarian structure, according to which things must be done at any cost . . . he did not understand that Congress's times are different from the Executive's.' For his part, Deputy Alberto Natale (1993: 91), a member of the *Partido Demócrata Progresista* and for four years the president of the State Reform Bicameral Commission, wrote in his memoirs that 'With Cavallo it is not always easy to have a dialogue. When he disagrees with something, he speaks up, blushes, and immediately transforms a conversation into a polemic.'

11 The National Direction of Political Affairs was created in the Ministry of Economy in 1991. 'There was the need to establish a communication between the two branches of government. The Executive realized that it had no information on congressmen's legislative proposals, and feared the political erosion that vetoes would cause. If no control was imposed on the rule-making processes, the veto was the only alternative to unwanted legislation. This was why this Direction of Political Affairs was born.' (Interview with Raúl López, National Director of Political Affairs since 1991). The Direction of Political Affairs depended on the Secretariat of Institutional Relations, which was structured to direct Cavallo's political operations.

12 *Ambito Financiero*, 27 June 1991.
13 *Ambito Financiero*, 25 October 1991; 18 March 1992.
14 In the case of electricity privatization, Murillo (1997: 86–7) has explained the several ways in which the Federation of Electricity Workers could profit from the participated property programme. The union bought 40 per cent of the stock in nine energy generators in the Argentine north-west, 33 per cent of the stock in four energy generators in the Argentine south, and 20 per cent of the stock in the Sorrento energy generator in Rosario. It participated in partnerships that bought 90 per cent of the stock in three energy generators in Santa Fé and Paraná, and the company that distributed energy in the Argentine north-east. Additionally, it bought a bank, organized a retirement fund with other unions that included insurance and automobile workers, reorganized its welfare fund, administered employee-owned stock of 15 privatized companies, and had a director in the energy transportation employers' association.
15 *Clarín*, 14 December 1991.
16 *Clarín*, 18 December 1991.
17 See Vidal (1995: 107–61).
18 Gerchunoff, P. and Cánovas, G. (1995: 502–03).
19 The legal framework invoked by the government to carry out this policy was the ruling Hydrocarbons Law (Act 17319) and the State Reform Law (Act 23696).
20 Decree 1055/89, *Boletín Oficial*, 12 October 1989.
21 Message and bill by the executive power, C.R.S., 18/19 April 1991, pp. 6561–3. Note that the government attempted to approach the oil company's privatization by means of a bill which showed that previous agreement with the oil unions had taken place.
22 *Ambito Financiero*, 14, 21, 22, 23 August 1991.
23 Message and bill by the executive power, C.R.S., 24 June 1992, pp. 1255–61.
24 As in other privatization cases, Congress also tried to extend its influence in the implementation stage. These movements were intended to enlarge the area of action that the State Reform Law had restricted to supervision. The bill (Article 17) enlarged the functions of the existing bicameral commission to include the obligation to issue a report about three matters: tender basis, assessment of offers, and final contracts.
25 The creation of this special commission was in addition to many other modifications that tried to emphasize the spirit of control present in the legislative branch. Amendments to the electricity and gas bills have already been mentioned as examples of this spirit.
26 Cavallo, D. (1997: 196).
27 Although some of the companies were profitable and suitable for the production of both civil and war material, many had only been destined to the production of war material. Consult the Appendices in Chapters 4 and 5 for details on the companies affected by the two laws.
28 *Clarín*, 5 September 1990.
29 Message by the executive power, C.R.S., 26/27 September 1990.
30 For instance, public statements by the Subsecretary of Production for Defence, Jean Charles Uranga, insisted on the use of privatization funds to satisfy the Armed Forces' needs. *Clarín*, 28 August 1990.

31 In an interview, Mario Rossi, advisor to Deputy Miguel Angel Toma in the Committee of Defence, stressed that nobody wanted to open another conflict with the military.
32 Cavallo, D. (1997: 31).
33 See minority report, C.R.D., 21 November 1991.
34 C.R.D., 21 November 1991.
35 Could these funds be used for modernization of the military? Sain (2000: 137) states that funds obtained from privatization were not used for the military reform, being this still a 'pending task'. On the other hand, in an interview, Admiral Molina Pico questioned that there was any privatization revenue at all. He suggested that only the Army, because many of its enterprises were suitable for a civil application, could probably have favoured. However, the three companies depending on the Navy did not have any possible market apart from the state. In fact, as a result of the privatization processes, the first company, Astilleros y Fabricaciones Navales del Estado, was partly transferred to Buenos Aires province (Astillero de Río Santiago) and partly to the Army's jurisdiction; the second, Astilleros Domecq Garcia, could not be sold as a submarine factory so its productive material was offered in auction sales; and, finally, Tandanor underwent a very difficult tender process from which the state has not yet received any payment.
36 *Clarín*, 30 April 1993.
37 Vidal, A. (1995: 231).
38 Isuani, A. and San Martino, J. (1995: 48–9).
39 C.R.D., 28/29 April 1993, pp. 6870–2.
40 See Madrid, R. (1996).
41 See Madrid, R. (1996: fn. 29, p. 23) and Vidal, A. (1995: fn. 7, p. 246)
42 Isuani, E. and San Martino, J. (1993: 117–19) and Isuani, E. and San Martino, J. (1995).
43 Isuani, E. and San Martino, J. (1993: 119).
44 *Clarín*, 5 March 1993.
45 *Observaciones al dictámen* by members of the Radical Party, C.R.D., 28/29 April 1993, p. 6907.
46 Vidal, A. (1995: 228).
47 Deputy Juan Manuel Moure to *Clarín* (25 February 1993).
48 Isuani, A. and San Martino, J. (1995: 66).
49 Specifically, the Executive vetoed the creation of the special commission to control YPF's privatization arguing that the existing Bicameral Commission for the State Reform Law had exactly the same function (Article 12). Neither did it wish to extend the powers of this bicameral commission, since this extension provided it with 'an implicit veto power that distorts the aims of its creation and encroaches on functions belonging to the executive power' (Article 17). Another vetoed article was number 23, which stipulated that the funds obtained from the sale of YPF would be destined for use in the pension system. However, the Executive explained that these funds were to be used to capitalize the system, and not increase pensions, as Congress was pretending to do. The partial veto also affected Article 93 of the electricity bill, which attempted to extend the powers of the bicameral commission in a similar manner as Article 17 of the oil bill had done. The Executive decided to veto this article as well. In the gas bill, Article 54 was regarded by the

Executive as a hindrance to the fulfilment of the privatization timetable because it demanded that two of the five members of the regulatory body be appointed by provincial governors. In the Executives' view, this procedure 'would delay the terms of Gas del Estado's privatisation as well as the constitution of the National Regulatory Body because securing the coordination, organisation and agreement among provincial governors would not permit the fulfilment of the timetable that had been fixed by the executive power.' Article 80 (10 per cent of the shares to be assigned to the participated property scheme), Article 92 (creation of a subsidy) and Article 95 (reimbursement of the provinces) concerned the policy itself and were seen as contradicting the economic programme.

50 As happened with the pensions law. Although private sectors publicly pressured the Executive to veto the controversial Article 40, this would not happen. Instead, the main point of the partial veto to this law was to stop the legislators' attempt to attach the minimum pension to the average wage (those should not be less than 40 per cent of the economy's average wage), while one of the ideas of the bill had been to separate the two issues and make pensions conditional to increases in the average individual contributions (Article 125). The veto would also point at restricting the type of investments that the *Banco Nación* was allowed to make (public works) as well as objecting to the fact that the employers' contributions could be reduced in case of an improvement in the state of funds (Articles 74 and 189, respectively).

51 The bill was submitted by deputies Santín, Dumón, Armendáriz and Tretell Meyer. However, it was only passed six months later on 23 June 1994.

52 Decree 660/94, *Boletín Oficial*, May 1994.

53 French-Davis, R. (1997: 203–06).

54 In 1995, the GDP fell by 4.6 per cent, aggregate domestic demand declined by 8.4 per cent, consumption decreased 6.1 per cent, and fixed gross investment by 16.3 per cent. See J. Fanelli and R. Frenkel (1997: 6).

55 Cavallo, D. (1997: 213–28).

56 Fanelli and Frenkel (1997: 7) have explained that 'Some of the more restrictive clauses of the convertibility plan regarding the lender-of-last-resort role of the Central Bank were flexibilised in order to soften the effects of the fall in reserves and deposits on the credit supply.... These measures and the external financial support obtained by the government prevented the collapse of the system. The government received financing for some eleven billion dollars in 1995... after reaching an agreement with the IMF in March 1995. As a result of these measures, the exchange rate crisis was avoided despite the net outflow of private capital.'

57 Decree 286/95, *Boletín Oficial*, 1 March 1995.

58 However, the Executive could not avoid the creation of a bicameral commission in charge of controlling the management of the Provincial Development Fund. Indeed, it tried to do so by vetoing the article establishing its constitution (Article 7, Act 24485), but Congress used its ultimate right of insisting on this procedure. The insistence was passed by the vote of the two-thirds of both Chambers, as required by the Constitution.

7 President, Congress, and Privatizations after Re-election

1 The Argentine Constitution of 1994. Article 90 also permits former presidents and vice-presidents to return to the presidential office after a four-year interval.

2 See Chapter 2 for further information on the distribution of congressional seats.

3 Torre (1996) has explained that 'the political game is developed within the confines of the ruling party, relegating the other political forces to the condition of secondary actors...'

4 *Ambito Financiero*, 10 July 1996, and *Clarín*, 11 August 1996. Similarly, Deputy Alberto Natale (PDP) explained the development of state accounts in these terms: 'Since 1991, with the approval of the Convertibility Law, and the achievement of balancing in the public accounts, the process of stability – that today all Argentinians are eager to defend – began; but, (recently) a dangerous tendency toward the increase of public expenditure began to creep in...(The budget) has been unbalanced from that distressing fourth trimester of 1994, when in the last days of December, we had to approve an increment of the budget for social security, until the dramatic first quarter of 1995, when we approved ostensible and important tax increases to avoid the flight of deposits that was taking place as a consequence of the end of the 1994 Mexican devaluation.' Discussion of the 1998 budget in the Chamber of Deputies, 27 November 1997, Shorthand Version.

5 For example, the privatization of the pension system was presented as a solution to the financial crisis of the present regime, and also it ensured some long-term macroeconomic benefits. In the short run, however, the reform reduced available funds because the gradual replacement of one regime by another meant that the state had to continue making payments without receiving equivalent contributions.

6 The fact that the Argentine state mainly relies on taxes on consumption makes it vulnerable to recessionary trends.

7 This poll did not include data on Alfonsín's popularity. This can be consulted in Chapter 3.

8 Llach, J. (1997: 218).

9 For details, consult Baylac (1996) and Felder (1997).

10 Article 8, Act 24629, *Boletín Oficial*, 8 March 1996.

11 It is also worth remembering that the only bill not approved concerned the privatization of the National Cattle Market. As explained in Chapter 6, this case only marginally met our definition of privatization since the case could also be considered part of the policy of deregulation. The Executive finally decided to approach it in this way. It discouraged the approval of this bill in Congress, and included it in the necessity and urgency megadecree that established the rules for the policy of deregulation. The decree was not the result of an institutional conflict since the debate of the bill had been initiated and was progressing smoothly.

12 *Banco Nación* is considered a giant in the local financial system, with a hundred-year existence in profitable and non-profitable places all over the country. It is the bank that assists rural producers in trouble, and grants credits to small and middle size enterprises both in rural and industrial areas. It has also been a state financial agent assisting the government and

other banks. During the second half of 1996, the press echoed the rumours about the forthcoming privatization of the National Bank, which the government denied on several occasions. Nevertheless, opposition and Peronist legislators expressed their negative attitude by submitting declarations and resolutions of rejection. See *Clarín*, 5 September 1996, *La Nación*, 8 December 1996, *Página 12*, 25 April 1997. A year later, the government began to discuss the topic more openly, and even expressed its political will in the letter of intent signed with the IMF. See *Clarín*, 4 December 1997. Then, it became obvious that this privatization was very unpopular. It generated all kinds of negative reactions. Important entrepreneurial entities, such as the Argentine Rural Society and the Argentine Industrial Union manifested their opposition. *Clarín*, 9 and 21 November 1997. Other organizations embracing small and middle size producers (Argentine Agrarian Federation, Argentine Rural Confederation) also expressed their total opposition. *Clarín*, 9 February 1998. Ahead of this, legislators confirmed their decision to reject the idea of a total privatization (for instance, *Clarín*, 8 November 1997). As a consequence, the government was not able to transform its initiative in a bill to be submitted to Congress.

13 The most controversial point appeared when, at the beginning of 1999, the government began to consider the possibility of eliminating the state's basic contribution, which had been arranged after the introduction of a pension system based on personal savings. The chief of the Peronist bloc in the lower house declared that 'there was no favourable climate to treat this topic in the bloc', *Clarín*, 24 June 1999.

14 Deputies Angel Abasto, Dulce Granados and Julio Migliozzi, *Orden del Dia* 309, from 14 June 1996.

15 Act 24804, passed on 2 April 1997.

16 *Clarín*, 15 April 1997.

17 Two senators were from Corrientes (Pacto Autonomista Liberal), and three ex-Peronists from Partido PAIS (José Octavio Bordón, Mario Fadel and Alfredo Avelín).

18 Letter from the undersecretary of Economic Deregulation and Organization, Jorge Ingaramo, to the president of the National Commission of Mail and Telegraphs, José Guillermo Capdevilla, 19 October 1994, reference: Note SSDYOE no. 404/94.

19 In his memoirs, Cavallo (1997: 108–09) wrote that the Ministry of Economy had prepared a decree to bid the postal service concession, using the privatization authorization that had been given by the State Reform Law. Then, he stated that 'Our intention was left unfinished because President Menem refused to sign the decree. At that moment, he argued that a group of legislators maintained that a new postal service law and a new regulatory framework were necessary before commencing the tender of the state post-office.'

20 *Página 12*, 22 November 1994.

21 This provision raised concerns in the United States. The Peronist senators denounced pressures from the US ambassador to kill the post-office bill. They reported that they had received a telegram from the American embassy expressing complaints about the post-office bill directly affecting the interests of American companies. Later on, Ambassador Cheek publicly declared

his position against the Senate's initiative and even warned the Senate that his government would respond to what was considered to be an attack on Washington's security policy in the region (*Clarín*, 23 and 26 November 1994). In this way, the American embassy sided with Cavallo, and somehow strengthened the idea that Cavallo was himself surreptitiously defending his own coalition. Senators made the point that since Cavallo was protecting the interests of foreign investors, he had been compelled to reject the clause that reduced their participation to 30 per cent (Senator Eduardo Vaca to *Diario Clarín*, 23 November 1994).

22 *Clarín*, 27 November 1994.

23 *Clarín*, 26 November 1994.

24 Minister Cavallo attended the meeting with all the secretaries of the Ministry of Economy, the president of the Central Bank, and the chief of cabinet. The minister's report lasted more than ten hours. C.R.D., 23 and 24 August 1995.

25 C.R.D., 23 and 24 August 1995, p. 3621.

26 C.R.D., 23 and 24 August 1995, pp. 3627–28.

27 *La Nación*, 8 December 1996.

28 Ramón Ortega had been Governor of Tucumán province, and had clear presidential aspirations. This group responded to his leadership in the Chamber of Deputies. *Ambito Financiero*, 4 November 1996.

29 Later on, the same entrepreneur became closely involved – as 'the brains behind' – in the still-unsolved murder of a journalist, José Luis Cabezas. Thus, Yabrán became the enemy of journalism and began to suffer a systematic media campaign against his activities. He committed suicide some time later.

30 The scandal started in late 1994 after the Senate passed the bill. But, at that time, any indication of instability in the Ministry created uncertainty in the business sector and cast a shadow over Menem's future re-election. Menem had based his re-election chances on the success and continuity of the economic transformation that he and Cavallo had started to consolidate a few years before. Then, Menem confirmed him until the end of the period, 'and if we win the elections on May 14, the minister will continue in office until 1999.' *Clarín*, 26 November 1994.

31 C.R.D., 23 and 24 August 1995, p. 3630.

32 C.R.D., 23 and 24 August 1995, p. 3630.

33 *Ambito Financiero*, 2 April 1997.

34 Some figures: debts with the Argentine state reached US dollars 7.5 billion; debts with other creditors, US dollars 1.5 billion. The Secretary of Energy estimated that construction projects had already cost around dollars 4.5 billion. *Clarín*, 17 February 1998.

35 *Clarín*, *Pagina 12*, *Ambito Financiero* from 26 July 1996; *Clarín*, 15 September 1996. Opposition concentrated on the following objections: 1) the dam was already working and its construction was soon to be finished, so that, with some extra financial help, it could begin to produce profits; 2) Yacyretá represented around 40 per cent of the country's electricity power. Since it began to operate, it significantly contributed to reducing tariffs in the wholesale market. Its privatization included the possibility of selling energy to Brazil where prices were higher, which would eventually push prices up in the Argentine market; 3) over decades, Argentine users were charged a 7 per cent additional tax in their electricity bills in order to finance the construction

of large power plants and, in turn, obtain a reduction of tariffs; 4) people living in the area of the dam had to suffer flooding of around 30 000 hectares, lose jobs and homes; 5) the government was planning to obtain 800 millions for the dam's privatization, but it agreed at the same time to cancel the dam's debts (including those of Paraguay).

36 It is worth noting that opposition in the Senate had also been significant. In this chamber, approval had only been possible with the drawing up of an 'additional protocol', in which some of the interests of the affected provinces were answered. This had been conditional in order to obtain a quorum for the bill's approval in this chamber.

37 *Clarín*, 17 February 1998.

38 *Clarín*, 4 April and 24 August 1997. It is worth noting that if the protocol had not been well received by Argentine legislators, neither had it been by the Paraguayans. However, it is probably true that Paraguay was waiting for some signals from Argentina in order to proceed accordingly.

39 *Clarín*, 17 February 1998.

40 For instance, Deputy Fernando La Hoz (PJ, from Corrientes province) stated that 'We do not agree with the sale of Yacyretá ... we believe that it is better to complete the projects first with obtainable domestic or external financial help.' *Ambito Financiero*, 20 August 1996.

41 *Clarín*, 16 April 1997.

42 Decree 265/97, *Boletín Oficial*, 25 March 1997. The decree established the concession of Encotesa in compliance with the requirements of the State Reform Law (Act 23696). The plan included a Participated Property Programme to give the workers an interest of 14 per cent of the social capital.

43 The winner was the group that offered the highest six-month canon. The companies forming the group were ITRON S.A., SIDECO AMERICANA S.A., Banco de Galicia and Buenos Aires S.A., with the technical assistance of the British Post Office. Decree 840/97, *Boletín Oficial*, 11 September 1997.

44 *Clarín*, 26 and 27 March 1997.

45 Decree 375/97, *Boletín Oficial*, 25 April 1997, was, then, regulating some existing laws.

46 *Clarín*, 14 May, 31 May, 9 July 1997; *Ambito Financiero*, 10 July 1997.

47 *Ambito Financiero*, 16 July, 21 August 1997.

48 Although Decree 842/97 invoked security problems in order to justify the need and urgency of this privatization, it surprisingly admitted, in another passage, that 'control over aeronautical activity and exercise of aeronautic police enforcement are state functions that can neither be delegated nor conceded.' *Boletín Oficial*, 28 August 1997.

49 Jorge Rottemberg, responsible for this privatization in the chief of cabinet's office. *Ambito Financiero*, 28 August 1997.

50 *Clarín*, 25 September 1997.

51 *Ambito Financiero*, 28 August 1997.

52 It was the not the first time that the Executive had resorted to this extraordinary method. As commented in Chapter 4, a previous case had concerned the privatization of the national airline.

53 Rafael Bielsa, constitutionalist, ex-advisor of the Ministry of Justice. *Clarín*, 18 December 1997. The Supreme Court supported the use of the *per saltum*

and the constitutional validity of the necessity and urgency decree with a five to four votes in favour. Details on this decision can be found in *La Ley*, 29 December 1997.

54 The expression 'weapons of the weak' was borrowed from Keeler (1993*b*: 526) who uses it to qualify the resources used by governments of the French Fifth Republic (package vote, the guillotine, circumvention of the Senate) when they face a weak majority in the National Assembly and/or have no majority in the Senate.

8 Conclusion

1 See, for example, Acuña (1994); Bresser Pereira, Maravall and Przeworski (1990); Haggard and Kaufman (1995); O'Donnell (1994*a*); Roberts (1995); Torre (1994).
2 Rockman, B. (1997: 49).
3 Margheritis, A. (1997: 175–6).
4 As was also maintained in Chapter 3, the Radical Party did not show much sympathy for the privatization bills. This party could be held responsible for the negative outcome of Alfonsín's first privatization bills in the lower house. The remaining three were, however, of much more relevance.
5 Charles Jones cited in Rockman (1991: 45).
6 Palermo, V. (1998); Palermo, V. (1995); Torre, J. (1998); Gerchunoff, P. and Torre, J. (1996).
7 Mustapic, A. (2000: 591).
8 Mustapic, A. (1999).
9 Etchemendy, S. and Palermo, V. (1998: 581–2).
10 Eaton, K. (1998).
11 Jones, M. (2001: 181–2).
12 Mustapic, A. (2000: 593).
13 Shugart, M. and Mainwaring, S. (1997: 49).
14 Ferreira Rubio, D. and Goretti, M. (1998: 59).

Bibliography

Acuña, C. (1994) 'Politics and Economics in the Argentina of the Nineties' in W. Smith, C. Acuña and E. Gamarra (eds) *Democracy, Markets, and Structural Reform in Latin America: Argentina, Bolivia, Brazil, Chile and Mexico*. New Brunswick (NJ): Transaction Publishers.

Acuña, C. and Smulovitz, C. (1995) 'Militares en la transición argentina: del gobierno a la subordinación constitucional' in C. Acuña (ed.) *La nueva matriz política argentina*. Buenos Aires: Ediciones Nueva Visión.

Adrogué, G. (1995) 'El nuevo sistema partidario argentino' in C. Acuña (ed.) *La nueva matriz política argentina*. Buenos Aires: Ediciones Nueva Visión.

Alberdi, J. B. (1981) *Bases y puntos de partida para la organización política de la República Argentina*. Buenos Aires: Plus Ultra.

Alonso, G. (1997) 'Democracia y reformas: las tensiones entre decretismo y participación. El caso de la reforma previsional argentina'. Paper presented at the III Political Science National Congress. Mar del Plata.

Alonso, G. (1998) 'Democracia y reformas: las tensiones entre decretismo y deliberación. El caso de la reforma previsional argentina' in *Desarrollo Económico*, 38 (150) 595–626. Buenos Aires: Instituto de Desarrollo Económico y social.

Ambito Financiero, national newspaper, Buenos Aires, several numbers.

Bates, R. and Krueger, A. (1993) 'Generalisations Arising from the Country Studies' in R. Bates and A. Krueger (eds) *Political and Economic Interactions in Economic Policy Reform: Evidence from Eight Countries*. Oxford & Cambridge: Blackwell.

Baylac, J. (1996) *Control y seguimiento legislativo sobre las privatizaciones*. Simposio Internacional. Buenos Aires: Auditoría General de la Nación.

Blondel, J. (1973) *Comparative Legislatures*. Englewood Cliffs: Prentice-Hall.

Boletín Oficial (Official Bulletin), Presidency of the Nation, Buenos Aires, several numbers.

Bonifacio, A. 'La Reforma del Estado y la modernización de la función pública en Argentina'. Compilación realizada para el Programa de Posgrado en Control de Políticas Públicas FLACSO-INAP-Poder Ciudadano-IDEA. Unpublished Paper.

Botana, N. and Mustapic, A. (1988) 'La reforma constitucional frente al régimen político argentino'. Working Paper no. 101. Buenos Aires: Instituto Torcuato Di Tella.

Bresser Pereira, L., Maravall, J. and Przeworski, A. (1990) *Economic Reform in New Democracies*. New York: Cambridge University Press.

Canitrot, A. (1992) 'La destrucción del Estado Argentino y los intentos posteriores de reconstrucción.' Paper presented at the Conference 'Democracia, Mercados y Reformas Estructurales' organized by Miami University North/South Center and CEDES. Buenos Aires.

Canitrot, A. (1994) 'Crisis and Transformation of the Argentine State (1978–1992)' in W. Smith, C. Acuña, and E. Gamarra (eds) *Democracy, Markets, and Structural Reform in Latin America: Argentina, Bolivia, Brazil, Chile, and Mexico*. New Brunswick (NJ): Transaction Publishers.

Canitrot, A. and Sigal, S. (1994) 'Economic Reform, Democracy, and the Crisis of the State in Argentina' in J. Nelson (ed.) *A Precarious Balance. Democracy and Economic Reform in Latin America*. San Francisco: ICS Press.

Cavallo, D. (1997) *El peso de la verdad*. Buenos Aires: Planeta.

Cavarozzi, M. (1994) 'Politics: A Key for the Long Term in South America' in W. Smith, C. Acuña and E. Gamarra (eds) *Latin American Political Economy in the Age of Neoliberal Reform: Theoretical and Comparative Perspectives for the 1990s*. Miami: University of Miami North/South Center.

CEPAL (1994) *La crisis de la empresa publica, las privatizaciones y la equidad social*. Chile: CEPAL.

Cerruti, G. (1993) *El Jefe. Vida y obra de Carlos Saúl Menem*. Buenos Aires: Planeta.

Clarín, national newspaper, Buenos Aires, several numbers.

Collier, D. and Levitsky, S. (1997) 'Democracy with Adjectives: Conceptual Innovation in Comparative Research' in *World Politics*, 49 (3) 430–51. Baltimore: The Johns Hopkins University Press.

Constitución de la Nación Argentina. Texto oficial de 1853 con las reformas de 1860, 1866, 1898, 1957 y 1994 ordenado por ley 24430 (1996). Buenos Aires: Editorial Astrea.

Corrales, J. (1998) 'Coalitions and Corporate Choices in Argentina, 1976–1994: The Recent Private Sector Support of Privatisation' in *Studies in Comparative International Development*, 32 (4) 24–51. New Brunswick (NJ): Transaction Publishers.

Corrales, J. (1999) 'Contribuyen las crisis económicas a la implementación de reformas de mercado? La Argentina y Venezuela en los '90' in *Desarrollo Económico*, 39 (153) 3–29. Buenos Aires: Instituto de Desarrollo Económico y Social.

Corrales, J. (2000) 'Presidents, Ruling Parties, and Party Rules. A Theory on the Politics of Economic Reform in Latin America' in *Comparative Politics*, 32 (4) 127–50. New York: The City University of New York.

Dahl, R. (1989) *Democracy and its Critics*. New Haven: Yale University Press.

Damill, M. and Frenkel, R. (1993) 'Restauración democrática y Política Económica: Argentina, 1984–1991' in J. A. Morales and G. McMahon (eds) *La Política Económica en la transición a la democracia*. Santiago: CIEPLAN.

De Riz, L. and Smulovitz, C. (1991) 'Instituciones y dinámica política. El presidencialismo argentino' in D. Nohlen and L. De Riz (eds) *Reforma institucional y cambio político*. Buenos Aires: CEDES-Legasa.

Diamond, L. (1996*a*) 'Is the Third Wave Over?' in *Journal of Democracy*, 7 (3) 20–37. Baltimore: The Johns Hopkins University Press.

Diamond, L. (1996*b*) 'Democracy in Latin America. Degrees, Illusions, and Directions for Consolidation' in T. Farer (ed.) *Beyond Sovereignty. Collectively Defending Democracy in the Americas*. Baltimore & London: The Johns Hopkins University Press.

Diario de Sesiones (Congressional Reports), Chamber of Deputies and Senate, several numbers.

Discursos Presidenciales (1988), vol. 5 bis. Buenos Aires: Secretaría de Información Pública.

Domínguez, J. (1998) *Democratic Politics in Latin America and the Caribbean*. Baltimore & London: The Johns Hopkins University Press.

Dromi, R. (1991) *Reforma del Estado y Privatizaciones*. Buenos Aires: Astrea.

Dromi, R. (1997) *Empresas Públicas. De estatales a privadas*. Buenos Aires: Ediciones Ciudad Argentina.

Ducatenzeiler, G. and Oxhorn, P. (1994) 'Democracia, autoritarismo y el problema de la gobernabilidad en América Latina' in *Desarrollo Económico*, 34 (133) 31–52. Buenos Aires: IDES.

Eaton, K. (1998) 'Fiscal Policy Making in the Argentine Legislature'. Unpublished Paper, Department of Political Science, Yale University.

Edwards, S. (1995) *Crisis and Reform in Latin America: From Despair to Hope*. Washington DC: Oxford University Press.

Ekmedjian, M. (1990) 'El instituto de la emergencia y la delegación de poderes en las leyes de la reforma del estado y de emergencia económica' in *La Ley*. Buenos Aires: La Ley S. A.

Escudé, C. (1992) *Realismo Periférico*. Buenos Aires: Planeta.

Etchemendy, S. (2001) 'Construir coaliciones reformistas: la política de las compensaciones en el camino argentino hacia la liberalización económica' in *Desarrollo Económico*, 40 (160) 675–706. Buenos Aires: Instituto de Desarrollo Económico y Social.

Etchemendy, S. and Palermo, V. (1998) 'Conflicto y concertación. Gobierno, Congreso y organizaciones de interés en la reforma laboral del primer gobierno de Menem (1984–1995)' in *Desarrollo Económico*, 38 (148) 559–90. Buenos Aires: Instituto de Desarrollo Económico y Social.

Fanelli, J. and Frenkel, R. (1997) 'The Argentine Experience with Stabilization and Structural Reform.' Working Paper no. 4. Buenos Aires: Universidad de Palermo/CEDES.

Felder, R. (1997) 'Las privatizaciones, ¿conspiración o estrategia política?'. Paper submitted at the XXI Congress of the Latin American Association of Sociology, Brazil.

Ferreira Rubio, D. and Goretti, M. (1995) 'La Reforma Constitucional Argentina: ¿un presidente menos poderoso?' in *Contribuciones*, 1, 69–89. Buenos Aires: Fundación Konrad Adenauer, Ciedla.

Ferreira Rubio, D. and Goretti, M. (1996) 'Cuando el presidente gobierna solo. Menem y los decretos de necesidad y urgencia hasta la reforma constitucional (julio 1989–agosto 1994)' in *Desarrollo Económico*, 36 (141) 443–74. Buenos Aires: Instituto de Desarrollo Económico y Social.

Ferreira Rubio, D. and Goretti, M. (1998) 'When the President Governs Alone: the *Decretazo* in Argentina, 1989–1993' in J. Carey and M. Shugart (eds) *Executive Decree Authority*. New York: Cambridge University Press.

Ffrench-Davis, R. (1997) 'El efecto Tequila, sus orígenes y su alcance contagioso' in *Desarrollo Económico*, 37 (146) 195–213. Buenos Aires: Instituto de Desarrollo Económico y Social.

Frenkel, R. and Rozenwurzel, G. (1996) 'The Multiple Roles of Privatisation in Argentina' in A. Lijphart and C. Waisman (eds) *Institutional Design in New Democracies*. Boulder: Westview Press.

Gerchunoff, P. and Cánovas, G. (1994) *Las privatizaciones en la Argentina: Impactos micro y macroeconómicos*. Santiago: CEPAL.

Gerchunoff, P. and Cánovas, G. (1995) 'Privatizaciones en un contexto de emergencia económica' in *Desarrollo Económico*, 34 (136) 483–512. Buenos Aires: Instituto de Desarrollo Económico y Social.

Gerchunoff, P. and Torre, J. (1989) 'Reflexiones sobre el papel del Estado en América Latina.' Document submitted at the International Symposium on Hirschman's work and a new development strategy for Latin America.

Gerchunoff, P. and Torre, J. (1996) 'La política de liberalización económica en la administración de Menem' in *Desarrollo Económico*, 36 (143) 733–68. Buenos Aires: Instituto de Desarrollo Económico y Social.

Gibson, E. (1997) 'The Populist Road to Market Reform. Policy and Electoral Coalitions in Mexico and Argentina' in *World Politics*, 49 (3) 339–70. Baltimore: The Johns Hopkins University Press.

Gibson, E. and Calvo, E. (2000) 'Federalism and Low-Maintenance Constituencies: Territorial Dimensions of Economic Reform in Argentina' in *Studies in Comparative International Development*, 35 (3) 32–55.

González Fraga, J. (1991) 'Argentine Privatization in Retrospect' in W. Glade (ed.) *Privatization of Public Enteprises in Latin America*. San Francisco: ICS Press.

Hachette, D. and Luders, R. (1993) *Privatisation in Chile. An Economic Appraisal*. San Francisco: ICS Press.

Haggard, S. and Kaufman, R. (1992) 'Institutions and Economic Adjustment' in S. Haggard and R. Kaufman (eds) *The Politics of Economic Adjustment*. Princeton: Princeton University Press.

Haggard, S. and Kaufman, R. (1994) 'The Challenges of Consolidation' in *Journal of Democracy*, 5 (4) 5–16. Baltimore: The Johns Hopkins University Press.

Haggard, S. and Kaufman, R. (1995) *The Political Economy of Democratic Transitions*. Princeton: Princeton University Press.

Huntington, S. (1993) 'Democracy's Third Wave' in L. Diamond and M. Plattner (eds) *The Global Resurgence of Democracy*. Baltimore: The Johns Hopkins University Press.

Huntington, S. (1997) 'Democracy for the Long Haul' in L. Diamond, M. Plattner, Y. Chu and H. Tien (eds) *Consolidating the Third Wave Democracies: Themes and Perspectives*. Baltimore & London: The Johns Hopkins University Press.

Ikenberry, J. (1990) 'The International Spread of Privatisation Policies: Inducements, Learning, and "Policy Bandwagoning"' in N. Suleiman and J. Waterbury (eds) *The Political Economy of Private Sector Reform and Privatisation*. Boulder: Westview Press.

Isuani, A. and San Martino, J. (1993) *La reforma previsional argentina. Opciones y riesgos*. Buenos Aires: Miño y Dávila Editores.

Isuani, A. and San Martino, J. (1995) 'El nuevo sistema previsional argentino. Punto final a una larga crisis?' in *Boletín Informativo Techint*, 282, 43–67. Buenos Aires.

Jaroslavsky, C. (1996) President of the Radical Bloc in the Chamber of Deputies (1983–91). Interview with the author, September.

Jones, M. (1997) 'Evaluating Argentina's Presidential Democracy: 1983–1995' in S. Mainwaring and M. Shugart (eds) *Presidentialism and Democracy in Latin America*. New York: Cambridge University Press.

Jones, M. (1998) 'Explaining the High Level of Party Discipline in the Argentine Congress'. Working Paper no. 14. Buenos Aires: CEDI.

Jones, M. (2001) 'Political Institutions and Public Policy in Argentina: An Overview of the Formation and Execution of the National Budget' in S. Haggard and M. McCubbins (eds) *Presidents, Parliaments, and Policy*. Cambridge: Cambridge University Press.

Keeler, J. (1993*a*) 'Opening the Window for Reform. Mandates, Crises and Extraordinary Policy-Making' in *Comparative Political Studies*, 25 (4) 433–86. London: Sage Publications.

Keeler, J. (1993*b*) 'Executive Power and Policy-Making Patterns in France: Gauging the Impact of Fifth Republic Institutions' in *West European Politics*, 16 (4) 518–44. London: Frank Cass.

Keeler, J. and Schain, M. (1996) 'Presidents, Premiers, and Models of Democracy in France' in J. Keeler and M. Schain (eds) *Chirac's Challenge. Liberalization, Europeanization, and Malaise in France*. London: Macmillan Press – now Palgrave.

Knight, Alan (1998) 'Populism and Neopopulism in Latin America, especially Mexico' in *Journal of Latin American Studies*, 30, 223–48. Cambridge: Cambridge University Press.

La Ley, jurisprudence magazine, several numbers, Buenos Aires: La Ley S.A.

La Nación, national newspaper, Buenos Aires, several numbers.

Larkins, C. (1998) 'The Judiciary and Delegative Democracy in Argentina' in *Comparative Politics*, 30 (4) 423–42. New York: The City University of New York.

Levitsky, S. (2000) 'The "Normalisation" of Argentine Politics' in *Journal of Democracy*, 11 (2) 56–69. Baltimore: The Johns Hopkins University Press.

Linz, J. (1994) 'Presidential or Parliamentary Democracy: Does It Make a Difference?' in J. Linz and A. Valenzuela (eds) *The Failure of Presidential Democracy: Comparative Perspectives*, vol. 1. Baltimore & London: The Johns Hopkins University Press.

Linz, J. and Stepan, A. (1997) 'Toward Consolidated Democracies' in L. Diamond, M. Plattner, Y. Chu and H. Tien (eds) *Consolidating the Third Wave Democracies: Themes and Perspectives*. Baltimore & London: The Johns Hopkins University Press.

Linz, J. and Valenzuela, A. (1994) (eds) *The Failure of Presidential Democracy: Comparative Perspectives*. Baltimore & London: The Johns Hopkins University Press.

Llach, J. (1997) *Otro siglo, otra Argentina*. Buenos Aires: Ariel S.A.

López, R. (1998) National Director of Political Affairs since 1991, direction depending on the Secretariat of Institutional Relations of the Ministry of Economy. Interview with the author, March.

Lowenthal, A. (2000) 'Latin America at the Century's Turn' in *Journal of Democracy*, 11 (2) 41–55. Baltimore: The Johns Hopkins University Press.

Machinea, J. (1990) '*Stabilization under Alfonsín's government: A Frustrated Attempt*'. Working Paper no. 42. Buenos Aires: CEDES.

Maclean, M. (1995) 'Privatisation in France 1993–94: New Departures, or a Case of *plus ça change?*' in *West European Politics*, 18 (2) 273–90. London: Frank Cass.

Madrid, R. (1996) 'The Politics of Social Security Reform in Latin America: Economic Pressures and Political Constraints.' PhD thesis working draft. Stanford University.

Mainwaring, S. and Shugart, M. (1998) 'Juan Linz, Presidentialism, and Democracy: A Critical Appraisal' in S. Mainwaring and A. Valenzuela (eds) *Politics, Society, and Democracy*. Boulder: Westview Press.

Manzetti, L. (1993) *Institutions, Parties and Coalitions in Argentine Politics*. Pittsburgh & London: University of Pittsburgh Press.

Maqueda, J. (1997) Peronist national deputy 1991–95; 1995–99. Also Vice-Chief of Cabinet (1996). Interview with the author, September.

Margheritis, A. (1997) 'Implementing Structural Adjustment in Argentina: The Politics of Privatisation'. PhD dissertation. Department of Political Science. University of Toronto.
Margheritis, A. (1999) *Ajuste y Reforma en Argentina (1989–1995)*. Buenos Aires: Grupo Editor Latinoamericano.
McBeth, B. (1996) *Privatisation: A Strategic Report*. England: Euromoney Publications PLC.
McGuire, J. (1995) 'Political Parties and Democracy in Argentina' in S. Mainwaring and T. Scully (eds) *Building Democratic Institutions: Party Systems in Latin America*. Stanford: Stanford University Press.
Molina Pico (1997) Admiral Molina Pico, *Jefe del Estado Mayor de la Armada* until December 1996. Interview with the author, December.
Molinelli, G. (1996) 'Las relaciones presidente-Congreso en Argentina '83–'95' in *POSTData*, 2, 59–90. Buenos Aires.
Murillo, V. (1997) 'Union Politics, Market-Oriented Reforms, and the Reshaping of Argentine Corporatism' in D. Chalmers, C. Vilas, K. Hite, S. Martin, K. Piester and M. Segarra (eds) *The New Politics of Inequality in Latin America*. New York: Oxford University Press.
Mustapic, A. (1984) 'Conflictos institucionales durante el primer gobierno radical: 1916–1922' in *Desarrollo Económico*, 24 (93). Buenos Aires: Instituto de Desarrollo Económico y Social.
Mustapic, A. (1988) 'Radicales y justicialistas frente al desafío de la renovación' in *Plural*, 10/11, 22–26. Buenos Aires.
Mustapic, A. (1995) 'Tribulaciones del Congreso en la nueva democracia argentina. El veto presidencial bajo Alfonsín y Menem' in *Agora*, 3, 95–113. Buenos Aires: Grupo Universitario de Estudios Políticos.
Mustapic, A. (1997) 'Las relaciones Ejecutivo-Legislativo en Argentina y Brasil.' Paper presented at the seminar Brazil–Argentina, Itamaraty Institute of International Relations, Rio de Janeiro, Brazil.
Mustapic, A. (1999) 'Oscillating Relations: President and Congress in Argentina' in G. Cox G. and S. Morgenstern (eds) *Legislative Politics in Latin America*. New York: Cambridge University Press.
Mustapic, A. (2000) 'Oficialistas y diputados: las relaciones Ejecutivo-Legislativo en Argentina' in *Desarrollo Económico*, 39 (156) 571–95. Buenos Aires: Instituto de Desarrollo Económico y Social.
Mustapic, A. and Goretti, M. (1991) 'Gobierno y oposición en el Congreso: La práctica de la cohabitación durante la Presidencia de Alfonsín (1983–1989).' Working Paper no. 117. Buenos Aires: Instituto Torcuato Di Tella.
Natale, A. (1993) *Privatizaciones en privado*. Buenos Aires: Planeta.
Nelson, J. (1994) 'Linkages between Politics and Economics' in *Journal of Democracy*, 5 (4). Baltimore: The Johns Hopkins University Press.
Nino, C. (1991) 'Presidencialismo y estabilidad democrática en la Argentina.' Working Paper. Buenos Aires: Centro de Estudios Institucionales.
Nino, C. (1996) 'Hyperpresidentialism and Constitutional Reform in Argentina' in A. Lijphart and C. Waisman (eds) *Institutional Design in New Democracies: Eastern Europe and Latin America*. Boulder: Westview Press.
Novaro, M. (1994)) *Pilotos de tormenta: Crisis de representación y personalización de la política en Argentina (1989–1993)*. Buenos Aires: Ediciones Letra Buena.

Novaro, M. and Palermo, V. (1998) *Los caminos de la centroizquierda: Dilemas y desafíos del Frepaso y de la Alianza*. Buenos Aires: Losada.
O'Donnell, G. (1994*a*) 'Delegative Democracy' in *Journal of Democracy*, 5 (1) 55–69. Baltimore: The Johns Hopkins University Press.
O'Donnell, G. (1994*b*) 'The State, Democratisation, and Some Conceptual Problems' in W. Smith, C. Acuña and E. Gamarra (eds) *Latin American Political Economy in the Age of Neoliberal Reform: Theoretical and Comparative Perspectives for the 1990s*. Miami: University of Miami North/South Center.
O'Donnell, G. (1997) 'Illusions about Consolidation' in L. Diamond, M. Plattner, Y. Chu and H. Tien (eds) *Consolidating the Third Wave Democracies: Themes and Perspectives*. Baltimore & London: The Johns Hopkins University Press.
O'Donnell, G. (1998) 'Horizontal Accountability in New Democracies' in *Journal of Democracy*, 9 (3) 112–26. Baltimore: The Johns Hopkins University Press.
O'Donnell, G. (2000) 'Teoría democrática y política comparada' in *Desarrollo Económico*, 39 (156) 519–70. Buenos Aires: Instituto de Desarrollo Ecómico y Social.
Orden del Día, Committe Report, Chamber of Deputies and Senate, several numbers.
Página 12, national newspaper, Buenos Aires, several numbers.
Palanza, V. and Sin, G. (1997) 'Partidos provinciales y gobierno nacional en el Congreso, 1983–1995.' Paper submitted in the III Political Science National Congress. Mar del Plata, Argentina.
Palermo, V. (1990) 'Programas de ajuste y estrategias políticas. Las experiencias recientes de la Argentina y Bolivia' in *Desarrollo Económico*, 31 (121) 125–39. Buenos Aires: Instituto de Desarrollo Económico y Social.
Palermo, V. (1995) 'Reformas estructurales y régimen político' in *Agora*, 3, 95–113. Buenos Aires: Grupo Universitario de Estudios Políticos.
Palermo, V. (1998) *Mares Agitados: interpretaciones sobre los procesos políticos latinoamericanos. Brasil y Argentina en perspectiva comparada*. First Meeting of the Brazilian Association of Political Science, Rio de Janeiro.
Palermo, V. and Novaro, M. (1996) *Política y poder en el gobierno de Menem*. Buenos Aires: Grupo Editorial Norma.
Paradiso, J. (1993) *Debates y Trayectoria de la Política Exterior Argentina*. Buenos Aires: Grupo Editor Latinoamericano S.R.L.
Peruzzotti, E. (1997) 'Post-Populist Democracies: Toward a Juridification of Politics? The "Delegative Democracy" Argument Revisited.' Paper submitted to the XX International Congress of the Latin American Studies Association. Guadalajara, Mexico.
Portantiero, J. (1987) 'La transición entre la confrontación y el acuerdo' in J. Nun and J. Portantiero (eds) *Ensayos sobre la transición democrática en Argentina*. Buenos Aires: Punto Sur.
Przeworski, Adam (1995) *Sustainable Democracy*. New York: Cambridge University Press.
Public Opinion Polls, *Centro de Estudios Unión para la Nueva Mayoría*.
Public Opinion Polls, *Estudio Sociológico y Político Mora y Araujo, Noguera y Asociados*.
Rausch, A. (1994) 'Monitoring and Regulating Aspects of Privatization in Argentina' in *Privatization and After: Monitoring and Regulation*. London: Routledge.
Reglamento of the Chamber of Deputies, National Congress, Buenos Aires.

Roberts, K. (1995) 'Neoliberalism and the Transformation of Populism in Latin America: The Peruvian Case' in *World Politics*, 48, 82–116. Baltimore: The Johns Hopkins University Press.

Rockman, B. (1991) 'The Leadership Question: Is there an Answer?' in C. Campbell and M. Wyszomirski (eds) *Executive Leadership in Anglo-American Systems*. Pittsburgh: University of Pittsburgh Press.

Rockman, B. (1997) 'The Performance of Presidents and Prime Ministers and of Presidential and Paliamentary Regimes' in K. von Mettenheim *Presidential Institutions in Democratic Politics: Comparing Regional and National Contexts*. Baltimore & London: The Johns Hopkins University Press.

Rossi, M. (1996) Adviser of the Peronist Deputy Miguel Angel Toma (1985–97) in the Committee of Defence. Interview with the author, October.

Rossiter, C. (1963) *Constitutional Dictatorship: Crisis Government in the Modern Democracies*. USA: Harcourt, Brace & World, Inc.

Sain, M. (2000) 'Quince años de legislación democrática sobre temas militares y de defensa (1983–1998)' in *Desarrollo Económico*, 40 (157) 121–42. Buenos Aires: Instituto de Desarrollo Económico y Social.

Schamis, H. (1992) 'Conservative Political Economy in Latin America and Western Europe: The Political Sources of Privatisation' in D. Chalmers, do Carmo Campello de Souza, and A. Borón (eds) *The Right and Democracy in Latin America*. Westport, Conn.: Praeger.

Schmitter, P. and Karl, T. (1996) 'Qué es... y qué no es la democracia' in L. Diamond and M. Plattner (eds) *El resurgimiento global de la democracia*. Mexico City: UNAM.

Serrafero, M. (1993) *Momentos Institucionales y modelos constitucionales: Estudios sobre la Constitución Nacional*. Buenos Aires: Centro Editor de América Latina.

Shugart, M. and Mainwaring, S. (1997) 'Presidentialism and Democracy in Latin America: Rethinking the Terms of the Debate' in S. Mainwaring and M. Shugart (eds) *Presidentialism and Democracy in Latin America*. New York: Cambridge University Press.

Síntesis Periodística (1983, 1985) Dirección de Información Parlamentaria, National Congress, Buenos Aires.

Smith, W. (1991) *Authoritarianism and the Crisis of the Argentine Political Economy*. Stanford: Stanford University Press.

Smith, W., Acuña, C. and Gamarra, E. (1994) *Democracy, Markets, and Structural Reform in Latin America: Argentina, Bolivia, Brazil, Chile and Mexico*. New Brunswick (NJ): Transaction Publishers.

Smulovitz, C. (1995) 'Constitución y poder judicial en la nueva democracia argentina. La experiencia de las instituciones' in C. Acuña (ed.) *La nueva matriz política argentina*. Buenos Aires: Ediciones Nueva Visión.

Snow, P. and Manzetti, L. (1993) *Political Forces in Argentina*. Westport, Conn.: & London: Praeger.

Socchi, H. (1993) Radical Deputy (1983–91), and President of the Industry Committee in the Chamber. Interview with the author, July.

Soria, D. (1994) 'Las privatizaciones y el control del Congreso' in *Revista Argentina del Régimen de la Administración Pública*, 191, 15–36. Argentina: Editorial Ciencias de la Administración.

Stallings, B. (1992)) 'International Influence on Economic Policy: Debt, Stabilisation, and Structural Reform' in S. Haggard and R. Kaufman (eds) *The Politics of Economic Adjustment*. Princeton: Princeton University Press.

Storani, F. (1996) Radical Deputy (1983–91; 1993–97), President of the Radical Bloc in the Chamber of Deputies (1995–99). Interview with the author, November.

Teichman, J. (1997) 'Mexico and Argentina: Economic Reform and Technocratic Decision Making' in *Studies in Comparative International Development*, 32 (1) 31–55. New Brunswick (NJ): Transaction Publishers.

Terragno, R. (1993) Alfonsín's Minister of Public Works and Services (1988–89). Interview with the author, August.

The World Bank (1993) *Argentina's Privatisation Program: Experience, Issues, and Lessons*. Washington DC: The World Bank, Development in Practice.

Tiempo Argentino, national newspaper, Buenos Aires, several numbers.

Torre, J. (1994) 'América Latina: el gobierno de la democracia en tiempos difíciles.' Working Paper no. 122. Buenos Aires: Instituto y Universidad Torcuato Di Tella.

Torre, J. (1996) 'Argentine: le pèronisme, solution et problème de la crise' in *Problèmes de Amerique Latine*, no. 20. Paris: La Documentation Française.

Torre, J. (1998) *El proceso político de las reformas económicas en América Latina*. Buenos Aires: Paidós.

Torre, J. and Palermo, V. (1992) 'A la sombra de la hiperinflación. La política de reformas estructurales en Argentina.' Unpublished paper, Buenos Aires.

Tsebelis, G. (1995) 'Decision Making in Political Systems: Veto Players in Presidentialism, Parliamentarism, Multicameralism and Multipartyism' in *British Journal of Political Science*, no. 25. Cambridge: Cambridge University Press.

Verbitsky, H. (1991) *Robo para la corona: Los frutos prohibidos del árbol de la corrupción*. Buenos Aires: Planeta.

Verbitsky, H. (1993) *Hacer la Corte*. Buenos Aires: Planeta.

Vickers, J. and Wright, V. (1988) 'The Politics of Industrial Privatisation in Western Europe: An Overview' in *West European Politics*, 11 (4) 1–30. London: Frank Cass.

Vidal, A. (1995) *El Congreso en la trampa: Entretelones y escándalos de la vida parlamentaria*. Buenos Aires: Planeta.

Weyland, Kurt (1996) 'Neopopulism and Neoliberalism in Latin America: Unexpected Affinities' in *Studies in Comparative International Development*, 31 (3) 3–31. New Brunswick (NJ): Transaction Publishers.

Williamson, J. (1993) *The Political Economy of Policy Reform*. Washington DC: Institute for International Economics.

Wright, V. (1995) 'The Industrial Privatisation Programmes of Britain and France: The Impact of Political and Institutional Factors' in P. Jones (ed.) *Party, Parliaments and Personality*. London: Routledge.

Index